BRAIN MOVIES

The Original Teleplays of Harlan Ellison®

Volume Seven

AN EDGEWORKS ABBEY OFFERING

BRAIN MOVIES
THE ORIGINAL TELEPLAYS OF HARLAN ELLISON®
VOLUME SEVEN
is an Edgeworks Abbey® offering in association with Jason Davis.
Published by arrangement with the Author and The Kilimanjaro Corporation.

BRAIN MOVIES
THE ORIGINAL TELEPLAYS OF HARLAN ELLISON®
VOLUME SEVEN

Harlan Ellison website: www.HarlanEllison.com
To order books: www.HarlanEllisonBooks.com

Editor:	Jason Davis
Assistant Editor:	Cynthia Davis
Designer:	Bo Nash

ISBN: 978-0-9895257-9-4

FIRST EDITION

Thanks to Steven Barber & Rod Searcey.

12062016

Contents

nota bene:

The documents in this book were reproduced from the author's file copies. They originated on a manual typewriter, hence the idiosyncrasies that set them apart from the sanitized, word-processed pages of today. The progressive lightening of the text followed by a sudden darkening of the same, indicates the author has changed the typewriter's ribbon; it is *not* a printing defect.

Throughout the works presented herein, there is evidence of the author's revision: struck-out text, handwritten emendations (sometimes right off the page), and typewritten text printed over passages that were cancelled with correcting tape. These artifacts have been maintained to preserve the evidence of the writer's process.

Esper

Editor's Note: Think Piece

The October 1968 issue of *The Magazine of Fantasy & Science Fiction*, wherein the short story "Try a Dull Knife" made its debut, tells us:

> Harlan Ellison's current projects include the following: scripting an sf film, *Esper*, for Universal Pictures (it is projected as a film-for-tv and later a series); putting together a second volume of DANGEROUS VISIONS...Ellison is presently crossing the country making tv and radio appearances to promote his new collection LOVE AIN'T NOTHING BUT SEX MISSPELLED...

Based on the references to AGAIN, DANGEROUS VISIONS and LOVE AIN'T NOTHING BUT SEX MISSPELLED, we know *when* Ellison wrote *Esper*—alternately titled *Foreseen* or *Wild Talent*—but the 70-page treatment remains something of an enigma, even to its author.

When asked what he remembered of authoring the pilot treatment, Ellison replied, "Nothing."

Upon being informed that the first nineteen pages of the treatment precisely prefigure the opening chapters of Stephen King's superlative 1979 novel THE DEAD ZONE as if Ellison foresaw—like Johnny Smith—the book King would one day write, Ellison laughed.

The similarities end there; Ellison goes a very different route once his protagonist is spurred to action, opening a detective agency with the requisite quick-witted girl Friday. When reminded of the supporting role, Ellison grinned, "Lurene Tuttle as Effie in *The Adventures of Sam Spade* was always my idol."

ESPER

a film by

HARLAN ELLISON

TREATMENT

FADE IN:

CLOSE ON NEWSREEL SHOTS of fighting in Viet Nam. OVER SHOTS we HEAR the deep VOICE of DEAN HERRON as he comments on the news. The film clip changes to a scene on a street with police cars and ambulance, crowd and police, tending over a sheet-covered figure, as Herron says:

"...Department of the Army statistics now bring the losses in the Danang Offensive to thirteen hundred Viet Cong dead or wounded; seven hundred fifty American and South Vietnamese killed or wounded in this latest thrust to reclaim the heavily-VC-infested territory... and for my editorial this evening, I want to draw a parallel between the staggering military mortality rate and this scene, which took place on West 82nd Street in New York City, at eleven O'clock this morning..."

3

ELLISON / 2

CUT TO FULL SHOT of Newscaster Dean Herron sitting behind his newsdesk, on-camera in a studio, TV cameras positioning around him. Behind him the New York film clip continues running, showing the procedure of Manhattan police as they tend to the body in the street. CAMERA MOVES IN on Herron as he speaks, giving us a prolonged and searching look at the man who will be our protagonist.

"Beneath this white sheet lies the body of Emil D'Angelo, 63, an Italian pastry chef who, this morning, returning from a night of preparing breads and rolls for the Plaza Hotel, walked into the middle of a gang rumble. D'Angelo was shot three times in the stomach by a member of one of the rival youth gangs feuding over the "turf" between Amsterdam and Columbus Avenues. Emil D'Angelo was a grandfather six times over, had lived in the same apartment on West 82nd for thirty years, and as far as Manhattan police have been able to establish, his only sin was coming home a little later than usual, and walking into the path of those three bullets. One more death in our city streets—even as senseless a death as this one—would rate little more than a passing note, were it not for the singular fact that Emil D'Angelo did not die immediately. Wounded, he managed to crawl almost two city blocks before expiring. Police on the scene verify that at least fifteen people witnessed D'Angelo's struggles...and made no move to assist him."

Herron's face displays pain and awe at the import of what he is saying. We can see genuine concern in his manner. He is not merely reporting the news, he is taking us somewhere inside the gut of events, to deal with the meaning. Not for the sake of sensationalism, but because there is a necessary involvement. He is by no means a handsome man, yet there is a charisma about him, a strength in his face, that belies his offtrail rugged appearance. His is the kind of face women mean when they say "an ugly beautiful". As the film runs behind him, he makes his point:

"Violence has become a kind of illiterate shorthand to express the dementia of our times. We, the average Americans, have no way of knowing if the deaths incurred in Southeast ▓▓▓ Asia are wrong or right, necessary or foolish, avoidable or inescapable...it is a matter we must leave to our national conscience and the judgment of history. But death in the streets...death we see and which we can prevent...this goes unchecked. And the fear of it, the inarticulate ▓▓▓ helplessness, these are the symptoms of a disease rapidly infesting the life of our country. What has happened to individual

conscience? What has become of simple _caring_? How much
longer will we see sights such as this on 82nd Street,
and fail to identify with them? At what point do we
realize it is for each of us for whom the bell tolls,
that the death of one Emil D'Angelo in this certain way,
this avoidable, preventable way, is the death of all of
us? How much longer can we chew the lie that we are a
compassionate people, an involved people, a moral people,
and let each other be butchered by the fifth horseman...
Fear?"

Herron pauses.

"This is Dean Herron, saying good night."

The broadcast ends, and Herron lights a cigarette,
pushes back from the desk, rises to go.

At the performer's exit of the television studio,
Herron is stopped by WILLIS DAMIAN, head of the network
news department. "We're getting calls on that editorial,
Dean," he says. Herron nods but says nothing. We can
see by his manner that he knows in his heart of hearts
that all the evangelical enthusiasm in the world will
not make people give a slightly larger damn about their
fellow man. Damian suggests joining Herron at the
bar across the street for a little talk and a few short
ones. To ease the tension. It is starting to rain.
Herron thanks him, but refuses, saying he wants to walk

in the rain for a while, walk to his nearby apartment and
do some~~tt~~ thinking. Damian is concerned. "You're looking
lousy, Dean."

"I'm getting weary in the yoke."

Damian tries to reach Herron. "You sure you don't
want to go and talk about it?"

Herron shrugs. "Talk about what? I've been pushing
news for seventeen years. London, Brussels, Teheran,
Washington. The one question I keep asking myself is,
'Why can't somebody do something, for God's sake?' When
does the world take a breather. Forget it, Will. I'm
developing a Christ complex. It'll pass. A good night's
sleep. See you tomorrow."

He slips into his trenchcoat, lights another
cigarette off the stub of the last, and slouches out into
the light, drifting rain.

CAMERA HOLDS on Herron as he walks away into dark.

SMASH-CUT TO NARROW STREET with windows dark,
buildings silent. Suddenly a light goes on in a window...
a WOMAN SCREAMS and a MAN SHOUTS undecipherable obscenities
as the Woman screams back at him. Their voices rise and
we HOLD on the EMPTY STREET as the SOUND of something glass
shattering follows the voices.

CUT TO HERRON WALKING in the rain, cupping the

cigarette to prevent its getting soaked. Head down, he is thinking.

HARD CUT TO narrow street again. Now a DOOR SLAMS and we HEAR a WOMAN'S HEELS on STAIRS. The DOOR SLAMS AGAIN and a MAN'S FEET thump heavily down the stairs, following her. The Woman rushes out onto the rain-swept street, wearing a bathrobe. The MAN emerges from the building. He sees the Woman standing in the middle of the street. They scream at each other. Their voices are lost in the wind. But there is anger and hatred and a kind of wild insanity in their tone. Lights begin to go on in windows all over the street.

CUT BACK TO Herron walking. On his feet, as he scuffs through pools of water, oblivious to the elements, lost in thought.

HARD CUT TO narrow street once more. The Man dashes into the street, grabs the Woman by the hair, and now we see he is brandishing a bread knife. The Woman screams, slaps his hand away, stands and curses him. Now windows are going up, lights are on, people are leaning out and watching the tableau. The Man's face is wild, insane, and his fury boils over. He lunges at the Woman and cuts her on the arm. The Woman screams and falls back, appalled at the sight of her own blood. The Man comes at her again.

INTERCUTS between Herron, obviously walking with predestined relentlessness into the scene of violence, and the Man and Woman as their senseless interchange moves more quickly toward death. People in the buildings are now shouting, "Leave her alone! Leave her alone!" and calling for police. Herron walks around the corner, into the street. He stops cold as we ZOOM IN FROM HIS POV to the enraged Man now slashing at the Woman who is helplessly trying to escape his psychopathic attack.

CLOSE ON HERRON'S FACE as we see him commit to this moment, totally, with rational awareness of the danger, but an overwhelming urge to intercede, to help, to <u>stop</u> <u>the violence</u>!

He charges the Man. They grapple. The Woman drags herself to safety in a doorway. The Man pushes Herron away from him, and then as Herron regains himself, the Man lunges...

The knife comes down in a glittering arc...

Light reflects in oil-rainbow patches from pools of rainwater...

The knife, the water, the light in the mad eyes of the assailant, all make a kaleidoscope of brilliance and emerging out of it is the blood-red reflector atop a screaming ambulance as it careens through traffic, weaves in and out of fire-lanes, races toward a receiving hospital. Ambulance doors crash open, a stretcher is lifted onto a meat wagon, the trundle pushes through pneumatic doors, down a corridor, someone shouts, "It's Dean Herron, the newscaster..." and then a wild montage of lights and whip-pans as scene dissolves through scene into an operating stage, and suddenly the face of DR. BENNO KEMP swims into view above Dean Herron.

"Quickly!" he snaps.

An operation. A long operation. The nurse swabbing Kemp's forehead, the flash of instruments, the pulse rate bobbing on an oscilloscope, and then Kemp looking desperate, cursing, struggling with Herron— "Hang on, damn you! Hang on! Adjust that oxygen flow. He's losing ground...more oxygen...slipping, slipping, damn you, don't die on me...I worked too long on you... don't die..."

Herron dies.

The oscilloscope sine curve is a straight line. Pulse: zero. Metabolic rate: zero. Respiration: zero. Kemp is a madman now! Everything he ever knew, everything he'd ever learned, frustrated, denied, useless. Cursing foully he continues to work over Herron's dead body. He won't give up. One minute...two minutes... almost three minutes...and then—a flutter, a short peak

on the scope, the respirator bulb twitches, light flashes
off Kemp's glasses and the shaft of light slides down
the blade of the scalpel as we CLOSE on the deathmask of
Dean Herron's face.

In a SERIES OF almost psychedelic TECHNIQUE SHOTS
we see the brain of Dean Herron, deprived of oxygen, the
encroachment of physical death, the shutdown of the
senses...and then a spark-gap as something unbelievable
explodes, and the brain awakens in its closed functions,
an electrical leap that expands the frontal lobe...a voice
calls down an endless passageway, a spinning downdrifting
flashing as Dean Herron struggles back across the river
Styx, as he fights his way back up the sheer ebony walls
of a bottomless pit, swarming toward the top, toward the
light, toward life...

"He'll live," says Kemp, pulling the face mask away.

"How long was he dead?" asks the anesthetist.

"Perhaps too long. He may live and be a
vegetable. I don't know."

And on the table, Dean Herron...once-dead, reclaimed
from a place for which there are no round-trip tickets.

Herron starts toward recovery. At first it seems
he may lose the use of his left side---paralysis. But he
pushes himself, and his strength asserts itself. Slowly,
with certain faculties lagging, he recovers. Lying in a
hospital bed, swathed in bandages, he is attended by
Kemp (who has become unaccountably fascinated by Herron's
case) and a special nurse on duty, MISS SMITH. From time
to time Herron drops into a dreamlike coma. His recovery
is fitful, erratic, he isn't emerging from it all at
once, there is concern. His systemic reactions to the
wounds and the peculiar, singular operation Kemp performed
on him, are strange.

Then, one night, with the hospital silent around
him, strange lights begin to invade Herron's mind...he
sees rushing vortexes of color...the insane sound of a
monster wind in his brain...everything goes negative...

As we will see often in our story, Dean Herron is
undergoing the first of his PSYCHIC FLASHES, the strange
halations and physical manifestations that precede an
imperfect glimpse into the near future. This is the first
time he---and we---begin to suspect he possesses one of the
rare ESP powers, that he is, in fact, an ESPER.

Mental images flow like hot wax. They come in a
jumble, unsorted, terrifying, breath-catching, and then

they slow, and hold. He SEES:

     Miss Smith working in the supply room.

     A shadow across the wall.

     Miss Smith turning in fear.

     A man lunging at her.

He SEES it all in his mind, all in slow-motion, all without
sound, surrounded by halations of light, the focus changing,
the images sometimes indistinct, and then...before the
scene can play itself out, the rushing of the wind and the
soundless lights again...

     Herron tries to rise, tries to summon help.

     "Smitty!" he calls.

     But no one answers.

     He falls back, unconscious.

     When he swims up through the coma once more, Kemp
is there, leaning over him. He tries to tell the Doctor,
with halting words, urgency. Kemp pushes him back on the
bed. "You've been under for two days," he tells Herron.

     "Smitty...?" Herron struggles with the word.

     Miss Smith leans in next to Kemp. A bandage on her
forehead.

     "Two nights ago," Kemp says, baffled, "an addict
managed to get out of the police detention ward. He
tried to steal morphine from the supply cabinet. Miss

Smith's struggle with him brought help. He was caught.
When she made her rounds an hour later, she found you in
a coma."

They stare at Herron. Haltingly, he tells them.

"Did you 'see' Miss Smith in the supply room before
she made her first rounds, or after?"

"After."

Miss Smith and Kemp exchange glances. It is obvious:
Dean Herron "saw" her being attacked by the addict before
the event took place.

Herron lies back. Only his eyes and mouth can be
seen through the bandages. But the eyes are frightened.

Weeks pass. Herron is allowed the run of the
hospital; for reasons he won't explicate, Kemp wants
the newscaster to stay within arm's reach. Herron is
not inclined to argue: the incident of the addict and
the first psychic flash has him unsettled. Naturally.

Finally, Kemp calls Herron into his offices, and
they talk. The surgeon tells Herron that the operation
has apparently been completely succesful, but the
technique he used, the manner in which he brought Herron
"back to life" has troubled him. He's not at all sure
there might not have been brain damage due to loss of
oxygen. He hints that possibly...maybe...the psychic

flash and the coma were a result of what Herron had been
through. He suggests that Herron's brain may have
been (and he pauses, to select the right word) "altered".
He says that humans use only one-fifth of their brain
to perform all the acts their body and mind require.
It is possible the unused, closed-off four-fifths of
Dean Herron's brain has been tapped, that another part
of it is functioning. He asks Herron to keep in close
touch with him when dismissed from the hospital.

Herron stares at him, not answering.

He is having another psychic flash.

He looks at Kemp and says, "Have you been painting
in your home?"

Kemp nods yes.

Herron tells him, "Your son, he's in danger."

Kemp lunges for the telephone, calls his home.
There is no answer. Kemp calls the police, but Herron
stops him before he has dialed: "No; you want the fire
department."

Kemp places an emergency call, and they wait.
Fifteen minutes later he receives word that his five
year old son has been saved from a burning garage where
cans of turpentine and thinner have been stored.

The fire had just started when the emergency squad

arrived. How had Herron known? What had he seen?

He describes to Kemp a series of scenes he had "seen" in weird montage: a garage with a car bearing doctor's license plates. A shelf of paint supplies. A small child playing with matches in the garage. A fire.

Kemp is naturally shaken. Herron is frightened. Kemp postulates that Herron can see into the future; such a talent is not unheard-of. But the power seems to have some rigid limitations. The focus of the psychic flash is someone near to Herron—Miss Smith who had been doting over him, taking care of him...Kemp who had saved his life—and the visions are imperfect. Had the car in the garage not borne medical license plates, and had Herron not equated the psychic flash with the man sitting across from him, Kemp's son would have burned to death.

Herron has "seen" into the future.

Only fifteen minutes, but fifteen minutes that had meant the difference between life and death for a five year old boy.

Kemp wants to keep Herron there, to experiment with him. Herron refuses. "I don't want any more of it; it hurt."

Herron is released from the hospital, and returns

to work at the network. But his days are filled with
"psychic static". Walking a city street, he culls
flashes off passersby. He sees bits and pieces of their
futures. A woman passing: he sees a wheelchair careening
down a flight of stairs. A man passing: he sees a ski
patrol bringing someone down off a mountain slope in a
stretcher. Another woman: he sees a hand throwing rice at
a wedding. Another man: he sees a stock market report
with figures circled in red. Another woman: he sees a
camera and pictures being taken. Another man: he sees
a pair of roller skates lying unseen on stairs. And it
goes on and on. Endlessly. Herron is receiving from
everyone. Jumbled broken bits of lives-to-come.

Liquor dulls the receptions. He starts drinking.

Willis Damian finds him in the bar across from
the television station, looking deeply into a glass of
bourbon, smoking and trying not to pick up the future
of the bartender. Damian tries to talk to him, tries to
find out what it is that has changed Herron since the
assault in the street that night. Herron will not
respond. He snaps at Damian, telling him that the first
time the drinking gets in the way of his newscasting,
Damian should cut him loose. Damian bristles and
reluctantly agrees that that will indeed have to be the

case. He leaves, and Herron continues drinking.

That night, when Herron reports the news, another psychic flash occurs. He is commenting on the lighter side of the news, noting that the Luxor Bros. Circus is opening in the city, and that just as in years past, even with the deteriorating condition of world affairs, people still like a good circus. The first performance of the circus will be for the benefit of the city's welfare fund, and the audience will include two hundred orphans from...

Herron stops.

The lights. The vortexes. The wind. Negative. Visions, surrounded by flickering light: a man dressed in the manner of a circus roustabout, drinking heavily from a bottle of liquor...tent-top rigging fastened insecurely...a high wire walker putting stress and tension on the rigging...a great tent collapsing...wild animals leaping into the midst of bleachers and people...

He stares into the camera and his eyes re-focus. "Oh, God!" he blurts. He cannot continue. They cut to a commercial. Damian stalks onto the set. He is furious; Herron brushes past him; Damian screams after Herron that he's fired, he'll worry about the Guild regulations when he has to.

Herron flees the studio. Into the night.

He rushes to the circus. The performance is in
progress. He finds the owner and tries to explain to
him what he has seen. The ~~manager~~ owner listens, and
because this is Dean Herron, he checks it out. He stops
the high-wire acts before they go on, sends men up into
the rigging, and they check it out.

Everything is double-checked. Everything is in
order. The roustabouts and riggers come back down and
report everything is cozy in heaven. The owner is furious
with Herron for wasting his time. When he demands to know
how it was that Herron "knew" the tent was unsafe,
Herron makes a stammering attempt to explain without
saying he has "seen" it in a precognitive vision. The
owner orders Herron off the lot.

Herron goes back to his apartment, sits and
broods. He was insane to think that the visions meant
anything. Obviously some lingering fault in the post-
operative condition. But he still has static from
the people in the streets, and he goes into the bottle
again. The night passes, and Herron, knowing he is out
of a job...tormented by his condition...lies in the
silent room, trying to find surcease. Night comes

again. Herron goes out, walks where no others walk, to taste the night air, be alone, and most important—not to have to glimpse what others will live.

The late night papers are out. Herron stops and stares with horror at the blazing headlines:

CIRCUS ACCIDENT CLAIMS 23 LIVES

Dean Herron rushes to see Kemp. He tells the surgeon he knew about the disaster at the circus, but he had no way of knowing it was twenty-four hours _further_ into the future. Kemp argues with him about Herron's feelings of guilt.

"Dean, for God's sake, man, what could you have done, even if you'd _known_?"

"I should have been able to do _something_!"

"But you _did_. You went there. You warned the man. He was a fool for not listening."

"Kemp, for Christ's sake, he wasn't a fool, _I_ was! How did I expect a man to react to a wild story like that? What would he have said if I'd told him I'd seen the future?"

Kemp cannot respond. He knows Herron is right.

"The only reason he listened to me at all was that he recognized me from television."

"You can't pillory yourself for this, Dean. It

isn't rational."

"Rational? Tell me about rational! I'm going out of my goddam mind with this thing. I walk down a street and I see them, all of them, what's going to happen to them...and it doesn't even make sense most of the time... I don't see something clear and simple so I can walk up and say, 'Hey, lady, don't go out for a hot fudge sundae with your husband tonight, because you're going to have a crack-up and get killed at the corner of State and Main.' All I see is the sundae, or her husband, or the street corner. I can't take any more of this, it's sending me up the wall. I have to drink myself blind every night just to get some sleep! You've got to <u>do</u> something!"

Kemp is dumbfounded. "<u>Do</u> something? Like what?"

"Operate again."

"Don't be ridiculous."

"I'm losing touch, Kemp, you've got to go into my head again, set it right, whatever you did in there."

"Forget it. No chance. Jesus, Dean, I don't even know what I did the <u>first</u> time! It was a fluke. I couldn't <u>do</u> it again in a million years...surgeons may not figure out <u>what</u> I did for another million years." (even)

"I'm telling you you've got to save me!"

Kemp screams back at him, "You lunatic, what the hell do you want me to do, <u>kill</u> <u>you</u> again?"

Herron stops cold. He realizes what Kemp is saying.

He hangs his head. If he were a weaker man, he might cry. Then the gentle voice of Kemp reaches through.

"You've got something, Dean. Now you've got to either learn to live with it or let it kill you."

It is the kind of challenge a Dean Herron can understand.

Now begins the climb back up.

FADE IN a small office in the downtown section of the city. The glass door bears the legend:

TOMORROW, LTD.

We come in on Herron, sitting behind a desk, talking to an extraordinarily attractive redhead. He is saying, "I want to thank you for answering the ad, Miss Folb. If I decide on you, I'll call you by the end of the week."

The redhead smiles with heavy killowattage, gets up and rotates out the door, Herron preoccupied but taking note of the action. There is a knock on the door, Herron tells the visitor to come in, and the door opens to admit THELMA TUTTLE. In her early fifties, grey hair, snapping bright eyes, a little woman in the mode of

#81129

ELLISON / 21

Thelma Ritter or Sam Spade's old secretary, Effie Clinker.

"You advertised for a secretary," ~~Miss~~ (Thelma) Tuttle advises Herron. She looks around the sloppy office with obvious distaste.

"Yes, that's right," Herron smiles. "Won't you sit down, Miss...uh..."

"Thelma Tuttle. Mrs. Widowed."

"Uh, yes, Mrs. Tuttle. Well, won't you sit down, please." She sits, continues to look around. Herron continues, "What I'll need is someone who can handle correspondence from all over the United States, very probably all over the world. There'll be considerable filing, I imagine, and part of the job will be scouring newspapers for certain items which I'll——"

Mrs. Tuttle has been perusing the disarray in the office with some distaste. Now she has run her white-gloved hand along Herron's desk. It comes away dusty, and she frowns.

"Is there something wrong?" Herron asks.

"This is how you run an office? All this dirt? No wonder you need a secretary. Look at that over there...half a pizza left from a lunch. When was the last time you had a regular meal, not some send-in

#81129

ELLISON / 22

garbage?"

"Well...I..."

"A man **cannot** work a full work-day, and perform the way he should, eating irregularly. Do you eat breakfast?"

"I usually only have a cup of coffee."

"Heartburn."

"I beg your pardon?"

"Heartburn. Coffee makes for heartburn. Everyone knows that. You've got heartburn, right?"

"Well, a touch, every now and then—" Herron catches himself. The insanity of the conversation suddenly dawns on him. The woman is interviewing **him**.

"Mrs. Tuttle, why don't you tell me a little about yourself."

"What's to tell. I'm fifty-three years old, true age. Both my children are grown up and married, Beth lives in Tucson and Paul is in Chicago. (And I don't make a big thing about their not writing; they write too much already; they can't get it through their heads they're grown up and should let me live **my** life for a change.) I have time on my hands and I don't like it. I type eighty-five words a minute, hunt-and-peck, but I don't make mistakes. I know the Dewey Decimal System for book filing, so I don't suppose what you'd have can

#81129

ELLISON / 23

bother me too much. Now. What do <u>you</u> do?"

Herron smiles, picking his words carefully. "I'm
something of a consultant. People come to me with a
special kind of problem, and I tell them what the future
potentialities might be for their situation."

"You're a fortune teller."

"Not exactly."

"Listen, Mr. Herron--you <u>are</u> the Herron from the
~~advertisement~~ want ad?--by me whatever service you offer
people is fine, as long as you're legal and you care
they should get their full dollar's worth."

"I'm quite legal, Mrs. Tuttle."

"Then that's fine. All right, the first thing is
I should clean up this rotten mess. I'll need about ten
dollars for cleaning supplies."

"But I haven't decided to <u>hire</u> you yet!"

Thelma Tuttle looks at him as if he were a small
child. "Mr. Herron, let me apprise you of a thing.
I saw that pretty girl who just left. Now we both
know, if you hire a young cupcake like that, she'll
be attractive, she'll get your head all confused, you'll
have an affair with her, she'll mess up the filing, then
you'll do three or four weeks of terrible ambivalence

#81129

ELLISON / 24

figuring out a way to fire her without being left holding such guilt you could die from it, and you'll xxxxght be right back where you started, needing a secretary. So why not save yourself the aggravation and do it right from the start. Ten dollars should cover all the dusting and cleaning supplies."

#

Dean Herron is aware that the only factor in his encounter with the circus owner that got him as far toward communication as it did, was his recognizability as a TV personality. But that wears thin when you aren't onscreen every night. And additionally, a newscaster is not the most instantly-recognized figure...as opposed to a film star. So Herron knows if he is to put his wild talent to its best use, if he is to be of some service to himself and to the world, he must get publicity. He must become as well-known as a Peter Hurkos or a Criswell or a Jeane Dixon or an Edgar Cayce. He must become a kind of celebrity. In that way, much of the distrust and obfuscation will be gone from any case he may care to take on. And--as with Hurkos--it will bring him into contact with police and government agencies that might consider him useful in their problems. He has a handicap that can easily be turned into a talent both rewarding to him personally, and financially. But to do this, he needs a base of operations--the office and Mrs. Tuttle take care of that--and he needs to be accredited.

How does a precognitive esper get himself accredited?

He solves a big-publicity headline-catching case that has the police stumped.

This is the first step on Herron's road.

He scans the newspapers and magazines for days, trying to find something that fits his needs. On the fifth day, he finds it:

A fire-bomb attempt has been made on the home of ASIVO, a forty-year-old man who has become guru and spokesman for the post-hippie segment of the city's underground community. Herron reads the newspaper item and goes to the home of Asivo.

Asivo lives in the hills, has a following of very clean, very groovy young people who live in the commune-style household. When Herron arrives, he finds TV cameras at the commune, police and a woman named JENNA BOWEN, a Joyce Haber-style reporter, magazine writer and columnist, in attendance doing a piece on

Asivo. The police are trying to initiate protective
custody over the guru, but Asivo refuses their help.
His philosophy of <u>passionate determinism</u> is one that
says what must be, will be--but that every man must
surge <u>toward</u> that inevitability. The police are finally
hipped that Asivo knows if he is killed, he will become
a martyr to his beliefs.

Herron gathers this information from the TV
men at the commune, covering the story for the news;
they still like Herron, and they help him slip through
the police on guard, using his still-valid press credentials.

~~But~~ Once in the house, Herron meets Jenna Bowen
and Asivo. He is impressed with the man, who has a
quiet power about himself. Asivo never demands, he
merely asks. People <u>want</u> to do for him.

Herron explains to Asivo why he is there, what
his power can do, and asks to be allowed to hang around
until he perhaps gets a flash. Asivo is intrigued, and
bids Herron stay around.

The commune is filled with pretty young people,
many of whom are engaged in determining their destinies
passionately. It is a colorful and exotic scene.

But Jenna Bowen is suddenly interested in Herron.

#81129

ELLISON / 27

She knows of his past career, his accident in the street, his subsequent drinking, and his mysterious firing from a highly-lucrative newscasting job and his "disappearance". She has heard his conversation with Asivo, and she now smells another story for her column. Herron has his first really upsetting contact with disbelief, as Jenna tells him she can understand his spilling such a load of nonsense to Asivo, in the mistaken belief that the guru is himself a charlatan, and will respond to the gaff...but if Herron himself believes that drivel, she can understand why he was fired.

Herron and the girl strike an instant antipathy, and he leaves her with bon mots as deadly and insulting as her own.

But she is on to him, watches him, waits for him to make an ass of himself.

In case it was not obvious, Jenna Bowen is enough female to take a very strong, very sure man to tame. And she is that fraction of a millimeter more than merely beautiful that stops regiments in their tracks.

Herron wanders through the scene, sits in on a determinism session with Asivo and his acolytes, and then--

It comes.

A psychic flash. Strong. Compelling. Nausea, rushing wind, spinning vortexes, everything negative, and then the visions, in disjointed shimmering series:

A tombstone with an angel on the headstone. The angel is a small child. Herron cannot make out the name on the headstone...

A hand with a long white scar on the back, reaching into a box of odds and ends, coming up with a hand grenade...

A telephone repair truck...

And then the visions fade.

A tombstone? Whose? What does it have to do with Asivo? A hand with a scar? How did the owner of the hand get the scar? How do you trace a scar in a city of millions? A hand grenade? From where? How long had it lain in that box? And where is that box now? A telephone repair truck? Was it a vision of Asivo's future? Was it the next attempt on Asivo's life?

It has to be. Herron knows. From the episode with Kemp's son, from the episode with the circus, from the incident with Smitty.

Herron calls Mrs. Tuttle. He tells her to get
everything she can from back date newspapers in the
city on Asivo. Then he queries Asivo about any enemies
he may have. Asivo swears his life has been led with
purity, that he speaks of love and trust and has no
enemies. Herron leaves him with the line, "You have at
least one."

Herron goes to Willis Damian. He tells him he
needs to know everything he can about Asivo and anyone
connected with him. Damian is at first infuriated at
Herron's temerity, to come to him and ask for help,
after what Herron did to him. But Herron says, "Will,
I'm trying to be of some use to myself. I'm trying to
climb out of a hole. Maybe I'll never really be able
to explain what happened that night on-camera, but
I need your help. Please."

Damian accedes to Herron's request. He has the
network morgue opened to Herron, who gets Mrs. Tuttle
down to scour the records. He returns to Asivo's
commune.

Unable to reach through the guru's placid exterior,
Herron confides in Jenna Bowen, asking her help. He
has to locate someone with a white scar on his hand
before the second attempt is made. Finally, he gets

the girl to help him. She makes some phone calls, gets
in touch with a friend in personnel at the telephone
company. They go through their records for a man or
woman working for them who has been injured on the job.

They come up empty.

Jenna Bowen castigates Herron for being a clown.

But Herron knows he is on to something.

He takes to lying in wait outside the house, in
thickets, waiting. Two nights later, the attempt comes.
A man parks a telephone repair truck down the road, and
comes through the woods toward the house. Herron jumps
him. They struggle. The hand grenade!

Herron grabs it even as the man pulls the pin.
But the latch and primer have not been released.
Struggling one-handed with the man, Herron yells for
help. People pour out of the house. Jenna Bowen in
the forefront. Herron manages to club the man down,
and then screams for everyone to fall flat.

Then he hurls the grenade into the woods.

It explodes before it even hits the ground.

When the police are summoned, the killer turns
out to be a fifty-ish man whose teen-aged daughter
had been a follower of Asivo. Though the guru had
been down on drugs, the girl had been flirting with

#81129

ELLISON / 31

many "mind-expanders"--the guru's philosophy being only
one of her routes to self-discovery. One night, under
the influence of amphetamines, the girl had wandered
into traffic and been killed by a truck. The father,
an ex-steel foundryman who had been injured many years
before, thus explaining the scar, had blamed Asivo for
"twisting his little girl's mind". Deranged with sorrow,
he had attempted to kill Asivo with a fire bomb, and
failing that, had searched through a box of World War
II souvenirs, and found the grenade...that afternoon.

After work (he was a telephone repairman) he
had driven around summoning up courage to use the
grenade, and had finally come to his preordained
assignation with Herron.

Asivo, of course, feels this is only verification
of his belief that Man Must Move Rapidly Toward His
Destiny. Jenna Bowen knows it is otherwise.

She wants to do a story on Herron and his
amazing precognitive talent. He is delighted.

Headlines soon proclaim Dean Herron the man who
can see tomorrow...

And Tomorrow, Ltd. is swamped with clients.

Most are fat old ladies wanting to know their

#81129

ELLISON / 32

future. A few are people who fear for their lives. One
or two have interesting problems. We see Herron on a
typical day in his office, turning away most of these
because he either gets no flash off them, or because he
is not in the business of fortune-telling...despite the
sly winks of Mrs. Tuttle, who still believes it is all
a lot of funny hokum.

Mrs. Tuttle shows in a thin, trembling man named
CASTEN. He has called several times for an appointment
and been unable to get in to see Herron. Now he practically
forces his way in. The instant he comes through the door,
Herron's face goes white, he clutches the edge of his
desk, and sweat breaks out on his face. We HEAR and SEE
all the manifestations of a flash, but we DO NOT SEE what
precognitive information Herron has gotten. Casten is
talking, saying all manner of mad things, crackpot ideas
about an invention he's devised, how The Establishment is
rejecting him, how everyone hates him, how he needs to
know if he's going to be a success, about spiders, about
terrible dreams, about pain. Herron can barely contain
himself: he is in pain, terrible anguish. He tells the
man he can do nothing for him, that he sees nothing, that
he must leave at once. Casten tries to stay, grows
frantic, in every way makes a demonstration of himself.
Herron finally summons enough presence to literally eject

him from the office. When Casten is gone, Herron faints.
Mrs. Tuttle brings him around and is deeply concerned for
her employer. Herron, weak, goes back into his office
and Mrs. Tuttle follows. He tells her if Casten ever
calls again, he is not, under any circumstances, to be
allowed in. She asks why.

"The man is going to die," he tells her.

"Why didn't you tell him that?"

"Because of what I saw."

Mrs. Tuttle is almost afraid to ask what he saw.
For the first time she begins to suspect he may not be a
flummerer. "Wh-what did you see?"

"The end of the world. For him."

He is shaking. She doesn't press it. We see that
Herron is still not free of the terrible burdens glimpsing
the future can bring.

"Do you want to see anyone else today?"

"How many more do we have?"

"Just one. He'll be here in an hour. Why don't
you lie down for a while?"

Herron agrees, and rests. An hour later Mrs.
Tuttle shows in a fat man; P.G. ROTHWELL, a businessman,
a man with many holdings, all interlocked, all dependent
one upon the other to keep his empire afloat. He wants
Herron to tell him what the stock market will be like the

following week...if it goes the wrong way, if the wrong stocks are up and the wrong stocks down, he can be wiped out. Herron, weary from his experience with Casten, tells him, "Mr. Rothwell, nothing would pleasure me more than being able to hit you with a stiff fee for keeping you in business, but what I've got...the 'equipment' I use... is chancy. Sometimes, yes. Sometimes, no. Right now, I get no buzz off you. I'm sorry."

Rothwell leaves and Mrs. Tuttle tells Herron that Jenna Bowen has called. He returns her call, and she asks him if he would consider a quiet evening with a home-cooked meal worthy of his presence. With almost religious relief, Herron tells her after the day he's had, nothing could be more desirable. They make the date.

Herron goes to Jenna Bowen's apartment. She makes dinner for him and they spend an evening working into a romantic relationship. It is a cautious pavanne, one which Herron dances with care, for it becomes obvious that he needs a woman like this--someone to whom he can talk, in whom he can confide the rigors and horrors of a life spent endlessly as a voyeur of the future. She begins to relate to him, and he spills some of his fears, recounts experiences such as the one with Casten, and tells her that sort of thing happens too often.

To relate to him, to show him he's not alone with
those kind of Christ-feelings, Jenna tells him about how
she gets involved in her newspaper stories...for instance,
at the moment she's doing a ~~frrrrqmrt~~ seven-part series
(culminating with a Sunday supplement section piece) on the
life of HOUGHTON VEDDER, the billionaire. She tells Herron
what it's like to be in the Vedder household, doing an
in-depth series such as this, while Vedder pursues his
empire-building. She tells Herron about Vedder's wife, a
former screen beauty whom Vedder had married years before
and who has never made another film, a woman Vedder is
systematically grinding into the ground. Of Vedder's
five children--three who are older, from previous
marriages, and the two youngest, very very young, by the
current Mrs. Vedder. She says that having been around for
almost a month, Vedder's wife has made a confidante of her,
and she is experiencing the same feelings of agonized
empathy that Herron feels for the people into whose
futures he peers.

Herron understands, but says, wisely, "Life isn't a
comparison of chamber of horrors."

The evening progresses, and finally, Herron makes
love to Jenna Bowen. Even as they embrace, Jenna looks
at him and with dead seriousness she says, "If you ever see

anything about me...don't tell me."

      FADE OUT.

      FADE IN: Herron's office, several days later. Mrs.
Tuttle shows in a dapper, tailored man; Saville Row suit,
radiating quiet strength, English, the man is ADRIAN NEVILLE.
He introduces himself as a liaison man for Houghton Vedder.
He tells Herron that Miss Jenna Bowen has recommended him
on a matter of utmost importance to Mr. Vedder, and will
Mr. Herron please come with him to see Mr. Vedder?

      "I usually see clients here in my office," says
Herron. "That's what paying rent is all about."

      Neville is bland but firm. "Mr. Vedder's business
entails his being at the hub of his own communications
network at all times. I'm sure you'll understand."

      "Do you mind if I call Miss Bowen first?"

      "She is at present with Mr. Vedder."

      Herron shrugs, rises, and goes with Neville.

      To the airport where a Lear Jet is waiting, already
cleared on the runway for takeoff. The Englishman and
Herron get in and the jet instantly climbs into the sky.
It is a brief flight, but a colorful one, up the
California coast to Carmel, where Vedder's immense,
sprawling, San Sebastian-like refuge perches amid gnarled
trees on a cliff--El Dorado in the sky.

#81129

ELLISON / 37

They skim past the eyrie, into the nearest airfield, where a chopper waits. The helicopter lifts them and back they whirl toward the house on the clifftop. They land in Vedder's private heliport, and an open touring car carries them to the house. Herron notices that the CHAUFFEUR has a black eye, and bandages over one side of his face. He doesn't say anything, but he notices.

In the house, guards are everywhere...and men on telephones. It is a scene of panic. Restrained, well-ordered, wealthy panic...but panic nonetheless. Jenna is waiting for Herron. She tries to brief him on what's coming down, but Neville interrupts, says Mr. Vedder wishes to see Herron.

Herron goes with him.

Out of the house, through the grounds with their lavish appointments, down past the Olympic-sized swimming pool, past the tennis and squash courts, to a small gardener's cottage into which disappear a skein of telephone wires as thick around as a man's wrist.

It is a humble dwelling indeed for Houghton Vedder. Neville ushers Herron in, and in a setting more reminiscent of an English country cottage than the hub of a multi-billion dollar empire, Herron meets Vedder.

Aside from the half dozen telephones--each with its own push-button console containing ten lines--the cottage

#81129

ELLISON / 38

is rustic and quiet. Vedder is a huge man, as lusty in appearance as myth would have us believe are his appetities. He instructs Neville they are not to be disturbed, and Neville leaves. When they are alone, Vedder studies Herron. Finally:

"Can you do what the Bowen woman says you can do?"

Herron bristles. He instantly despises Vedder's manner. It is impossible for Vedder to speak to anyone as an equal. Herron stares at him.

"Well?"

"You mean Jenna Bowen, don't you?"

Vedder is incapable of understanding the gaucherie he has committed. "What...?"

"The Bowen woman. Jenna."

"Jenna."

"I don't know...what did she tell you I could do?"

"She says you can see the future."

"Sometimes. Imperfectly."

Vedder seems to be having difficulty asking what it is he needs to ask Herron. It becomes apparent that Vedder does not really credit Herron with the abilities Jenna has touted; he is a hard-minded businessman, and consulting

an esper is outside his ken. Finally, he muses, "Well, I've
used Rand to extrapolate for me, I've used water dowsers
and they've worked, I've got whole buildings of computers
that tell me which way to shake the tree...I suppose it isn't
any more fantastic to try you."

    "If I let you 'try' me."

    Vedder raises an eyebrow. "The check is blank."

    "I can be rented, Mr. Vedder. I can't be bought."

    "This is a personal matter."

    "Then why not tell me about it, and forget the clout."

    Vedder tells Herron that his wife has left him.
Herron is not entirely sympathetic; he can understand a
woman's rejecting a life peopled with Vedder, his toadies
and telephones. Vedder adds the woman has taken the two
youngest children with her. Herron suggests Vedder ought
to let her go: a woman who takes her children with her
when she goes is likely a woman not intending to return.
Herron suggests rudely that Vedder can afford the loss.

    "She tried to kill the children once," Vedder
says, softly. Herron glimpses what may be genuine concern.
"She tried to make it a triple, once. Herself and the
kids. The pulmotor squad got here in time."

    "And you think she may be trying again?"

    "I don't know. That's the future, isn't it?"

#81129

ELLISON / 40

"It might already have happened."

Vedder agrees, reluctantly. But he adds that none of **his** considerably able sources have been able to locate her, and if there's still a chance, he wants to take it. Herron asks when it happened, and what Vedder has done so far. Vodder says at first he thought it was a kidnap, and he "questioned" his own personnel, thinking it had to be an inside job. Herron remembers the battered chauffeur, and says wryly, "Yes, I saw your chauffeur. You have a lumpy way of questioning your hired hands." Vedder does not explain or apologize.

"And what makes you think **I** can find her when your other operatives haven't?"

"I don't know that you can. **Miss** Bowen suggested you. I'm willing to try anything at this point."

"I don't read minds. I'm not a clairvoyant, or a telepath, or a people dowser. I see the future...sometimes."

"Would it help if I took you to her room, to see her clothes, the things she left behind?"

"I don't know. It's always worked in the presence of the party I'm precoging."

They decide to try. Vedder takes Herron to the house and accompanies him as Herron submerges himself in the world of BETH VEDDER. Finally, he tells Vedder he wants to see anything Beth has written. A diary, letters, anything. Vedder is reluctant to acknowledge that there is anything of that sort around the house. Herron tells him to stop screwing around, if he wants Herron to try, he had better shape up. Herron isn't kidding. Vedder calls in Neville, tells him to go to the safe and get the diary and the note.

Neville brings them to Herron, who sees that the "note" is a suicide note left by Beth when she took the children and fled. The diary has been opened. There are pages missing. He demands the missing pages. Vedder puts up a fight, but finally gets them. Then Herron tells him to leave him alone in the library, so he can have a placid scene in which to try and obtain a flash.

Then with Vedder and Neville gone, Herron reads the note. It says explicitly that Beth has had enough, that she would rather see herself and the children dead than let them grow up under the same kind of torment Vedder has used on her for so many years.

The diary is a compendium of horrors. Vedder has, of course, been cheating on his wife, with an endless string of beauty contest winners, starlets, debauched nobility and casual strangers. As he reads the diary, evening falls, and finally Herron, sitting in the dusky library begins to get his psychic flash...

#81129

ELLISON / 42

The negative zone and the screaming winds and the
vortexes whirlpooling and the sounds of damned folk in a
black place, and then he sees:

A short order grill, with grease spattering on it...

The unmistakable shape of a giant brontosaurus, in
shadow, suddenly lit by flashes of light...

A woman's hand, stretched out on a floor, in a welter
of paper clips, clawing at the carpet in anguish...

A Raggedy Ann doll, being crushed underfoot by a foot
wearing a heavy lumberjack's sod-boot...

Herron comes back from that other place where his
psychic eyes have gone, and breathing heavily, tries to
regain himself. Save for the experience with Casten, he
has never had such an overpoweringly oppressive vision of
violence and imminent danger. He calls for Vedder, tells him
he has gotten a flash, says he doesn't know if he can locate
Beth, but it will cost the man a thousand a day, plus
expenses. Vedder agrees. Herron seeks out Jenna, and they talk.

He tells her what has happened, what he has seen,
and asks her help. She agrees. He tries to find out
from whatever clues she's amassed in the process of
writing the articles on Vedder, what leads to take.

Jenna is a thorough researcher, a good reporter.
She offers the following:

#81129

ELLISON / 43

Beth's last living family is her mother, now residing
in some small Southern town, Jenna doesn't know which.

Jenna has overheard Vedder talking to one of his
many mistresses, a girl in Los Angeles named HEATHER--no
last name--asking her to keep on the lookout for Beth.
Why Vedder should alert one of his paramours is something
Jenna cannot comment upon.

There are three older Vedder children, by previous
marriages. One of them, KATRIN, works in Las Vegas, at
one of the hotels. HOUGHTON JR. is in New York. VINCENT
is in Paris. Beth was close with at least two of them...
Vincent and Katrin.

Herron asks Jenna to get her locations on Beth's
mother and the older children. Without Vedder's knowing
of the inquiries. He stresses that this is of utmost
importance. Jenna says she will do it.

Herron then asks for and gets transportation back to
Los Angeles. Using his network associations he contacts
a gossip columnist named OLIVE FREED (we can substitute
a Rona Barrett or Army Archerd if we need this kind of
shtick). Calling in a favor, Herron wangles from her
the last name of the Heather Vedder had called. It is a
small-time actress known more for her commercials than her
acting ability, named HEATHER CLARET. Herron gets the

name of her agent from ~~Saxtx~~ the Actors Guild, and when he
calls, on the pretext of doing an interview, he is told
she is making a commercial that day at one of the studios.
Herron drives to the studio and we do a parody scene on
a popular commercial.

When Herron is finally alone with the girl, he does
not reveal why he is asking her questions, but he tells her
he is from Vedder, and he suggests she talk. She plays
very dumb indeed, says she doesn't know anything about
anything, and Mr. Vedder is wasting his time, as is Mr.
Herron.

When Herron shocks her with the note Beth left,
however, the girl breaks down and tells him what she knows
about it all. The year before, Beth Vedder had discovered
that Vedder was having an affair with her, and she had
come to the actress to...to what? Heather doesn't really
know. She suspects it was not to ask them to break it off,
because with Vedder's proclivities it would not matter
that he stopped seeing one girl, when there were so many
millions of others available to Vedder. Perhaps it was
to torture herself...or to firm up a resolve Beth had
made. Because the next day, ~~BXXX~~ Beth had made the suicide
attempt Vedder mentioned to Herron.

Then, a few days before, Beth and the children had

#81129

ELLISON / 45

appeared on Heather's doorstep. She wanted to borrow money
to get away from Vedder. Far away. Heather had given her
as much as she could spare—two hundred dollars. Then
—when Beth had left—two of Vedder's "associates", who had
obviously been trailing Beth, came to Heather. They
called Vedder, and Heather talked to him for only a few
minutes (the call Jenna had overheard), in which time
Vedder had warned her to be quiet about what had happened,
not to tell anyone that she had been visited by Beth.
A check for ten thousand dollars had been left by the
Vedder men.

Now Herron understands that Vedder <u>let</u> Beth go. That
he had tracked her—at least as far as Los Angeles. Why
is he now trying to find her? Did she slip his tail?
Is he genuinely concerned for the welfare of the children?
Herron doubts it, but he hasn't enough to go on. He
knows, though, that he is now being tracked himself...
that Vedder is behind him, watching him. To what end,
he does not know. But he decides not to let Vedder use
him as a pawn any longer.

How far will two hundred dollars carry three people?
Herron decides to find out...after he's made some small
arrangements.

He calls Mrs. Tuttle, tells her to get in touch with

#81129

ELLISON / 46

Jenna and to set up some way in which Jenna can transmit the names and addresses he'll be needing without Vedder's tracing the route of the information. Mrs. Tuttle says they'll use the one of her married children, Paul in Chicago, as a go-between. She gives Herron Paul's phone number. She assures Herron that she'll communicate with Jenna in a terribly circumspect manner.

Herron hangs up and addresses himself to the problem at hand: shaking the Vedder tail he knows is on him.

First he goes to his bank and withdraws enough cash to finance his peregrinations. Then he goes to his apartment and packs a bag. He calls Mrs. Tuttle again and tells her the bag is in the apartment, to get it to their go-between, and not to convey any further information over the office phone. From this point on, it will be all too easy for Vedder to tap the line—if in fact he has not already done so. Herron must gamble that it hasn't happened yet.

Then he changes into old clothes, almost derelict garb, and goes out the rear entrance of the building. He manages to establish that he is, indeed, being followed, and leads his stalkers to the downtown skid row of Los Angeles, where he manages to stage a fight in a soup kitchen bread line that allows him to slip away without a tail. Now he has to follow Beth Vedder's trail.

#81129

ELLISON / 47

Herron gets to Chicago, where Mrs. Tuttle's son,
PAUL, has word for him from Jenna, via Mrs. Tuttle.
Beth's mother is working in a diner in Stoneman, Georgia.
Herron leaves at once, after changing into the clothes in
the suitcase sent by Mrs. Tuttle. Remember this suitcase.

Stoneman, Georgia is a slat-back town of red mud
and rural prejudice. Jenna has traced Beth's mother
accurately, and Herron finds her slinging hash in a diner
at the edge of one of those concrete and chrome shopping
centers featuring 19¢ hamburgers, bowling alleys, food
giants, and tastee-freezi emporiums.

LUCY SEAMAN is a faded woman almost in her sixties.
Well-preserved, but held together by cooking grease and
the flickering hope that some day, maybe, a big man will
get down off a 16-wheel cab-&-hitch and see her, and take
her off to find a few remaining years of happiness.

The diner is a local hangout for the kids, and they
refer to Lucy as "Mom". When Herron approaches her,
asking for aid in locating her daughter, Lucy grows cold,
somewhat frightened, and refuses. Herron persists, saying
if she knows anything to please help him. She tells him
to go away. He refuses. One of the kids overhears. He
starts to brace Herron. Herron, not realizing either
the affection in which they hold Lucy, or the toughness

of these rural kids, fends the kid off. He is set upon by the entire bunch, and they beat him badly...carting him to the edge of town in their cars, and dumping him.

Later that night, Herron comes to in a ditch, and starts back for the diner. He arrives as the place is closing...and sees through the window, Lucy being talked to by two men. Well-dressed men.

They grab her and start to maul her. Obviously they, too, want information. And Herron sees the reality of part of the psychic flash he had in Beth Vedder's bedroom: Lucy Seaman suddenly flinging a scoop of hot grease from the griddle on one of the men. He falls back and the other pulls a gun. Herron crashes through the door. He manages to take out the two men, but they escape.

But because he has come to her rescue, Lucy Seaman is now prepared to listen to Herron. He convinces her he is out to <u>help</u> Beth, and her mother says Beth called from Chicago, asking for money for a long trip. Beth has been sending money regularly to her mother, and Lucy has been laying it aside for just such an emergency as this: she has known in her heart that Vedder was not the sort of man with whom her daughter could live a lifetime in safety. She had sent the money...several thousand dollars. And Beth was to call the tomorrow morning, to

#81129

ELLISON / 49

let her mother know where she was going, that she got
the money, that everything is all right. Herron asks if
Lucy will let him talk to Beth when she calls. Lucy says
yes. That means Herron has to spend the night in Stoneman.
But he now knows that someone is trailing him again. Very
probably Vedder's men. He cannot stay with Mrs. Seaman...
but he has to be near enough to help her in case of
trouble.

She says she may be able to solve the problem, and
calls one of the tough kids who had done in Herron earlier.
Several of them arrive at the diner, she tells them that
Mr. Herron is a friend, that she might need some of them to
stay at her home for the night, and would they mind helping?
They look on Herron with suspicion, but agree.

Herron goes to the home of the one of the kids, sacks
out, and the others stay with Lucy Seaman. Next morning
Herron is there to take the call when Beth checks in.
She is in Chicago. He begs her to wait there for him,
that he will be there that day, first flight in, where
can he meet her.

She says the Chicago Museum of Natural History,
he tells her what he looks like, and because her mother has
vouched for him, she agrees to meet him. Herron leaves,
with the kids racing their cars to the nearest airport

so he can make the next flight.

Chicago. Herron checks in with Paul, finds a series
of messages from Jenna and Mrs. Tuttle. Among the messages
is the information that the deranged—seemingly deranged—
man who had come to Herron's office just before he met
Neville, the man Casten, the man whose death Herron xxxxxxx
foresaw with such terror, the man who ranted and tried to
tell Herron something...this man, this little man, is dead.
XXXXXXXXXXXXXXXXXXXXXXXXXXXXXXXXXXXXXXXXXXXXXXXXXXXXXXXXXXXX
XXXXXX Died in a terrible way, amid flames and molten
metal, in a factory. They were unable to even recover the
body from the slag bucket. Herron finds it difficult to
draw a breath for one moment. He knew. Could he have
done something? No, probably not...not without staying
with Casten full-time...not without getting another flash
than the one he had had: the flash that showed only bubbling
lava and the sound of a man dying...hideously.

He cannot think about it now. He has to meet
Beth Vedder.

He goes to the Museum. XXXXXXXXXXXXXXXXXXXXXXXXXXXXXXX
He meets Beth Vedder.

She says she doesn't want any help, that she was
about to disappear, never to be seen again, and had it
not been for her mother asking her to see this Herron,

#81129

ELLISON / 51

she would now be long-gone like a big-bottomed bird.
Herron insists he can help her...but the strange thing is
that he was <u>certain</u> he would get a precognitive flash from
her; but he is receiving nothing like that. Perhaps her
way <u>is</u> best. She starts to walk away, and Herron sees,
past her, coming through the gallery featuring the
coelacanths, the two men from the diner in Stoneman.
He dashes for Beth Vedder, grabs her, even as the two men
see her, and pulls her through a service door.

They hide out in the Museum. (This can be mocked-up
or location-shot, but either way I need to get in touch
with Chicago's Museum to effect a <u>modus operandi</u> for this,
mechanically.) When they emerge, night has fallen, and
Beth Vedder has told Herron no more about her reasons for
running away than he knew already. Save now he is sure
she will not kill the children. He cannot say why he knows
this, but the woman seems too rational, too well-
ordered for anything as insane as infanticide.

They emerge into the Museum and walk silently through
the darkened galleries. Suddenly, Herron stops.

He looks up at the shape of a giant brontosaurus.
And the psychic flash he had in Beth's bedroom asserts
itself. "Drop!" he commands her. They fall to the floor
even as the gunshots ring out. His vision...a saurian...
flashes of light...gunshots...

#81129

ELLISON / 52

A running and hiding, seek-and-destroy scene ensues, among the bizarre shapes and reconstructed horrors of the Age of Reptiles. Herron manages to get Beth Vedder out through a window, even as night guards rush to the scene and shoot down the two stalkers. Herron is taken into custody, and instead of calling an attorney, calls Vedder in California.

He is out in a matter of hours, and winging his way back to California. Beth Vedder is gone once again. Vedder's car is waiting for Herron at the LA International, but Herron puts the chauffeur up against the side of the vehicle and tells him, "Go back and tell The Man I'll get to him when I'm ready. And if he puts anybody else on my back, I can't guarantee the shape he'll be in when he crawls back."

Then he goes with Jenna—whom he had called to pick him up—and they start trying to put the puzzle together.

Hip-deep in clippings and wirepress stories on Vedder, they look for a clue...something...with the sure knowledge that there are still two scenes out of that first psychic flash that have not yet occured.

One of the news items is the story of a raid Vedder had made into a small munitions and arms company, and how he had taken it over. The firm was DRAKE & CASTEN,

ELLISON / 53

MUNITIONS. The name Casten again. Again and again and
now for the third time, again. Casten...dead...let's check
the records and find out if...ah, there it is...the other
two partners in the original firm, WALLACE DRAKE and JOSEF
LA BADO...their obituaries...both dead...now, Casten is dead...

Herron calls Mrs. Tuttle, to find out if there
was any possible way that Vedder could have traced him.
There is an audible click on the line. Herron hangs up.
He doesn't need to know anything more. The line had been
tapped when he had called to tell Mrs. Tuttle to pick up
his bag. Vedder's men had trailed him to Lucy Seaman.
They had gone on back to Chicago and waited. He had turned
up there, and they'd followed him to the Museum.

Okay. Now it's irrefutable. He'd known it all
along, but it had seemed Vedder had reasons other than
mayhem for following Herron. Now that is ruled out.
Vedder wants Beth dead. And the children? And Casten?

Herron goes to Vedder.

He broaches all of it. He says he wants to know
what is behind it all, or he goes to the police. Vedder
gets very nervous, tells Herron he has it all wrong.
He tells him that he, Vedder, had entered into some, uh,
rather "questionable" dealings with some gentlemen of
The Syndicate, to purchase property in Nevada, and to
cover his own ground he had had it signed into Beth's name,
through a series of interlocking companies. Now, with

#81129

ELLISON / 54

Beth gone, and her record of instability since the suicide attempt, and the nervousness of his "partners", Vedder has gotten word that The Syndicate is _itself_ looking for Beth. In desperation, _he_ _says_, he has been trailing Herron and hoping for his talent to stumble on his wife. But the strongarm tactics were by The Syndicate's men, whom he now ---reluctantly---must assume, are trying to kill Beth.

Herron doesn't buy it. Not for one moment. But he listens.

When Vedder is finished, Herron says, "I'm done."

Vedder is amazed. "What?"

"I said: I'm done. You'll get a bill from my office. It's going to be a stiff bill."

"But---"

"Goodbye, Vedder."

And Herron walks.

But Vedder watches.

FADE OUT.

FADE IN an EXTREME CLOSEUP of an alley mouth, dark and silent. Then suddenly, the brief xxxxxxxxxxxxxx brightness of a cigarette's glowing tip as it flares. CAMERA IN and IN till we get a CLOSER SHOT of a section of that darkness, and in the next light of cigarette we see a man's face. A hawk face. Alert. Predatory. The HAWK

#81129

ELLISON / 55

watches. CAMERA PANS AWAY from the Hawk, across the street.
To a car. CAMERA ZOOMS IN on a man sitting behind the wheel
of the car, apparently sleeping. But as CAMERA CLOSES we
see the man is only feigning sleep. His heavily-lidded
eyes, like those of a FERRET, are slitted, watching. The
Ferret is watching the street. CAMERA RISES and we see
the legend on the window of one of the offices:

TOMORROW, UNLIMITED.

CAMERA LOWERS and we have a LONG SHOT down the
silent street. Silent, save for the sharp clacking of
a woman's heels on concrete. And we watch as Beth Vedder
emerges out of the darkness, passes through a pool of
street lamp light, and comes toward Herron's office
building.

The Ferret emerges from the car. The Hawk emerges
from the alley. She sees them. She starts to run. She
makes the entrance of the building, just as they both
fire. She is caught in the crossfire, and falls. The
Hawk and Ferret jump back into the car, and are gone.

The body stirs. It moves sluggishly.

Beth Vedder drags herself into the building, and
into the stairwell. Up the stairwell as we CUT TO HERRON
sitting at his desk, tie askew, collar open, poring over
news items. There is a sound. He goes to the connecting
door to the outer office and pulls it open. Beth lies on

the floor, dying. The sound Herron heard was her fall as
she stumbled against the desk, knocking over a tea saucer
filled with paper clips, sitting on Mrs. Tuttle's desk.
She lies there, face down, her hand stretched out, lying
in a welter of paper clips. It is the third vision of his
psychic flash. The woman's hand in the paper clips, clawing
at the floor.

Herron goes to her, gets down on his knees, and
cradles her head in his lap. She's dying.

She stares up at him, and past him. Her eyes are
already glazing, she is blind, cannot see him. "Dean...?"

"I'm here."

"Th-the chil-dren..." she mumbles. "They have...
wh-what I g-gave them...Dean...ask Kit...Kat...the logging
c-camp...please, Dean...save themmmm..."

And she dies.

Dean Herron crouches there on the floor of his office,
memories whirling about in his head, the inert form of
a woman with whom he had shared a past slack in his arms.
And once again he realizes that even for a man who can
see the future, that future is too often immutable. He
was helpless to save her, to do anything.

Covering Beth Vedder's body with his jacket,
Herron calls Jenna, tells her what happened. Soon, she

arrives with a friend from the Homicide Squad, LT. RICHARD
FEE. Herron tells Fee only that he was working late, heard
a sound, and came out to find this woman dead. Jenna
looks at him oddly, but keeps silent. Fee says he will
take care of the body, but that Herron should keep
himself available for questioning. When the meat wagon
and the police have left, Herron relates to Jenna what
Beth said just before she died. Now, apparently, the
children are the key to the mystery; and if Beth Vedder's
dying tone can be taken as any gauge, they are in danger.

Herron runs the dying woman's last words past
Jenna again, and for some time they are stumped by the
reference to "Kit Kat". Then Jenna remembers that Beth's
--and the children's--nickname for Vedder's oldest
daughter (by the previous marriage), Katrin, was "Kit Kat".

They drive for Las Vegas immediately, knowing that
when Fee comes looking, Herron will be gone.

In Vegas they find Katrin Vedder singing in one
of the lounges at one of the major Strip hotels. (This
occupation can be altered to fit needs, but if she is as
stated above, we can use this as a guest vignette for a
star/singer.) She has changed her last name. Known as
KATRIN VALLEY, she has divorced herself from any contact
with her father. Though it is obvious she can never

ELLISON / 58

really escape her father, that he can buy whomever and whatever he wants, she has separated herself as much as possible. Herron tells her that Beth is dead, and katrin looks sad...but not terribly startled. She says k she knew it was bound to happen. Her step-mother was doomed, she says, ever since the suicide attempt the year before; then she confides in Herron and Jenna that she was never really sure it __was__ attempted suicide. The circumstances (from inside the house, where matters looked very much different from the way they looked to investigating police) were suspicious, and katrin had suspected for some time that her father had for some inexplicable reason tried to kill her step-mother and the two younger children.

Herron asks her about the logging camp, and katrin says it is an abandoned x camp in upstate California where Beth and she and the kids had once gone with Vedder's oldest son, Vincent, now in Paris.

Herron rushes to the airport with Jenna, and urges her to return to L to cover for him with the police while he goes to the logging camp.

But as they leave the Vegas Hotel, we see Vedder himself...what is he doing here? It can only mean he has tracked Herron once more. He enters the hotel.

#81129

ELLISON / 59

DISSOLVE TO Herron driving a rental car up through the backwoods of upstate California, toward the logging camp. When he arrives there, he finds Heather with the two youngest Vedder children. It is now apparent that Heather knows a good deal more than she was saying.

She breaks down and tells Herron that Beth had returned from Chicago--where she had secreted the children while meeting Herron at the Museum--and given her two thousand dollars, telling her to take the children to the logging camp, that someone who could be trusted would come for them. The person was Vincent Vedder, the millionaire's son, who would be coming from Paris.

Herron has spent time mulling the entire situation, as he drove to the logging camp, and he has constantly returned to the matter of Casten. What was it that brought the man into Herron's office, shortly before Herron had taken on the case? Was it coincidence? Herron thinks not. He doesn't fully understand the psychic nature of the power he now possesses, but he has now come to believe that there is a strange magnetism in his visions, a pull and tug that ties things together. If this is so, then Casten, Vedder, Beth, the children, all of it tie together in some weird limbo where his

mind makes connective linkages he cannot consciously
understand.

But what he knows now is that he must get the children
out of there, even before he can find out from them what
secret it was that Beth entrusted to them...knowing
she was marked, and hoping to reach Herron with the
final answers before Vedder could get to her.

He piles the two children, Heather and himself
into the car, and starts back down the corduroy road
to the outside world. The only road out of this
God-forsaken outback.

He feels they are safe now, that they've made it.

But as he drives, he remembers there is still one
section of the vision that he got in Beth's bedroom that
day now so long ago. One vision that does not fit in,
that cannot fit in. Beth is dead. Her life is ended,
so how could a psychic flash off her still be unfulfilled?

Is it possible...

His thoughts of Casten tie in suddenly, and he
realizes that yes, his powers are more complex. He
had received a flash not only of Beth Vedder's future,
but of the future of the children...by refraction!
The children are flesh of her flesh! They are still

#81129

ELLISON / 61

in danger. And as he realizes this, he suddenly shouts
to Heather in the back seat to jump, with one of the
children. He pulls open his own door and plunges out of
the slowly-moving car, even as a great tree at the side
of the road, half-sawed, topples, crushing the roof of
the car.

There are shots from the side of the road, and
as Herron grabs up the two small children and the four
of them plunge into the forest, he sees Vedder and his
Hawk and Ferret, dressed in woodsman's clothes, wearing
sod-boots and carrying rifles, dashing after them.

Once again, Herron's uncanny power has saved his
life.

Vedder comes after them, intent now upon closing
off the last exits to his secret, and his problem...
whatever that may be.

Herron now understands that Vedder will kill
anyone in his way, even the two small children.

And as they dash for safety, we begin the final
phase of the story, with Vedder and his assassins
stalking Herron and his group, playing the most dangerous
game of all.

#81129

ELLISON / 62

One of the children carries a Raggedy Ann doll, and
Herron recalls the final flash of the precog vision he had
gotten in Beth's bedroom: a sod-boot crushing a Raggedy
Ann doll. He ~~now~~ knows that whatever ~~the~~ secret Beth held,
~~now~~ the children now possess it...so Vedder will be tracking
them <u>first</u>, and Herron second. He throws the doll in one
direction, and they flee in the opposite.

Herron secretes Heather and the children in the
high branches of a felled tree. It forms a kind of nest
in which they are unseen from the forest surrounding.
Then Herron sets out to track the trackers.

The Hawk, the Ferret and Vedder are stalking them
through the snaggletooth stumps of a worked-over logging
preserve. And we see the final image of Herron's precog
vision as Vedder and his men come to a fork in the path,
see the Raggedy Ann doll, pick it up, look in the direction
Herron intended them to look, drop the doll, and start
down the trail. Vedder's foot crushes the head of the
doll...what Herron saw...

ARRIFLEX SHOTS with Vedder and his men as they
plunge through the underbrush, leaping over stumps,
casting this way and that for the slightest trace of the
quartet quarry. But Herron is in the opposite direction,
and we see him wrench a great branch free of its parent

#81129

ELLISON / 63

stump, frantically pulling the leaves and twigs off its length, sharpening the end of the now-recognizable spear against a stone. He turns, the shaft in his hands, a long, thick spear at the ready. Now he lopes off in the direction of the trail where he left the Raggedy Ann doll.

SERIES OF MOVING SHOTS showing Herron moving-in on the stalkers from a right angle, Vedder and his men fanning out. Then QUICK INTERCUTS as the Hawk and Herron approach one another, come closer, closer, and then break through a stand of foliage at the same time, each at the ready, very close. The Hawk glances back to see where either the Ferret or Vedder may be, then realizes Herron is dashing toward him across the open space, the spear aimed at him. He brings down the rifle to fire, but Herron has gotten the jump, and using the spear like a quarterstaff he slams the rifle up and around. The Hawk fires wildly, the shot caroms off a tree...

CUT TO Vedder, turning at the sound of the shot, calling for the Ferret, and plunging back the way they have come, to cross the Hawk's trail once more.

There is a scream from the ft forest, Vedder dashes toward the sound, breaks into the clearing and we see...

The Hawk, impaled by the spear, dead. Herron is gone.

#81129

ELLISON / 64

A voice from the forest: "It's not going to be that easy, Vedder!"

Vedder motions for the Ferret to go around to the right, as he goes around to the left. They'll encircle Herron, who <u>must</u> be in that stand of short timber ahead, for there is an escarpment rising up behind it. He has to be trapped between them.

CAMERA WITH FERRET as he breaks out parallel to the escarpment, trots through the woods and suddenly breaks right, heading straight for the timber stand and the rock wall. He reaches the escarpment, starts edging along to the right, bound to meet Vedder. CAMERA TILTS UP and we see Herron in the rocks above him, waiting. Herron hefts a rock. Then, as the Ferret—out of sight below camera —moves past Herron, he hurls the rock. There is a thunk! and Herron leaps down. He picks up the rifle. And he looks for Vedder.

But there is no Vedder. He has grasped Herron's strategy. He has gone the other way, toward the hiding place of Heather and the children.

Herron takes off at a dead run.

He emerges into the area of felled trees, just as one of the children, TEDDY, steps out of the hidden nest, followed by the other child, JULIE, and Heather. The child sees Herron and starts across the open space to him, when Vedder steps out of the trees.

They face each other, rifles lowered. Deadlock.

The child stops.

Vedder calls to the children. "Come here, kids. Come to daddy."

Teddy and Julie start toward their father. He holds the rifle ominously. Herron calls to them. "No, kids...we're still playing the little game...hide and seek with Daddy...come on over here with me..."

They stop, wavering, undecided.

Vedder calls them again.

They start toward him. Herron calls to Vedder. "Drop it, Vedder. Don't do it. Don't make me kill you."

Vedder laughs. "You're not going to kill me, Herron. How do you explain to the authorities that you killed one of the ten richest men in the world...in a backwoods accident? Don't be ridiculous. Back off, drop the rifle and go your way. I won't press you, and I won't follow you. It begins and ends right here."

"I'm serious, Vedder."

"I can see that, Mr. Herron. It doesn't impress me." He smiles at the kids. "Come on, Teddy, Julie. Come on to Daddy."

At that instant Heather emerges from the nest. "I can tell the authorities, Houghton."

He turns to see Heather...suddenly realizing who

#81129

ELLISON / 66

the woman in the car with Herron was...he turns the rifle
on her...is about to fire...Herron yells at Vedder...then
when Vedder does not lower the weapon, fires himself.

The blast catches Vedder in the side, the rifle
is spun out of his grasp as the shots hurl him across the
clearing. Vedder manages to get to his feet, takes off
into the woods, with Herron close behind. Herron tracks
him by the sound of crashing underbrush. Then there
is silence, and Herron has lost him.

Behind Herron, we see Vedder moving slowly toward
the esper, having slipped off the trail to ambush him.
Vedder pulls back a thick branch just as Herron turns...
and lets it fly. It cracks Herron in the face, and he
goes down. Vedder grabs up the rifle and is about to
shoot Herron when there is a sharp report, and Vedder
pitches forward. Heather comes out of the woods, holding
a smoking rifle.

"Now you'll have to explain," she says to Herron.
FADE OUT.

FADE IN Herron's office, days later. Herron is
giving the final story to Jenna, for the capper to her
xxx series. "Vedder had bought into the munitions firm.
The design for the automatic rifle xxx belonged to
Drake and La Bado. Casten was the wheeler-dealer.

#81129

ELLISON / 67

Vedder wangled the government contract, and it wasn't till
they were ready to ship the first batch that Casten and
Drake discovered the rifles had a flaw in the ejection
mechanism. They jammed. XXXXXXXXXXXXXX Drake and La Bado
wanted to pull them back, but Casten told Vedder, and
Vedder couldn't afford to lose the contract--and his reputation.
He let them go through. A company was wiped out in
Viet Nam. La Bado couldn't handle the guilt. He killed
himself. Then Vedder got nervous, and Drake was disposed
of. We'll never actually know if Vedder had a hand in it,
but the odds are yes."

Beth had found out about the awful thing Vedder had
done, and confronted Vedder with it. He said nothing at the
time, but later arranged what was to look like a suicide
for both Beth and the children. But at the last minute
Vedder found that the evidence that could reveal the
whole story--ballistics reports, La Bado's memos telling
of the testing results, other correspondence--had been
taken from the safe. He managed to save Beth before
the "suicide attempt" could be carried out. But Beth had
known her days were numbered, if Vedder ever got his hands
on the papers. X Where were the papers? She had given
them to Heather, days before Vedder tried to kill her.

#81129

ELLISON / 68

Beth had, of course, known Vedder was sidelineing
Heather; he had had many mistresses. But the years of
torment with Vedder had finally taken their toll, and
Beth had gone to see Heather...to see who she was...to
confront the failure of her marriage. It had been one of
those inexplicable female reactions, without logical
explanation, without authentic purpose. And somehow,
they had liked each other, had compared the unhappiness
each had known at Vedder's hands, and become friends.
So it had been in Heather's care that Beth had left the
papers: it would have been the last place Vedder would
have looked for them.

Beth had been saved by her forethought. By only
a matter of days...and when Vedder had realized the
papers were missing, by only a matter of minutes. Time
had passed...not much time...but enough to allay Vedder's
suspicions about Beth. He had been unable to extract
from her the location of the papers, and with that
uneasy truce Beth had thought she could at least raise the
children.

Then she had finally found love. With Vedder's
oldest son, Vincent. They had planned somehow to be
together. Perhaps in Europe, where Vedder would have a

more difficult time of locating them. Then Beth had
overheard Casten and Vedder in conversation---the former's
growing fear that though they had rectified the rifle
malfunction, and covered their tracks, that someone was
bound to investigate a debacle as awful as the one in
Viet Nam that had wiped out an entire company. And she
had heard Vedder order Casten's death. And known she
was now the last link with his secret...a link not even
her stand-off over the papers would permit to exist.

  So she had fled with the children.

  And Herron had found her for Vedder. Unwittingly.
She had left the children with Heather, told her to go
to the logging camp where Vincent would find them, and
sought out Herron, to seek his help and protection. She
had never made it.

  Now. Now, Vedder was dead. The entire story
was out. Now Vincent had come from Paris to get the
children, to try and piece together a life for them out
of the remains of the evil Vedder had used to hold so many
in thrall for so many years.

  And now Herron's first case was ended.

  Herron concludes his narration and Jenna suggests
they take a rest...together. The idea sounds fine to

#81129

ELLISON / 70

Herron, and they discuss it as they leave the office, descend to the street, and start toward an evening of good food and relaxation.

But as they walk toward Herron's car, they are passed by an extraordinarily good-looking young woman. As Herron turns to watch her pass, we suddenly get the precog vision starting again. The rushing vortexes, the screaming winds, the negative look of the scene, and then we get brief flashes of an apartment building on fire, a hand in a black glove reaching for a circuit-breaker, a mad dog leaping toward us with saliva and bared fangs, a jetliner taking off from an airfield...

And Herron leaves Jenna, rushes after the girl, yelling, "Miss! Miss, stop a minute, I want to talk to you..."

And Jenna watches as Dean Herron, the esper, moves through the now--toward someone's deadly tomorrow.

FADE TO BLACK

and

FADE OUT.

The Tigers Are Loose

Editor's Note: Not a Speck

"*The Tigers Are Loose* came in the wake of the murders of eight nurses in Chicago by Richard Speck," recalls Ellison. "There was a book done on [Speck] by the psychiatrist who had overseen his work-up, and who was—more or less—defending him." Ellison fashioned a fictional movie-of-the-week based on the penal psychiatrist's work, and even used his name for that of his protagonist.

"I wrote the screenplay as a pilot for an ongoing series, which would feature the psychiatrist who would go from prison to death-cell to murder-scene," said Ellison, who considers *The Tigers Are Lose* a forerunner to the countless television crime-procedural series now in evidence. "It was a new idea and everybody loved it," he recalls.

Ellison spent a year writing the movie, waging war with NBC Broadcast Standards and Practices, which considered the story too grisly for 1975 sensibilities.

"How about we just have [the killer] standing on a rooftop shouting, 'You're all dead now!'" Ellison volunteered eventually.

"Are you serious?" asked NBC.

"Abso-fucking-lutely," replied Ellison, "And that was the end of that; we came to a dead end. After years, the option ran out and I had a complete movie sitting there, so it went back into the drawer...until now."

"In retrospect, it drains the blood out of my head. I had been honed on the hard-boiled writers—Raymond Chandler, Dashiel Hammet, James M. Cain—and I knew the difference between reality and mushy, soft-heartedness. Boy gets girl, boy loses girl, boy gets girl; that's all [the network] really wanted, but they wouldn't tell you that."

Reflecting upon his screenwriting career, Ellison thinks, "I would have done much better in French film; the *nouvelle vague*. The films of that time all had an amazing edge to them—Godard was brilliant, Jules Dassin, Truffaut's adaptation of Woolrich's *The Bride Wore Black*—they all affected me deeply. I was mesmerized by their ability to do the dark side of the streets.

"Everybody over here was doing la-de-da. Very frustrating," he concludes.

ACT ONE

FADE IN:

1   LIMBO SHOT - BLACK FRAME

CAMERA MOVING IN THROUGH DARKNESS as we HEAR the VOICE of
Dr. Marvin Ziporyn OVER. All we can see is a faint ball
of light in the far distance, but the CAMERA SWEEPS IN
STEADILY till we perceive the light to be a man, standing
in the darkness that cloaks him.

                    ZIPORYN OVER
              (No echo chamber; Voice as
               though he was right beside
                         you)
          In Book IX of "The Republic," Plato warns
          there is a sleeping beast in each of us.
          When the beast is roused, suddenly we learn
          the name of the place where it slept.
                    (beat)
          Names like Attilla, Genghis Khan, Cesare
          Borgia, Adolf Hitler, Eichmann...
                    (beat)
          Less well-known names. Charlie Starkweather,
          nineteen years old; when the beast shook
          itself awake he went on a killing spree and
          slaughtered eleven people in less than a
          week in 1958.
                    (beat)
          Charles Whitman killed thirteen people from
          a clocktower in Austin, Texas. 1966. Richard
          Speck tied and murdered eight student nurses
          in Chicago. 1966. Charles Manson's beast
          was roused in 1969, and ordered up an orgy of
          murder that may have claimed as many as 35
          to 40 lives.
                    (beat)
          Lee Harvey Oswald, James Earl Ray, Sirhan
          Sirhan, Edward Bremer. Tigers. Wakened
          beasts.

                                        (CONTINUED:)

1   CONTINUED:

CAMERA HAS MOVED IN STEADILY throughout this DIALOGUE OVER.
Now the CAMERA MOVEMENT SLOWS so we have an opportunity to
see this man who has been speaking: DR. MARVIN ZIPORYN,
mid-forties, tall; a vitality, an energy, lying just below
the skin; regular features but hardly handsome; memorable,
yes, but hardly handsome. The jaw is strong. The eyes
seem capable of humor, but there's none of that now. He
looks directly at us. At you.

> ZIPORYN (CONT'D.)
> Kill them, you tell me. Strap them in
> electric chairs, slip nooses over their
> heads, burn them out, gun them down...
>   (beat)
> Put them away forever, you tell me. Pen
> them up. Send them into darkness. Get
> them out of my sight.
>   (beat)
> You're beautiful...all of you. There you
> sit, your gut rumbling from dinner, the
> dishwasher running in the kitchen, you can
> read and write and add a column of numbers,
> and you tell me kill them, jail them, keep
> them off the streets...
>   (beat)
> It's not that easy. I know you like easy
> answers, simple solutions, everything tied
> up by the final commercial so you can get
> some sleep. But it's not that easy.
>   (beat, angry)
> I have to deal with them! Not you. I have
> to talk to them, listen to them, see them
> in their cells, try to find out what woke
> the beast in them...otherwise none of you
> will ever be able to sleep.
>   (beat)
> But this time you're going to be responsible.
> This time you'll see it all, and you'll
> understand there is no one simple answer.
>   (beat)
> Here. Look at this. I'll show you how
> this story ends. You'll see it now and
> you can remember it...and we'll find out what
> you would have done...

Ziporyn looks to his right and CAMERA PULLS BACK so we
HOLD him DIMINISHED IN LIMBO, but a SPLIT-SCREEN INSERT
LIGHTS UP and Ziporyn talks OVER as we WATCH THE ACTION
in the INSERT:

2
thru
15

INSERT ACTION – MONTAGE – VARIOUS CAMERA SPEEDS

(NOTE: careful attention to good taste in the direction
of these scenes will substantially soften the
physical aspects of the action. This is of utmost
importance! While we are dealing with relatively
violent material, we must never glorify or "feed the
need" for violence. The very essence of this script--
and these insert scenes particularly--is the attempt
to demonstrate the roots of violence in our time without
promoting it in even the vaguest way. Camera technique,
blurred shots and misdirection--subtlety, if you will--
must be uppermost in the mind of the director and film
editor. It is a tightrope we must walk if the content
of social consciousness in this script is to be maintained.)

WHAT WE SEE: (pastiches of scenes we will see in their
entirety in scenes 158 through 182) A young man, attractive,
flashily-dressed, but possessed by a madness, a demon
of anger, rough-housing a young woman who clutches a
blanket around her as he hits her. The scene is dimly
lit, though it is daytime; floor-to-ceiling drapes are
closed, and sunlight filters through in an amber wash,
distorting the clarity of our vision. He picks up a
table lamp, almost without realizing it, and strikes
her. She falls. While it is clear she is unclothed,
the blanket covers her discreetly so only a long, naked
leg protrudes from under the oddly-tumbled heap. She
is dead, but we have avoided the blunt show of murder.
Suddenly a woman screams, the young man turns his head,
we see another young woman just coming through the
apartment door; police and Ziporyn rushing up a flight
of stairs; the young man dragging the screaming girl
toward the blanketed shape on the floor; he turns away
from her, drops her, at the sound of people running; he
rushes into the bathroom, locks the door; police and
Ziporyn as they break down a door; the young man
opening a small window in the bathroom, trying to
climb out; police at the bathroom door about to kick
it in; the young man crouched in the window estimating
the distance to the next building, the five-story drop
looking down to the glass skylight of a first-floor
roof; cops kick in the door; Ziporyn fights through,
sees young man; the young man jumps, grabs edge of
next building; Ziporyn reaches through window, trying
to grab him; a bandage wrapped around Ziporyn's hand;
young man slipping, turns at last moment, flings back a
hand, touches Ziporyn's hand, clutches at the hankie
or bandage wrapped around Ziporyn's hand; then he
falls; CAMERA TILTS CRAZILY as the INSERT FRAME NARROWS
TO A SLIT and vanishes and LIMBO EXPANDS to bring
ZIPORYN BACK INTO FULL FRAME.

(CONTINUED:)

2   CONTINUED:
thru
15   Throughout preceding action we HEAR ZIPORYN OVER:

                          ZIPORYN OVER
                His name is Lyle Simon. Twenty years
                old. I met him, I interviewed him, at
                the STATE   Training School at OAK
                MEADOWS a few weeks ago.
                          (beat)
                I've only seen him three times in my
                life, only talked to him once, but I
                knew he'd do something violent and
                terrible if he was turned loose.
                          (beat)
                I made a mistake, a stupid, tiny
                clerical error...an oversight...
                that's all it was...but he got out...
                          (beat; softly)
                A little mistake...
                          (beat)
                and he beat a girl to death with his
                fists, with a table lamp.
                          (beat)
                So why didn't I listen to you, why
                didn't I keep him penned up? Why
                didn't I keep the streets safe for
                you? Well, my friend, I'm not God.
                I'm only a psychiatrist; a prison
                psychiatrist, that's true, but only
                a human being. I make terrible tiny
                errors, like you.
                          (beat)
                And it would take a God to solve
                this problem...violence all around
                us.

16   FULL FRAME OF ZIPORYN IN LIMBO

as we return to the psychiatrist in full with the insert
gone.

                    ZIPORYN (CONT'D.)
                    (cynically)
Did you know that there are over ~~26,000~~ 25,000
psychiatrists in the United States and
the sad, sorry fact is that out of those
25,000 ~~~~ wizards only 200 or so do any work
in the field of penology or corrections?
                    (beat)
I'm a bloody expert at my profession...by
default. No one else'll go <u>near</u> it.
                    (beat)
Let me show you why. Then maybe you'll
understand why Lyle Simon is going to
slaughter an innocent girl and then fall
to his death by the end of this story.
                    (accusing)
And you'd damned well better stay there
and try to follow this. It's maybe the
first time in years someone's gone out of
his way to tell you the whole truth...even
when he knows you'll hate him for it.

This last remark is delivered almost resignedly, as Marvin
Ziporyn turns AWAY FROM CAMERA. As he does, the LIMBO
LIGHTS UP behind him and as he turns into the LIGHTED
SCENE, CAMERA DOLLIES IN RAPIDLY PAST HIM to HOLD on:

17   INT. CORRIDOR - DYKEMAN PENITENTIARY - DAY

Gray flat paint, very clean floors, well-lit. A series
of closed doors on the right side, a blank wall on the
left. Three PRISON TRUSTYS are down soaping and swabbing
the deck, two blacks and a white. As we HOLD MEDIUM
SHOT of this scene, a form walks INTO CAMERA and AWAY
from CAMERA. For a moment we think it's Ziporyn, but
then we realize it's a much bigger man, dressed in
prison gear. He walks toward the three trustys. One
of them, a skinny black dude named FRISKY sees him and
gets to his feet, drying his soapy hands on his pants.

                    FRISKY
Heyyyy, it's mah main man, the
mighty Moo-hahm-ed! Wass happ'nin'
Danny, m'man?

18   REVERSE ANGLE - ON DANNY

UPTILT ANGLE of the CAMERA gives the impression of Colossus
of Rhodes enormity of DANNY DARK. Ex-prizefighter, kisser
a triptych of every club brawl he ever had, nose skewed off
in the direction of Skokie, bright eyes, big hands like
catcher's mitts. He smiles at Frisky, they do a mock dodge-
and-feint.

                    DANNY
          Told you once, Frisky, I told you <u>several</u>
          times, my name's Cash-ee-us Clay.

                    FRISKY
          I got'chur Clay, baby!

                    DANNY
          You're too STONE skinny to run your
          mouth at me thatway. You better
          get back to your knees before they
          take away your trusty.

He moves on past Frisky, who grins and resumes cleaning.
CAMERA MOVES PAST WITH DANNY as we HEAR ZIPORYN OVER.

                    ZIPORYN OVER
          Take a look at Daniel Joseph Darckowski;
          used to fight under the name Danny Dark.
          Pretty fair light-heavy, worked smokers
          and prelims around the Chicago area till
          one night he had a couple too many
          boilermakers and used those clubs of his
          to break a guy's face in a bar on the
          South Side. He's just now finishing up
          the fat part of a 5-to-10 for manslaughter.

Danny comes to a door, stops, and starts to knock. The
plaque on the door reads:
                    MARVIN ZIPORYN, M.D.
                    Chief Psychiatrist

He's about to knock, when we HEAR the SOUND of hideous
screeching from inside the room. It sounds like banshees
who haven't had a good bowel movement since Dante took
his trip through Hell. Danny hesitates, screwing up his
face, but the noise goes on. Finally, he knocks. The
VOICE of Ziporyn from inside:

                    ZIPORYN O.S.
          Come on in!

                              (CONTINUED:)

18   CONTINUED:

Danny opens the door and steps through as CAMERA GOES WITH.

19   INT. ZIPORYN'S OFFICE – DANNY'S POV – WHAT HE SEES

Marvin Ziporyn, behind his desk, which is piled high with
case folders, a tape recorder, a dusty pipe rack filled
with battered pipes. A pair of skis leans against one
wall, which more or less explains the cast on Ziporyn's
right leg, propped up on some books on the desk. File
cabinets all over the room, pictures on the wall--Picasso's
"Guernica," Max Ernst's "The Nymph Echo," a detail from
Dali's "The Burning Giraffe," several others, all hanging
crooked. Ziporyn is trying to play a recorder, which
accounts for the screeching. Danny stands stunned, in
pain. Ziporyn catches the look, stops blowing, waves
Danny to a seat. Danny sits as Ziporyn tries once more,
gives it up as a bad deal and tosses the recorder onto a
window ledge.

                    ZIPORYN
          You know something, Danny? Vivaldi
          and Pergolesi were bloody geniuses.

                    DANNY
          I don't know them.

                    ZIPORYN
          They shared a ten-round card at the
          Masonic once.
                    (beat)
                    (almost to himself)
          Eleven-year-old girls in the court of
          Louis VII and Eleanor of Aquitaine
          could play better than Jean-Pierre
          Rampal...nuts!

                    DANNY
                    (very friendly)
          You pick that up on your vacation,
          Dr. Z.?
                    (he points to cast)

                    ZIPORYN
          I schussed when I shoulda slalomed.

                    DANNY
          Y'know, Doc, there's sometimes I don't
          understand a thing you say.

                              (CONTINUED:)

19   CONTINUED:

> ZIPORYN
> I had a wife once who said the same
> thing, Danny. So don't feel like
> the Lone Ranger.
> (beat)
> Now. What's up with you?

> DANNY
> (earnestly)
> Doc, I got your problem all figured
> out.

> ZIPORYN
> (amused)
> Yeah, huh?

> DANNY
> Right. I got your situation down tight.
> Look, it's like this: I'm up for parole,
> right? And I've gotta have your okay on
> my skull chart to get an early out, right?
> But you're worried if you put me on the
> street I'm gonna go out one night and beat
> somebody into the sidewalk, right?

> ZIPORYN
> So many rights couldn't be wrong.

> DANNY
> Okay. So how about this: I been here
> over eight years...I've had it. I max
> out in a year and eight months; a year
> from next Labor Day I walk out that
> gate free, no matter who don't like it.
> (beat)
> So I herewith make you a solemn and
> solid promise. If you clear me and the
> board okays the parole, I guarantee
> for a year and eight I don't touch
> but nobody. After that, it's my own
> time, I wanna clean some dude, it ain't
> gonna make you look like a bum.

Ziporyn looks at him with bemusement. He laughs lightly.

> ZIPORYN
> Danny, I'm going to miss you. You've
> been in the joint so long you're even
> thinking like a shrink.

> DANNY
> That mean you'll okay me?

(CONTINUED:)

19   CONTINUED: - 2

                              ZIPORYN
                    It means I'm inclined to think
                    you've smartened up pretty good
                    around here, Danny. Chances look
                    good. Anything else?

Danny stands up. Grinning. He extends his hand.

                              DANNY
                    Thanks, Dr. Z.

                              ZIPORYN
                    Don't thank me yet. You're still inside.

Danny shakes his hand, walks to door. Opens it.

                              DANNY
                    You ain't gonna be sorry, Doc. I won't
                    make you look like a bum.

                              ZIPORYN
                    That's the only thing that was worrying
                    me, Danny. Take it easy, I'll see you at
                    the hearing.

Danny starts to go, stops, turns back.

                              DANNY
                    I wouldn't mess with that flute no
                    more, Doc. It'll make your head hurt.

He goes out, closes the door. Ziporyn grimaces. He sits
thinking about Danny for a moment, pulls over his file
folder, makes a notation. Then, heaving a sigh, he gets
up and walks around the desk. He seems to be walking
well for a man with a skiing cast on his leg. He stomps
it several times, seems satisfied with the healing progress
and goes to the door. He goes out, carrying a folder.

20   INT. CORRIDOR - DYKEMAN PENITENTIARY - DAY

As he starts down the corridor toward a barred door at
the other end, a woman emerges from another office.
Ziporyn stops and the woman catches up with him. It is
ELIZABETH DE MARCO, 33, slightly taller than Ziporyn,
very serious features, conservatively dressed in a
pantsuit; not flashy or expensive. They nod at each
other.

                                        (CONTINUED:)

20   CONTINUED:

                              DE MARCO
              Marvin.

                              ZIPORYN
              Liz.

They walk side-by-side down the corridor as CAMERA GOES
WITH. There is obviously tension between these two. But
not animosity. Wariness, perhaps. But respect.

                              DE MARCO
              You going to see Berghoff?

                              ZIPORYN
              That's where I'm headed now. Need a
              lift?

                              DE MARCO
              If you don't mind seeing him together.

                              ZIPORYN
              Not a bit. It's a drive, why don't
              we get something to eat near the jail.

                              DE MARCO
              If you've found a decent restaurant
              within walking distance of the XXXX Scott
              County Jail, I'll buy.

                              ZIPORYN
              Nolo contendere.

They reach the barred door, each reaches for a key to
open it, they fence for a moment, then De Marco moves,
and opens it.

                                        CUT TO:

21   SERIES OF SHOTS - ARRIFLEX - WITH ZIPORYN & DE MARCO
thru
26   In the car, driving. Sitting across from one another in
      a small restaurant eating. Walking across a street to
      the XXXX County Jail. Being admitted to the security
      (Scott) section. Walking down a corridor side-by-side. Coming
      up to a locked door with a small window in it.

      Throughout this sequence of SHOTS we HEAR the VOICE of
      Ziporyn OVER:

                                        (CONTINUED:)

21   CONTINUED:
thru
26

ZIPORYN OVER

Elizabeth De Marco. Thirty-three years
old, married, three kids. Master's in
Social Work, wrote two standard texts
on socio-economic aspects of the penal
system, one on the psycho-history of
the criminally insane, working on a
fourth book about aversion therapy.
Chief Sociologist for the State.
            (beat)
Statistics prove the best prisoner
counseling relationships are a man
talking to a man; next best are man
to woman; next best woman to man; and
worst is woman to woman.
            (beat)
I'd like to be able to say Elizabeth
De Marco holds her job because of the
need for token women in traditionally
male jobs...but I can't. I'm not only
a sexist pig, but I've seen how badly
some women handle interviews vis-a-vis
male prisoners who've been locked up
without a woman. Unfortunately for
my chauvinism, it doesn't apply to Liz.
            (beat)
One afternoon I saw a hardcase rapist
make a grab for her across an interview
table. They took eleven stitches in
his right temple. She's a remarkable
human being.   (beat)
We don't see exactly eye-to-eye on what
prisons should do, what they're for and
what place prison shrinks have in the
correctional set-up. Liz really believes
all people are born beautiful, healthy,
good and loving and the only cause for evil
people is an evil society. She's hip to
genes and biology, but they're myths to
her, like the Great Pumpkin. I don't
know, maybe she's partially right; she
does a helluva job working her way.
            (beat)
I just wish I could be as sure of anything
as she is of everything. But I like her.
Probably more than she likes me; but that's
okay, too. It's not that we're on opposite
sides of the fence...we're just not on the
same side.

27   INT. SECURITY CELL - SCOTT COUNTY JAIL - DAY

CLOSE SHOT on the inside of the steel door with the tiny
window, as the door opens, revealing Ziporyn and De Marco
standing there. CAMERA PULLS BACK into cell as they
enter. It is dimly-lit inside the cell, and as the door
swings shut and locks, they stand there a long moment,
squinting, trying to see through the murkiness. Then,
slowly, Elizabeth De Marco exhales a word that is more
a sound than actual syllables:

                    DE MARCO
                  (unbelieving)
          Geeeeee-zussssss...

CAMERA COMES AROUND THEM as they stand there shoulder-to-
shoulder, staring at something. As CAMERA COMES AROUND
we see a tiny cell with a trough metal bunk bolted to the
wall, a lidless toilet, a sink with one cold water push-
button and a roll of toilet paper on the edge. A holding
cell in a big city lockup. A small window, screened and
high up, and a protected light bulb dimly burning in the
ceiling provide the only light. There is a resident in
the cell. It is the sight of that resident which has
them speechless.

                              (CONTINUED:)

27   CONTINUED:

EMIL BERGHOF is somewhere between thirty and forty. It's
impossible to tell. His hair is gray and lank, but his
gray face is that of a younger man. He stands facing the
east wall of the cell, holding a blanket up under his
chin with both hands in such a way that the first finger
of his left hand is free. With that free finger he is
making arcane motions toward the corner where ceiling and
wall meet. He is mumbling words we cannot make out, very
softly. He does not stop when Ziporyn and De Marco enter.

                    ZIPORYN
          Mr. Berghof?

No response. He continues his incantations. Ziporyn nods
to De Marco.

                    DE MARCO
          Emil? Emil Berghof?

No response. The two ~~men~~ look at each other, clearly asking
silently if Berghof is faking it. Ziporyn shrugs. He
walks to the bunk and sits down. De Marco leans against
the wall. After a few moments Berghof walks to the east
wall, rubs his hands and the blanket along the wall, says
more inaudible things, and then goes straight to the
toilet and gets down on his knees. He drops the blanket
and cups water into his hands from the bowl, and drinks.
Then he gets up and turns to them.

penologists

                    BERGHOF
          ˙Who sent you here?

                    ZIPORYN
          We're ~~psychiatrists~~, Mr. Berghof. We
          were asked to come and talk to you.

counselors,

                    BERGHOF
          There are people here...

He pauses too long.

                    DE MARCO
          People here...who...?

                    BERGHOF
          They're trying to get me. Maybe even
          poison me.

                              (CONTINUED:)

27   CONTINUED: - 2

                    ZIPORYN
The people who put you here?

                    BERGHOF
                   (affronted)
Of course not, don't be stupid! I was
put here by the police. Say, who the
hell are you? You're too dumb to be a
psychiatrist!

                    ZIPORYN
~~Then, you, understand, why you've been put here.~~

No one's too dumb to be a psychiatrist. Do you know why you've been put here?

                    BERGHOF
I'm supposed to've killed my friend.

                    DE MARCO
Alan Tattler? you mean

                    BERGHOF
That's my friend. I'm thirsty.

                    ZIPORYN
Did you do what they said? Did you kill
your friend Alan Tattler?

                    BERGHOF
Did I kill Alan?

                    ZIPORYN
Yes, did you do that?

                    BERGHOF
They say I did that.

                    ZIPORYN
Is that correct?

                    BERGHOF
Is it correct? Is it? Where's George,
and Bobby Harmon? Are they here, too?

                    DE MARCO
Yes, they've been charged, too.

                              (CONTINUED:)

27   CONTINUED: - 3:

> BERGHOF
> That's dumb. I'm supposed to've beat Alan
> to death, is that right? Boy, are you dumb!

> ZIPORYN
> Can you tell me about that, Mr. Berghof?

> BERGHOF
> Can I tell you about that? We were friends
> for a couple of months, we used to go out
> drinking a little. He lived with me over on
> Shattuck Street for a while, how about that?
> I'm thirsty.

> ZIPORYN
> Do you still live on Shattuck Street?

> BERGHOF
> Yes. I've lived there a long time.

> ZIPORYN
> Is that where you and George and Bobby Harmon
> had the fight with Alan Tattler?

> BERGHOF
> Where?

> ZIPORYN
> On Shattuck Street.

> BERGHOF
> I've been working at Lake Bend in Sloatsburg
> for the last couple of months.

> DE MARCO
> I thought you said you've been here in
> ~~Sloatsburg~~ *the city* for the last couple of months,
> where Alan lived with you on Shattuck Street?

> BERGHOF
> I don't want to talk to you two any more.

He goes to the blanket, lifts it, begins facing the east
wall and making his obscure circling finger-movements.
Ziporyn and De Marco heave sighs. They wait.

> ZIPORYN
> It'll be a long interview.

DISSOLVE THRU:

28   INT. CELL — DUSK

as the light dims in the window. They sit and watch Emil
Berghof as we

DISSOLVE THRU TO:

29   EXT. CORRIDOR — [Scott] COUNTY JAIL — EVENING

as De Marco and Ziporyn emerge from Berghoff's cell.
Ziporyn is rubbing his eyes with weariness. De Marco is
shaking HER head. The GUARD locks the door behind them
as they come TO CAMERA.

                    DE MARCO
          He wasn't faking it.

                    ZIPORYN
          No.

                    DE MARCO
          What's your recommendation?

                    ZIPORYN
          Not competent to stand trial. Commit
          him to maximum at the psychiatric facility
          so they can work with him, try to get
          through.
                    (beat)
          God, I'm beat.
                    (beat)
          You know the part I liked best?

De Marco looks at him with confusion.

                    ZIPORYN
                    (with a tone)
          After he killed him, how he asked George
          and Bobby Harmon if Alan would like a
          beer.

They walk toward CAMERA and INTO CAMERA as FRAME GOES
BLACK and we

                              FADE TO BLACK

                              and

                              FADE OUT.

                    END ACT ONE

ACT TWO

FADE IN:

30   SOLARIZED IMAGE - EXT. OAK MEADOWS CORRECTIONAL - DAY

The state youth correctional facility at Oak Meadows (in
an unnamed Midwestern state). It's a nice-looking place,
if you've ever been there; like a rustic summer camp.
That is, if you don't notice the maximum security building
off to one side, and the great gray laundry block. Dorms,
a lake with ducks and swans, fields, horse paths, kids
walking around. If you had to go to the slam, Oak Meadows
would be your choice. But OPEN on a SOLARIZED VIEW to
give it the momentary misdirected feel of "magic realism."

> ZIPORYN OVER
> This is the State Training School for
> Male Incorrigibles at Oak Meadows. I'm
> here three times a week. If it doesn't
> look like a prison, that's because the
> people here try to make it look like
> anything but a prison. It doesn't work:
>> (beat)
> Prison is any place you don't want to be,
> even if it's got a nice gym and cute swans.

As Ziporyn speaks OVER, the SOLARIZATION TRANSLATES INTO
NORMAL SHOT and we have an ESTABLISHING as Ziporyn's not
so late model car drives through the entrance and swings
around the winding road through the stately oak trees
toward the Medical Facility Building. CAMERA ON CAR as
it passes and we see Ziporyn driving, then CAMERA PAST
CAR to HOLD the Medical Building as we

DISSOLVE TO:

31   INT. CORRIDOR - OAK MEADOWS MEDICAL - DAY

CAMERA TRUCKING down corridor as Ziporyn walks into
SHOT and assays the benches on both sides, and a dozen
young boys, black and white but predominantly black,
just sitting and waiting. They wear regular street
        (CONT'D.)

                                (CONTINUED:)

31   CONTINUED:

(CONT'D.)

clothes, not prison uniforms. Among the boys is LYLE
SIMON. CAMERA HOLDS AN EXTRA BEAT on him, then moves
on having allowed us time to identify him as the young
man in scenes 2 through 15. Like Simon, all the boys
sit silently as Ziporyn and CAMERA PASS DOWN CORRIDOR
toward the door to Ziporyn's office. Ziporyn's VOICE
CONTINUES OVER all this action as he enters and door
closes behind him.

(CONTINUED:)

31   CONTINUED: -2

                              ZIPORYN OVER
                                (Cont'd.)
                    Do you still live at home with your
                    parents when you want to be out on
                    your own? You're in prison. Are you
                    married to someone you can't stand?
                    You're in prison. Do you spend all day
                    working in a windowless box, making
                    money for someone else? You're in
                    prison. It's anyplace you don't want
                    to be.
                    ~~OAK MEADOWS~~   (beat)
                    gets them as juveniles.
                    We're required by law to let them go
                    at age 21. That's my job here; to
                    see if they're ready to go...

CAMERA TO OFFICE DOOR, no name plate, as a young black boy
moves INTO FRAME and knocks.

                              ZIPORYN O.S.
                    Come on in.

                                              CUT TO:

32   INT. ZIPORYN'S OFFICE - DAY

Stark, empty, just a desk and a couple of chairs. A file
cabinet, some paintings obviously done by inmates. Ziporyn
is behind the desk, soaking his now-cast-less foot in a
tub of water. Desk piled high with file folders. Door
opens and the boy stands there. LESTER COOPER is 18, tall,
gangly, surly and hidden emotions all at once.

                              ZIPORYN
                    Come on in and sit down, Lester.

The boy sits down across from Ziporyn. He says nothing, has
his hands folded in his lap, looks at floor.

                              ZIPORYN
                          (opens folder, reads)
          MOUNTAIN   I understand you want to be transferred
                    over to ████ View, is that right,
                    Lester?

                              LESTER
                          (softly, doesn't look up)
                    Yessuh.

                                        (CONTINUED:)

32   CONTINUED:

Get Ziporyn's manner: he doesn't press. He talks softly,
without much inflection, takes everything that's said,
even contradictory, without vocal judgment. He draws out
the boy, lets him weave his own story. Lester is sullen,
slow, thick-voiced, as though he's just wakened from sleep
or is, in some emotional way, stunned. *Ziporyn plays casual
by continuing to soak his foot.*

> ZIPORYN *(MOUNTAIN)*
> It's nice over there at ~~Valley~~ View,
> is what I hear, Lester.

> LESTER
> Yessuh, it's nice.

> ZIPORYN
> You ever been there, Lester?

> LESTER
> Nosuh. I heard.

> ZIPORYN
> Well, that's a minimum security farm,
> Lester. Experimental. You know what
> that means?

> LESTER
> Yessuh.

> ZIPORYN
> What?

> LESTER
> (long pauses, slow)
> Nice.

> ZIPORYN
> Uh-huh.
> (beat)
> Nice. Well, that's a new facility,
> Lester, and they're taking over the
> people they think have the best chance
> of making good. You think that's you,
> Lester?

> LESTER
> Yessuh.

They continue talking in b.g. as ZIPORYN'S VOICE SPEAKS
OVER explaining what's happening, as though reading from
what will be his report on Lester Cooper.

                              (CONTINUED:)

32   CONTINUED: - 2

                    ZIPORYN OVER
          Lester Cooper is just eighteen, had his
          birthday here in ~~Oak Meadows~~ two weeks
          ago. Lester has been here almost two
          years. He's in for rape-murder. One
          afternoon when he was 16 he raped his
          sister and her girl friend when they
          came home from school. Then he used a
          paring knife to stab the girl friend
          to death. I once asked him how he thought
          the dead girl's family felt about it...
          meaning, didn't he think they'd be sad
          at the loss of their child.
                    (beat)
          You know what he answered me?

OAK MEADOWS

                    LESTER'S VOICE OVER
                (obviously a memory voice)
          Oh, they cant's fine me. Mah fam'ly they
          moved t'nother neighbuh-hood.

                    ZIPORYN OVER
          Among my fellow wizards, we call that
          ~~disorientation reaction.~~ You might call
          it amoral. Lester doesn't <u>know</u> he's
          been a bad boy.
                    (beat)
          And before some one or the other of you
          starts running changes on how we ought
          to "put all them niggers in chains," you
          ought to know Lester's got an IQ around
          73. His EEG is normal for a 12-year-old.
          Only trouble is, Lester's 18. The fact
          is Lester has serious brain disturbance,
          probably because of malnutrition when he
          was a baby, not to mention lousy prenatal
          and obstetrical care. The fact is, Lester
          had eight major concussions before he was
          fourteen. You know what that means? Listen
          to this.

the ego defense of isolation.

brain wave

33   ANOTHER SHOT - FAVORING LESTER - REAL TIME - REAL VOICES

                    ZIPORYN
          Lester, can you spell "tiger" for me?

                                        (CONTINUED:)

33   CONTINUED:

Lester doesn't look up. He sits and is obviously thinking.
Hard. Finally, still staring at his folded and twisted
hands, he says, softly:

                    LESTER
          No suh.

                    ZIPORYN
          How much is five and five, Lester?

                    LESTER
                (long pause)
          Ten.

                    ZIPORYN
          Fifteen and eleven.

                    LESTER
                (longer pause,
                 painful)
          Twenny-six.

                    ZIPORYN
          How many states are there in the union,
          Lester?

                    LESTER
                (long pause)
          I dunno...some.

                    ZIPORYN
          Name me some of them, will you, Lester.

This is a long, painfully drawn-out answer.

                    LESTER
          Chicagos, Los Angeles...the United States.

                    ZIPORYN
          Can you spell "house" for me, Lester.

                    LESTER
          H...o...m...e...

They continue talking in b.g. as ZIPORYN'S VOICE OVER.

                    ZIPORYN OVER
          When you tell me to "put this nigger
          in chains," you're asking me to lock
          up a human being. One who cannot
          read, or write, or think complex
          thoughts. He is damaged. We stopped
          punishing damaged creatures hundreds
          of years ago.
                    (CONT'D.)

The only reason
he can add and
subtract is he needs
it for a job or to
buy dope on the
street.

                              (CONTINUED:)

33   CONTINUED: - 2

ZIPORYN OVER (CONT'D.)
None of which means a ~~damn~~ to the family
of that girl who was raped and butchered.
(beat)
So what's the answer? Where does the
main responsibility lie? To society,
that big wonderful nebulous thing that
collects our taxes and sends us off to
fight wars in muddy places? Or to the
individual? Or both? Or neither?
(beat)
Remember I told you ~~that~~ De Marco and I
had differing opinions? ~~De Marco~~ stand
is for the prisoner first, society next.
Mine is society first, the prisoner
next. Who's right? Neither of us.

Liz

Liz's

Return to REAL VOICES as Ziporyn and Lester finish their
talk.

ZIPORYN
Well, Lester, I don't believe I'll
okay this transfer.

LESTER
(surly)
Why?

ZIPORYN
Because you've been here close on two
years and you've been sent to isolation
11 times for causing trouble in school.
(beat)
Miss Unger has a lot of hobbies, but
getting her head slammed into the
blackboard beacuse she told you to
zip up your pants and sit down isn't
one of them. And I understand Miss
Horwitz had to hit the deck pretty fast
when you threw the eraser at her head.
(beat)
You're going to have to learn that you
can't clobber a woman just because she
doesn't hop when you say froggie.

Lester sits surly, staring at floor. Finally, he gets
up and goes to the door, stops, turns back, still stares
at floor.

LESTER
I ain't never gonna get outta here,
am I?

(CONTINUED:)

33   CONTINUED: – 3

>   ZIPORYN
>   (up front)
>   Probably not till you're 21, Lester.
>   Then we have to let you go.

Lester opens the door and goes out.

>   ZIPORYN OVER
>   And then you'll be back on the street,
>   Lester, no better than you are today.
>   And God help the girls who cross your
>   path three years from now.

>   CUT TO:

34   SHOT DOWN LENGTH OF BENCHES IN CORRIDOR

as Lester comes out, moves PAST CAMERA and the CAMERA
HOLDS the scene. Then, one by one, as the light begins
to dim in the corridor, one boy after another slowly
FADES OUT, giving us the sense of the passage of time
and the passage of interview cases in and out of Ziporyn's
office, until there is only one boy left. LYLE SIMON.
As he rises and goes to the door of Ziporyn's office we

>   CUT TO:

35   SAME AS 32

On Ziporyn, as he sits at the desk, rubbing his eyes.
All the file folders that were in one stack are now in
the "Out" basket. Only one remains in the old stack.
He is speaking into a Stenorette recorder. His voice
is dry and weary. It is dusk outside, as opposed to
bright, sunlit day as we began this sequence. The tub
of now-cold water sits untended beside the desk.

>   ZIPORYN
>   Despite Mrs. De Marco's recommendation,
>   I must strenuously disagree with the
>   findings on Joseph Evans. Technically,
>   my diagnosis is psychoneurotic depressive
>   reaction. His compulsive pattern of theft
>   and burglary is related to his need to
>   obtain dependency gratification by giving
>   himself objects since the world, in his
>   opinion, has refused to give him anything.
>   (beat)
>   From a psychodynamic point of view...

There is a knock on the door.

>   (CONTINUED:)

35   CONTINUED:

ZIPORN

I'll be with you in a minute. Please
wait.
              (beat; to machine)
...from a psychodynamic point of view,
Walter has never recovered from the shock
of his mother's death during his infancy.
In the perverse world of unconscious
thinking he has laid the blame for this
"desertion" on his mother in particular
and women in general. This feeling of
parental rejection has caused strong
feelings of inadequacy. What he's saying,
in effect, is that he was abandoned because
he was unworthy of continued affection
and deserved to be cast aside by his mother.
The domineering attitude of his grandmother,
with whom he lived, has compounded his
difficulty so that Walter has evolved a full-
fledged case of hatred for the opposite sex.
              (beat)
This is why he acts out against them by rape
and assault. The pattern is set. He has
raped three women and been apprehended each
time. Clearly, he wants to be caught and
punished. If released, he will continue to
assault women until he kills one, or may
develop into the kind of deviant who looks
to women for punishment: spanking, whipping.
              (beat)
He needs intensive individual psychotherapy.
In a separate facility. Here, he sees me as
a representative of the penal authority,
rather than as a doctor. He lies, gives me
the answers he thinks I want, and cannot
relate to me other than as One of Them.
              (beat)
Please talk to me about what facility would
be best suited for breaking through in this
case.
              (beat, wryly)
Not to mention which facility has a spare
broom closet or cubbyhole that isn't occupied.

He turns off the machine, rubs his eyes wearily, sighs
deeply, then takes the final folder. He glances at it,
then calls out.
                      ZIPORN
Okay, come on in now.

36   SHOT ON DOOR

as it opens and LYLE SIMON stands there. He is a very
good-looking white boy. Curly hair, bright eyes, a
ready smile, intelligent appearance, no animosity.

                    LYLE
          Hi. Doctor Ziporyn? I'm Lyle Simon,
          I was supposed to see you about a
          furlough.

                    ZIPORYN
Man,   Come on in. ~~Boy,~~ you're patient. How
          long've you been out there?

                    LYLE
          Since about two this afternoon.

                    ZIPORYN
          You're probably as tired as I am.

                    LYLE
              (sitting down)
          No, you're probably a lot more beat
          than I am. I counted. You interviewed
          seventeen guys before me.

                    ZIPORYN
          Well...you're the last. After we have
          a talk I can go home and collapse.

                    LYLE
          I know how you feel.

Ziporyn consults the folder.

                    ZIPORYN
VALPARAISO. They just transferred you over from
          ▮▮▮▮▮▮▮▮

                    LYLE
          Right. I was up for furlough there,
          but when I heard there was space here
OAK MEADOWS at ▮▮▮▮▮▮▮, I jumped to come on
          over.

                    ZIPORYN
          Oh? Why's that?

                    LYLE
          Everybody knows you got that new
          chassis dynamometer in the auto
          shop.

                              (CONTINUED:)

36   CONTINUED:

                    ZIPORYN
          You want to be a mechanic?

                    LYLE
          Beats running the streets.

                    ZIPORYN
          Beats somebody pee'ing in your pocket.

They both laugh.

                    ZIPORYN (CONT'D.)
          Tell me some stuff.

                    LYLE
          You tell me what, I'll be glad to tell
          you what you want to know.

                    ZIPORYN
          Well, your file isn't too complete.
          What about your family?

                    LYLE
          Seven kids. I'm number four. Two older
          brothers, one of 'em is doing time at
          Joliet. Four sisters, one three years
          older than me, two younger.

                    ZIPORYN
          That's only six.

                    LYLE
          Oh. Yeah. Uh, who'd I forget? Uh,
          Denise. Yeah, she's two years younger
          than me.

                    ZIPORYN
          Your father?

Lyle's face tightens slightly.

                    LYLE
          He took off.

                    ZIPORYN
          When?

                    LYLE
          When I was six. Good riddance to bad
          rubbish.
                              (CONTINUED:)

36   CONTINUED: - 2

As Lyle speaks, the ROOM BEGINS TO DIM until all we see is
Lyle sitting in the chair, in the faint light, while behind
him, where the office was a moment before, we SEE the
facts of Lyle's life acted-out as he remembers them. But
Lyle's VOICE FADES OUT as the room dims and we HEAR the
VOICE of ZIPORYN OVER, while we watch the action, Lyle in
the f.g.

> (As this scene-
> within-a-scene
> is played in the
> background,
> surrounded by
> shadows, we will
> be unable to make
> out details; merely
> suggestions of the
> violent activity.)

                         LYLE
                    (fading off)
               He was a real winner. Last of the
               gandy-dancers, you know what that
               was, a gandy-dancer? Railroad stiff.
               Wander from place to place working on
               the tracks...
                    (fades off as)

                    ZIPORYN OVER
               Case profile, Lyle Simon.
                    (beat)
               Father an alcoholic given to extremes
               of brutality when drunk...

We SEE the FATHER, a thin but muscular man with a nasty
smile, holding a YOUNG LYLE, perhaps four or five years
old, ~~the body had on side~~, meaty hand wrapped in the
lad's shirt. Holding him against a wall and ~~jerking~~ shaking
him ~~against it~~ as LYLE'S MOTHER, a sharp-featured, slight
woman, tries to interfere, to save the child. Father
backhands the mother and she falls among a group of LYLE'S
BROTHERS AND SISTERS. Lyle is ~~semi-conscious,~~ stunned.

                    ZIPORYN OVER
                    (CONT'D.)
               Father deserted the family when subject
               was six years old...sense of rejection
               in subject was profound though he hated
               the father. Saw strength in the way
               the father reacted to mother and sisters.

We SEE Father getting into stake-bed truck as Lyle bursts
out of screen door of house, chasing him. As truck starts
and tears out of the yard in a cloud of dust, Lyle tries
to jump on the bed, slips, falls, is left in the dirt as
truck vanishes, its tail-lights fading away. CAMERA IN
ON LYLE'S dirt-streaked face, age six.

                              (CONTINUED:)

36   CONTINUED: – 3

                        ZIPORYN OVER
                          (CONT'D.)
        Mother highly emotional, given to shouting
        and crying. Hypochondriac. Disciplined
        children using an ironing cord used as a
        whip. Favorite tactic: humiliating the
        boys by taking down their trousers for
        whipping.

We SEE the Mother throwing a tantrum because Lyle has
broken a jar of cooking fat all over the kitchen floor.
She goes for the ironing cord hanging inside the door
of the ironing board closet. One of the older boys
tries to get between her and Lyle, but she shoves him
aside, yanks down Lyle's pants—the boy is screaming *she raises the*
and trying desperately to keep his pants up—and ~~lashing~~ *cord to strike*
~~flashing him across the buttocks with the cord~~ *him; but*
before we see
it fall we slid
to the next
scene.

                        ZIPORYN OVER
                          (CONT'D.)
        Subject began petty thefts at age seven.
        Behavior in school violent and anti-social.
        Attacked a female teacher, became utterly
        uncontrollable, had to be restrained.

We SEE a seven-year-old Lyle stealing from the toy counter
in a Woolworth's, bracing a kid in the schoolyard for his
lunch money, running down an alley. We SEE a shrike-faced
TEACHER ordering Lyle to hold out his hands for a slapping
with a ruler, and Lyle grabbing the ruler, ~~swinging it~~ *flailing*
wildly, ~~against the teacher's arm,~~ the Teacher grabbing him.

                        ZIPORYN OVER
                          (CONT'D.)
        Subject placed in a foster home at age
        9 by court order. Attacked foster
        mother; punished by being dressed in
        skirts of step-sister and sent to school.

We SEE a nine-year-old Lyle being led out of the house of
his family, into the darkness. CAMERA INTO DARKNESS and
as it comes out we see Lyle attacking fat FOSTER MOTHER.
He is grabbed by a man, obviously FOSTER FATHER and is
slapped. CAMERA INTO AND OUT OF DARKNESS and we SEE
LYLE entering a school room dressed in a little girl's
blouse and skirt, CHILDREN laughing at him, Lyle's
face genuinely hateful, tears held back.

                                        (CONTINUED:)

36   CONTINUED: - 4

All through this SEQUENCE we SEE the present-time Lyle
sitting in his chair in Ziporyn's office, his mouth
moving, the DIM B.G. SOUND of HIS VOICE, but we cannot
make out distinct words. The only light is on the past-
time scenes behind him. He grips the chair's arms, his
knuckles white and CAMERA ROAMS LYLE so we see his face
at one point, his hands at another, tense, strained.

> ZIPORYN OVER
> (CONT'D.)
> Returned to real mother at age 10,
> continued getting in trouble...

And the CAMERA HOLDS LYLE as the B.G. SCENES FADE OUT and
we return to present-time.

37   ON ZIPORYN

As he sits back in the chair, obviously having been on
the edge of the seat listening to Lyle's story.

> ZIPORYN
> Your records aren't back yet from
> ~~Williamsville~~ Valparaiso. You'll have to fill me
> in on what they got you for.

> LYLE
> Oh, I was a jerk. I stole a car.

> ZIPORYN
> That all?

> LYLE
> (embarassed)
> Uh, no. This girl, it was her car,
> she came along while I was scoring
> it. She gave me a hard time...

> ZIPORYN
> And...

> LYLE
> I busted her nose.

> ZIPORYN
> Spell tiger for me.

> LYLE
> Huh?

> ZIPORYN
> How do you think she dug having her
> nose busted?

(CONTINUED:)

37   CONTINUED:

                    LYLE
Not much I guess. I'm sorry I did
it. I was a jerk.

                    ZIPORYN
Spell tiger for me.

                    LYLE
T-i-g-e-r. What's that for?

                    ZIPORYN
Just a thought.
          (beat)
Okay, Lyle, that's it for today.

                    LYLE
What about that furlough?

                    ZIPORYN
Not right now. I've got to go out to
Nebraska to testify at a trial. I'll
be back next Thursday; by that time
your records'll be here from ~~Nebraska~~ Valparaiso
and we can take a look at the situation
then. Okay?

                    LYLE
Well, I was hoping...

                    ZIPORYN
Best I can do m'man.

Lyle looks annoyed, then quickly covers it with his Mr.
Charm smile. He nods, stands.

                    LYLE
Okay, Dr. Ziporyn. I guess I can
wait. Thanks for taking so much
time with me.

                    ZIPORYN
Say hello to the dynamometer for me.

Lyle smiles, gives Ziporyn a buddy-bye gesture with
thumb&forefinger, and goes out. Ziporyn sits staring
at the closed door. The office is almost dark now,
as the sun disappears in the window behind him. He
clicks on the Stenorette, speaks briefly.

                                        (CONTINUED:)

37   CONTINUED: - 2

                          ZIPORYN
          About this Lyle Simon. No furlough for
          him yet.

As he speaks, light dims and dims in the office until we
can barely see him. Only the angry red light on the
Stenorette's off-on control, as CAMERA MOVES IN on that
red light.

                          ZIPORYN (CONT'D.)
          Couldn't get a handle on it, he didn't
          really tell me that much, just hints,
          some random, free-floating hostility,
          but I want to get into this kid's case
          a lot more before I turn him onto the
          street...
                          (beat)
          I'm whacked out; I wish ~~to get that~~ I
          didn't have to run my group tonight,
          but I suppose they want some attention,
          too...

As he is saying this last, the CAMERA MOVES INTO EXTREME
CLOSEUP of the red light and as Ziporyn's VOICE CONTINUES,
carrying over into the next SHOT we
                                        MATCH-CUT TO:

                      (MID-CITY)
38   INT. ZIPORYN'S ~~CHICAGO~~ OFFICE - NIGHT

MATCH ON EXTREME CLOSEUP of RED LIGHT. As Camera PULLS
BACK we see it's a flame in a cigarette lighter being
applied to a cigarette in the mouth of a woman, ELSA, a
group therapy patient of Ziporyn. CAMERA BACK to FULL
SHOT ESTABLISHING of the medium-sized office, from the
big window of which we can see ~~████████████~~ Avenue.   *a busy metropolitan*
The office is furnished with a random selection of sofas
and comfortable chairs that look rummage sale friendly.
In the chairs and on the sofas are eleven "patients."
All members of the Group. They will be identified as
we go along. The one who is speaking, whose VOICE FADES
IN as Ziporyn's voice talking about being exhausted
fades out, is LEO. Leo is about forty-eight, balding,
portly, a plumbing equipment salesman in a midtown store.
He has a Babbit-like manner, very authoritative.

                          LEO
          Well, I think Elsa's problem is very
          common. She doesn't like to be
          embarassed in public. I hate scenes,
          too, so I know how she feels!

39 SERIES OF INTERCUTS - ON GROUP MEMBERS
thru
44   as each one speaks, CAMERA CUTS to him or her in CLOSEUP.
~~Marsha~~ SHERRI answers Leo. She is in her late twenties, made
up rather flashily. Pretty under it all. Sensual, but
with the click of granite in her words. Chilly eyes.

                              ~~MARSHALLYN~~ SHERRI
SHERRI   You feel nothing, you fat clown!
                 The best you can feel is your own
                 lack of ego. How ~~would~~ would
                 you know how Elsa feels? Elsa's
                 what slobs like you call "plain,"
                 man, and that's—

ELSA is thin, waspish, archetypically a cliche of what
uptight librarians used to be. Thin lips, flat face,
no pazazz at all. About forty.

                 (Sherri)   ELSA
            Now, ~~Marshallyn~~, don't talk to Leo
            like th—

                              ~~MARSHALLYN~~ SHERRI
            Shut ~~Marshall~~ up, Elsa. You're not
            so damned disturbed, you're mostly just
            a bore. So you got embarassed at the
            party last week? So what?

DANIEL is a dapper little guy. He's been trying to raise
a mustache since he was fifteen. He's now thirty-five.
He thinks he's got good moves, but he's strictly zero.

                              DANIEL
            Oh, listen to the party girl. Just
            because you're a hooker, love, doesn't
            mean you understand human nature, right
            Dr. Z.?

CAMERA BACK as they all look at Ziporyn. He's obviously
got his thoughts elsewhere. He realizes they're looking
at him and snaps into focus.

                              ZIPORYN   (Sherri)
            How come you've got it in for ~~Marshallyn~~
            tonight, Daniel?

                              ~~MARSHALLYN~~ SHERRI
            Right at it, Marvin! This little creep
            tried to hustle me at the party; when I
            told him I'd charge him double the
            going rate, he went off and cried.

                                        (CONTINUED:)

107

39
thru
44 BEVERLY is about twenty-two, college-girl sort of thing.
    Pleasant, a bit chubby and worried about it, the sort
    of nice girl who makes herself a victim for guys. Obviously
    envies and despises ~~Marilyn~~ [sherri] for what she is.

> CONTINUED:

                         BEVERLY
            I'd cry too if someone wanted to charge
            me double for getting v.d.

And they all have at one another, all eleven of them
howling and shouting and rat-packing one another. And
as their VOICES FORM A B.G. DRONE we HEAR OVER a reprise
of the conversation from scene 33, the VOICES of Lester
Cooper and Marvin Ziporyn.

                         ZIPORYN OVER
            Lester, can you spell "tiger" for me?

                         LESTER OVER
            No suh.

                         ZIPORYN OVER
            How much is five and five, Lester?

                         LESTER OVER
            Ten

                         ZIPORYN OVER
            Fifteen and eleven.

                         LESTER OVER
                    (longer pause,
                        painful)
            Twenny-six.

                         ZIPORYN OVER
            How many states are there in the union,
            Lester?

                         LESTER OVER
                    (long pause)
            I dunno...some.

                         ZIPORYN OVER
            Name me some of them, will you, Lester?

                         LESTER OVER
            Chicagos, Los Angeles...the United States.

                                        (CONTINUED:)

39   CONTINUED: - 2
thru
44
                              ZIPORYN OVER
          Can you spell "house" for me, Lester?

                              LESTER OVER
                          (as voice fades)
              H...o...m...e...

Lester and Ziporyn's VOICES FADE OUT as the hullabaloo
of the group therapy patients rise up over. CAMERA FULL
as Ziporyn stands up, raises a hand. They all fall silent.

                              ZIPORYN
              That'll be it for tonight, people. I
              have to get up early for a trip to
              Nebraska in the morning. Why don't
              you all go on over to the Chinese place
              and have some coffee and talk over
              what went down in here tonight.

They all start to rise and leave, ~~some of them~~ stopping
to make some final teacher's pet remark to Ziporyn. As
they leave, in twos and threes, the SOUND IN THE ROOM
FADES INTO B.G. NOISE and we HEAR ZIPORYN OVER for the
last time.

                              ZIPORYN OVER
              God help them, they all need something,
              too. I just wish I could take their
              loneliness as seriously as they do.
                          (beat)
                          (angrily)
              Who the hell's in charge of this
              lunatic asylum?

He stands there behind the desk as we HOLD HIM and

                                      FADE TO BLACK

                                      and

                                      FADE OUT.

                    END ACT TWO

ACT THREE

FADE IN:

45   CITY STREET – NORTH PLATTE, NEBRASKA – NIGHT – ESTABLISHING

(WHAT WE SEE is all FLASHBACK, events that have taken
place eight months earlier, but we need not demonstrate
that at this time; it will become obvious in Scene 47.)

LONG SHOT ZOOMING IN STEADILY on a small restaurant amid
a group of other commercial buildings that are closed.
As CAMERA MOVES IN the front door of the middle-income
restaurant opens and a black man and woman, HARRY and
WILLA JOHNSON, emerge. They are in their sixties, and
they help each other as they walk, two elderly people
who have spent most of their adult lives together, in
love; companionable. They are kindly-looking and have
great poise, though they're obviously not too well off
financially. They walk down the front of the buildings
toward the parking lot. CAMERA IN ON THEM and HOLDS in
MEDIUM SHOT with them.

46   ANGLE ON JOHNSONS

as they near their car, an older model two-door. As
Harry starts to unlock the car door for Willa, a man
and a woman come out of the shadows between parked
cars. They are white, young, and they each have a knife.
They are GERDA and ALEX FOUCHE. They move swiftly and
silently to the Johnsons. Suddenly ALEX grabs Harry
Johnson pushes him up against the car. Willa is already
inside. As Gerda makes a move toward Willa, Harry shoves
the door shut, and Willa locks the door from inside.

                    HARRY
          Lock it! Lock it!

                    ALEX
          Gimme your money, nigger.

                    WILLA
              (muffled, from inside)
          Leave him alone! He has a bad heart!

                    GERDA
          Open that door!

                                        (CONTINUED:)

46   CONTINUED:

Throughout this scene, the sense of "distance-from-reality" is maintained by diffused light in the far b.g. that forms a bright fog of brilliance (as if we had placed several large kliegs or arcs in a wooded area and high-key lighted directly into the camera, thus throwing a nimbus of silver fog around the car that would tend to glare-out in specific areas. (NOTE: this technique of backlighting would assist greatly in masking the specific action that follows.)

     HARRY
     (terrified)
  Leave us alone, we got nothin' for you!

     ALEX
  I said give me what you got, boogie, or
  I'll cut your black throat!

     HARRY
    (scrabbles in pockets)
  Here...here...take it all...take it,
  jus' leave us be.

Through the brilliant light-ball streaming at us from the b.g., Gerda has rushed around to the other side of the car while preceding action and dialogue hold in f.g. The silver light shines through the car windows, making everything look ethereal. The other door is locked. Willa is inside, terrified, but yelling for them to leave Harry alone. Gerda comes dashing back around.

     GERDA
  How much?

     ALEX
    (viciously disgusted)
  Seven dollars, some change, and a lot
  of dust.

Gerda flies into a rage.

     GERDA
    (wildly)
  Dust! Dust, you cheap, lousy nigger!
  Dust to dust...

She lunges at him with the knife as CAMERA WHIPS ACROSS to Willa in the car and we see all of the action with Harry, Alex and Gerda as twisted reflections in the brilliantly-lit glass of the rolled-up car window. We do not, at any time, see the murder directly. But what
     (CONT'D.)

       (CONTINUED:)

46   CONTINUED: - 2

(CONT'D.)

we see--backlit and luminescent--is Gerda attacking Harry.
We HEAR Harry scream. And as though the scream has
triggered a response in Alex (which, as we will shortly
discover, it has in psychiatric terms), we see a movement
in the window of the car that could be Alex swinging his
knife-arm hard, underhand. We see no entry, but the
forms in the window clearly interpret as Harry slumping
over Alex's wrist, and we perceive the stabbing has been
fatal. A blur of movement as the two assailants continue
working over Harry (in the way psychomotor epileptics will
continue performing a given action with endless repetition)
as the CAMERA MOVES OFF REFLECTIONS IN GLASS and COMES IN
CLOSE on Willa's unbelieving face as she witnesses the
death of her husband. Yet all we see are the rapidly-
moving shadows in the window, played against that silvered
arc lighting in the far b.g. and the SOUND of Willa
screaming and crying. Finally, the action outside the car
ceases and CAMERA SLOWLY COMES BACK to FULL SHOT of Gerda
and Alex standing over the body.

ALEX
Get his watch...

Gerda bends, pulls the wrist watch off the dead man. She
holds it up to her ear to ascertain if it's working--cold,
chill, amoral--more frightening than even the murder--and
then looks directly at Willa.

As CAMERA MOVES IN PAST GERDA she slams her fist against
the rolled-up car window. Again and again. CAMERA IN
TIGHTER on the window and Willa's face until all we can
see of Gerda is her reflection superimposed over Willa's
face, highlighted by that faerie light from the b.g. and
we HEAR OVER the VOICE of the DISTRICT ATTORNEY (a very
distinct voice we have never heard before).

D.A. OVER
And all this happened eight months
ago, is that correct?

HOLD SUPERIMPOSE of Gerda's face over Willa's face as we
HEAR the speech above and we

MATCH LAP-DISSOLVE TO:

~~[scribbled out text]~~

~~[several lines of scribbled out text]~~

47   INT. COURTROOM – DAY – ESTABLISHING

    EXTREME/
MATCH-DISSOLVE TO CLOSEUP OF WILLA JOHNSON as the last
scintillas of reflection of Gerda's face fade from her
eyes and we HEAR the VOICE of the PROSECUTING ATTORNEY
OVER as CAMERA PULLS BACK out of EXTREME CU OF WILLA to
show us the courtroom in the North Platte jurisdiction.
Jam-packed courtroom, press reporters and photographers,
full jury, and Marvin Ziporyn sitting in the first row
behind the defense counsel's table. On the stand, a
uniformed police officer is answering questions asked
by the D.A. The cop is MEDEARIS. Fortyish, reliable.

                    D.A.
          Now, Officer Medearis, when Miss
          Milgrim and her fiance hailed your
          patrol car near the intersection
          of Phillips and South Jeffers, tell
          us what happened, if you will.

                    MEDEARIS
          Well, they said they saw this man
          and woman assaulting someone and
          it looked like a robbery.
                    (beat)
          So Officer Thatch and I proceeded
          to the parking lot next to Willoughby's
          Steak House where we found Mrs. Johnson
          locked in her car, and Mr. Johnson, the
          victim, lying on the ground.

                    D.A.
          What condition was Mrs. Johnson in?

                    MEDEARIS
          Hysterical. She was scrabbling at the
          car window like she was trying to claw
          through the glass but was afraid to
          open it.

                    D.A.
          And Mr. Johnson?

                                        (CONTINUED:)

47   CONTINUED:

                    MEDEARIS
          He was dead.

                    D.A.
          Were you able to ascertain from what
          cause?

                    MEDEARIS
                    (starts to answer)
          Multiple...

The DEFENSE ATTORNEY leaps up.

                    DEFENSE ATTORNEY
          I object, your Honor. Calling for a
          conclusion on the part of the witness
          that is more properly the province of
          an autopsy.

                    D.A.
          Your Honor, by virtue of the witness'
          eight years experience on the police
          force, he is an expert witness on such
          matters. It is my attempt here to
          illustrate that the very nature of this
          crime was so clearly brutal, even to a
          casual observer--and Officer Medearis is
          hardly that--

                    JUDGE
          All right. Prior testimony by the
          Coroner lays groundwork for such a
          line of questioning. But I caution
          the witness against overcharacterizing
          what he saw. Objection overruled.

                    D.A.
          To your trained eye, Officer Medearis,
          how had Mr. Harry Johnson met death?

                    MEDEARIS
          Multiple stab wounds in the stomach,
          chest, back, neck, groin, shoulder and
          face.

                    D.A.
          The Coroner has testified these repeated
          wounds were inflicted by more than one
          person. Do you agree?

                    DEFENSE ATTORNEY
          Objection!

                    MEDEARIS
                    (quickly)
          Had to be. High and low entries, front
          and back. Had to be!

48   ANGLE ON GERDA AND ALEX

at the Defense Table, Ziporyn behind them in the audience.
They look humble, quiet, hardly criminal, hardly killers.
CAMERA HOLDS THEM SEVERAL BEATS as we HEAR JUDGE'S VOICE
O.S. and the Defense Attorney sits down.

> JUDGE
> Objection overruled.

49   ANOTHER ANGLE PAST MEDEARIS TO D.A.

> D.A.
> Now, Officer Medearis, would you
> describe what happened next?

> MEDEARIS
> I called in for a backup and when it
> arrived about three minutes later,
> we left Mrs. Johnson and the dead man
> with the backup team.
>   (beat)
> We began a sweep of the immediate
> area and intercepted the Accuseds
> three blocks away, attempting to
> break into a parked car.
>   (beat)
> We apprehended the suspects and took
> them into custody.

> D.A.
> And what caused you to think the
> Accuseds were the assailants of Mr. and
> Mrs. Johnson?

> MEDEARIS
>   (amazed)
> You're kidding.

> JUDGE
> Just answer the question, Officer.

> MEDEARIS
> This guy here...
>   (he points to Alex)
> he was bloody all the way up to his
> armpits, and her...
>   (at Gerda)
> she still had the knife and the old
> man's watch! ~~And everything.~~ We had
> 'em dead to rights.

> DEFENSE ATTORNEY
> Objection, Your Honor!

SMASH-CUT TO:

50   INT. JUDGE'S CHAMBERS — DAY

Ziporyn sits opposite the Judge, who has his robes off.
The Judge is lighting a pipe. Ziporyn sits quietly,.
waiting. Finally:

                    JUDGE
          Dr. Ziporyn, you understand that
          if you testify as you intend, I
          will be forced to direct the jury
          to bring in a verdict of not
          guilty by virtue of insanity?

                    ZIPORYN
          I understand perfectly, Your Honor.

                    JUDGE
          You know these people are guilty.

                    ~~ZIPORYN~~
          ~~[struck out]~~

                    ~~JUDGE~~
          ~~[struck out]~~

                    ZIPORYN
          ~~[struck out]~~ I'd have to
          agree, from the evidence, ~~which is quite~~
          It's clear and full, ~~and~~ in no way even
          remotely circumstantial. ~~[struck out]~~ The Fouches
          slaughtered that old man. They are killers.
                    (beat)
          They are also ~~[struck out]~~ psychotic.

                    ~~JUDGE~~
          ~~[struck out]~~

                    ~~ZIPORYN~~
          ~~[struck out]~~

                    ~~JUDGE~~
          ~~[struck out]~~

                    ~~ZIPORYN~~
          ~~[struck out]~~

                                        (CONTINUED:)

50   CONTINUED:

                         JUDGE
                       (angrily)
          Don't play semantics with me, Doctor!
          Call it what you like, but it still
          means you're forcing me to put two
          butchers back on the street!

Ziporyn has pulled out his pipe and his pouch, makes a
motion indicating he'll accept the Judge's verdict on
whether or not he can smoke it in chambers. The Judge
glares at him angrily for a moment, then waves away any
objection. In this silent exchange we perceive the
relationships of power between the two men, and that the
Judge is the sort of man who probably will not let personal
pique affect his judgments. Ziporyn tamps the pipe full,
lights up, exhales a cloud of blue smoke that rises out of
the frame.

                      JUDGE (CONT'D.)
                    (half to Ziporyn,
                     half to himself)
          You wouldn't believe the sand they raise.
          "Why did you let that crook go free, why
          did you turn that monster back into the
          streets?" I'm even past worrying about
          what's going to happen at election time.
                       (beat)
          I tell them we're a nation ruled by laws,
          not by men...and they tell me about
          Watergate. I tell them it's not our
          right to judge by personal prejudice...
          and they tell me there's a 17% rise in
          crimes against property...
                       (beat)
          Do you know the latest? Eh? People are
          breaking and entering to steal <u>food</u>.
          Not a thing stolen, no TV sets, no stereos,
          just food. And sometimes they eat it
          right there in the kitchen of the home
          they've broken into. 17% in one year.
                       (beat)
          And you'll force me to let these two
          sick animals loose!

Ziporyn gets up, walks around the chamber, goes and stands
against the far wall, smoking, talking softly.

                        ZIPORYN
          Your Honor, the law in this state says
          very specifically that if an individual
          cannot conform his conduct to the
          requirements of law, by virtue of mental
          disease or defect, he shall be found not
          guilty.

                              (CONTINUED:)

50   CONTINUED: - 2

The Judge stares at Ziporyn with open hostility now.

                    JUDGE
          By God, Ziporyn, you've got more gall
          than any punk law student I've ever
          had in here!

                    ZIPORYN
          I'm not trying to quote scripture to my
          own ends, Your Honor. I'm merely saying
          you and I are agents of the law you
          represent, and I've bloody well got no
          choice in this! I'm a pathologist looking
          at a slide: cancer is cancer! I didn't
          make them sick, but the fact is that those
          two creatures out there are mentally ill!

The Judge's face sags. He is a man overworked, understaffed,
caught on the inescapable horns of a terrible dilemma.

                    JUDGE
                   (softly)
          This is a terrible thing, Doctor.

                    ZIPORYN
                   (just as softly)
          Do you want me to perjure myself?

                    JUDGE
                   (harder now; he's made
                    up his mind to confront)
          Don't push me, Doctor.
                   (beat)
          Just do what you have to do.

HOLD their faces in lines of resignation as we

                                        DISSOLVE BACK TO:

~~50 CONTINUED:~~

~~JUDGE~~
~~Irresistable impulse?~~

~~ZIPORYN~~
~~That is what my interviews with them convince me was the case. They know the difference between right and wrong, Your Honor, but their psychosis is mutually shared, they would have done it if there'd been a cop at their elbow. And that establishes prima facie case for irresistable impulse.~~

~~JUDGE~~
~~This is a terrible thing, Doctor.~~

~~ZIPORYN~~
~~I'm not terribly happy about it myself, Your Honor. Would you have me perjure myself?~~

~~JUDGE~~
~~We don't have to get smart-ass, Doctor. Just do what you have to do.~~

~~HOLD their faces in lines of resignation as we~~

~~DISSOLVE BACK TO:~~

51 INT. COURTROOM - DAY

CLOSE ON A PAIR OF LINED, WRINKLED BLACK HANDS as we PULL BACK and see they are Willa Johnson's hands, clasped on the table as she stares at the man in the witness chair. CAMERA PULLS BACK TO FULL SHOT so we see Ziporyn is that man, and the Defense Attorney approaching him.

DEFENSE ATTORNEY
All right then, Dr. Ziporyn, we've established your expertise. And you've said, in your opinion, Gerda and Alex Fouche could not help themselves, that they were driven by what you call an irresistable impulse. Would you explain what you mean by that?

ZIPORYN
What we're dealing with here, is the concept of "Folie a Deux." [pronounced: foe-lee ah dew]

(CONTINUED:)

51   CONTINUED:

Defense Attorney, feigning ignorance, leads Ziporyn to
elucidate the term.

> DEFENSE ATTORNEY
> Folie a Deux...I'm afraid I don't...would
> you explain that for us, Doctor?

> ZIPORYN
> Folie a Deux is a state of mental disorder
> in which two individuals share the same
> psychosis, the same world-view. In the case
> of the Defendants, it is a manifestation of
> mutually-shared paranoid schizophrenia.

> DEFENSE ATTORNEY
> And how is this condition manifested?

> ZIPORYN
> It can surface in many ways, depending on
> the relationship of the partners. It
> is common among siblings, father-and-son,
> and in this case, between lovers. Even in
> a common-law marriage relationship such as
> the one the Defendants share.
> (beat)
> The Fouches see themselves as "agents of
> justice." They truly believe they act in
> the name of God and society when they
> attack black people. Clearly, this is a
> derangement, but they think they're doing
> good. But there's something else even
> more important operating in their relationship.

> DEFENSE ATTORNEY
> And that is...?

> ZIPORYN
> A strong sexual imbalance.

> DEFENSE ATTORNEY
> I'm not sure I understand.

> ZIPORYN
> Well, consider several aspects of the
> crime itself. The female member of the
> partnership struck the first blow; later
> she cut off the tie of the deceased.
> (beat)
> These are manifestly indications of her
> attempt to impugn the sexuality of her
> lover, Alex Fouche. He, in response,
> was triggered by her actions, and in an
> attempt to assert his masculinity in her
> eyes, struck again and again.

(CONTINUED:)

51   CONTINUED: – 2

                    DEFENSE ATTORNEY
          Then you're telling us that a hatred of
          blacks and a castratory attitude lie at
          the core of this relationship?

                    ZIPORYN
          What I'm telling you is that the
          Defendants have elevated racial prejudice
          to a holy cause. Thus, they cannot, they
          are unable to conform their conduct to
          the requirements of law.

[handwritten margin note:] If there had been a police officer at their elbows they would have done exactly what they did. They are mentally ill.

Defense Attorney turns to the D.A. His look is tight,
but assured.

                    DEFENSE ATTORNEY
          Your witness.

                                        CUT TO:

52   ANGLE ON DOOR TO JURY ROOM – DAY

       as the jury files back in. They get seated.

                    JUDGE
          Have you reached a verdict?

                    FOREMAN
          We have, Your Honor.

                    JUDGE
          How say you?

                    FOREMAN
          Not guilty by virtue of insanity.

                    JUDGE
          So say you all?

                    FOREMAN
          Yes, Your Honor.

                    JUDGE
                (looking at Ziporyn)
          The Court thanks you and, under the
          circumstances, commends you on your
          verdict. While I'm not certain justice
          has been served in this matter, you
          have followed my instructions and, again
          with the Court's thanks, you are free to
          go.

53   ANGLE FROM ZIPORYN ACROSS COURTROOM

as the Jury files out. Gerda and Alex wait, with their
Defense Attorney. The D.A. is shoving papers into his
attache case angrily. Willa Johnson sits stunned, too
brutalized by events to move.

> JUDGE (CONT'D.)
> Now, with respect to the disposition of
> this case, it appears to the Court from
> the testimony I have heard, and from the
> pivotal report of the psychiatrist, Dr.
> Ziporyn, and from my own personal observation
> of the Defendants, that they are, indeed,
> mentally ill. Seriously so. So seriously,
> that returning them to society at this time
> would constitute a clear and present danger.
> (beat)
> I therefore commit them to the Dept. of
> Mental Hygiene, where they shall be placed
> under intensive psychiatric observation,
> care and treatment until, in the evaluation
> of this Court, they have recovered.
> (beat)
> And if I may add a personal comment...this
> day, and this verdict, will stay with me
> for a long time, and though the memory will
> sicken and sadden me, I suspect it will only
> be a shadow of the torment this poor woman
> has sustained, and will continue to suffer.

As he has been speaking, CAMERA HAS COME ROUND to HOLD
on Ziporyn, who now looks across to the prosecution
table, where Willa Johnson still sits, her eyes dulled
with tears, her hands twisted together like ropes, as
though she has been bludgeoned with a hammer and can
contain her anguish no longer. CAMERA MOVES IN STEADILY
ON HER FACE as we:

LAP-DISSOLVE TO:

54   INT. ZIPORYN'S ~~CHICAGO~~ [MID-CITY] OFFICE - NIGHT

LAP-DISSOLVE permits us to see the image of Willa Johnson's
blasted expression as a shadowy form in the window that
overlooks ~~Michigan~~ [the busy metropolitan] Avenue. CAMERA BACK SLIGHTLY to show
us Ziporyn sitting in the darkness, staring out at the [smoking his pipe]
lights of the Shore Drive, and Lake. ~~Michigan~~ Silence.
Then we HEAR O.S. the SOUND of the office DOOR OPENING.
It is closed, softly. Footsteps. A woman's VOICE.

> MARILYN O.S.
> Marv? Where are you?

55   MEDIUM SHOT - ACROSS OFFICE FROM MARILYN

It is Ziporyn's ex-wife, MARILYN. All we see of her at this point is a tall, slim figure, waiting beside the door, staring at the silhouette of Ziporyn, his back to her, staring out the window.

                ZIPORYN
                  (softly)
Don't turn on the light.

                MARILYN
What's the matter, are you ill? I came as soon as I got your message from my service.

                ZIPORYN
It was a long plane ride from Nebraska. I had too much time to think.

She picks her way through the office furniture, to the desk. She doesn't quite know how to respond, whether to touch him or just sit down and wait for him to talk.

                MARILYN
One of the bad ones?

                ZIPORYN
Yeah. I turned a couple of stone crazy killers back onto the street.

                MARILYN
                (familiarly)
Oh.

                ZIPORYN
You've heard this song before.

                MARILYN
                (gently)
Not in a while.

He turns in the chair to look at her, and the light from the street falls across her face and we see she is quite remarkably beautiful, the face of a model perhaps. The poise is there, the grace, the elegance. *He puts down his pipe carefully.*

                ZIPORYN
How've you been?

                          (CONTINUED:)

55   CONTINUED:

>   MARILYN
>   Okay. I'm working too hard, but that's
>   a song you've heard before.
>
>   ZIPORYN
>   Heard you were engaged to a cattle baron
>   from Argentina. Buenos Aires.
>
>   MARILYN
>   Copper. From Catamarca.
>
>   ZIPORYN
>   I must have missed a ~~New-Times~~ social
>   section one week. Sorry.
>
>   MARILYN
>   No need for sorry. It was over six
>   months ago.
>
>   ZIPORYN
>   How long's it been since we were over?
>
>   MARILYN
>   Don't take it out on me, Marvin.
>
>   ZIPORYN
>   That's twice I'm sorry.
>   (beat)
>   ~~Perhaps~~ Sometimes I don't know if any
>   of it makes sense. They were guilty,
>   red-handed guilty. I talked to them
>   in their cells; mad as mudflys. And
>   in a year, maybe less, they'll be out *of the nut-house,*
>   and doing it again, sure as God made
>   little green apples.
>
>   MARILYN
>   Have you eaten?
>
>   ZIPORYN
>   Something on the plane.
>
>   MARILYN
>   Come home with me, Marvin; I'll make
>   you something Julia Childs never heard
>   of and you can get some sleep.
>
>   ZIPORYN
>   How'd you like to take a trip?
>
>   (CONTINUED:)

55   CONTINUED: - 2

> MARILYN
> (after a pause)

Where?

> ZIPORYN

I don't give a damn. Anywhere. We'll
drive up to ~~Mondvachary, Lake Winnebago~~
maybe keep going right into Canada,
maybe keep going right to the North Pole.
A trip. Some air. Get away.

[handwritten: Silver Springs, Lake Laurette,]

> MARILYN
> (another pause)

All right.

He looks at her with pleasure. He wasn't expecting her
to agree. He reaches for her hand, she takes it.

> ZIPORYN

You don't have to get anything sorted
out, no meetings to put off, no deals
to stall, no showings to postpone...?

> MARILYN

My car's in the underground right across
the street; tank's full.

> ZIPORYN

Let me call Kenny, tell him I'll be
gone for a week or two, set him up to
take my interviews.

> MARILYN

I think this is why we got divorced in
the first place.

They laugh. Not hysterically, just with great resignation
that they are both career-people and if it wasn't one, it
was always the other. Marvin picks up the phone, dials a
number, waits.

> ZIPORYN

Kenny? Marvin.
> (beat)
Yeah, I got back about three hours
ago. Listen, I was thinking of cutting
out for maybe a week, ten days. Can we
rearrange my schedule, particularly at
~~Brownchardon~~ OAK MEADOWS?
> (he listens)

125

56   CLOSER ANGLE ON ZIPORYN - FACE LIT BY STREETLIGHT

> ZIPORYN
> Uh-huh. Uh-huh. That's good, yeah.
> Oh, and listen, get Lyle Simon put
> over till...
> > (beat)
> What!?! He was what!?! And who the
> hell authorized a furlough? I didn't
> want that kid out on...
> > (beat)
> De Marco. Yeah, right. Right. Okay.

He hangs up. He sits silently, staring at the phone.
CAMERA ANGLE WIDENS to include Marilyn.

> MARILYN
> I feel the cool breezes of the North
> Pole receding.

> ZIPORYN (REVERENTIALLY)
> ~~Holy Moses,~~ Dear God.

> MARILYN
> What?

> ZIPORYN
> I've got a time bomb out there at ~~the~~ OAK MEADOWS.
> ~~Christian~~ Kid named Lyle Simon.
> > (beat)
> > (angry with himself)
> ~~God,~~ What a jerk I am! I made notes on
> his case, recommended he not be given a
> furlough, then I went off and left the
> ~~damned~~ belt on the machine and didn't *leave a note to have*
> have it transcribed.
> > (beat)
> You remember ~~De Marco?~~ (Liz)

> MARILYN
> The ~~social worker?~~ State sociologist?

> ZIPORYN
> *Yeah. She* ~~Rep from the John Howard~~ okayed the
> furlough. Saw the kid's record was up
> for it and turned him loose.

> MARILYN
> And that's got you upset?

Ziporyn looks at her levelly.

> ZIPORYN
> I turned two killers loose already this
> week; I've got to make sure the count
> doesn't go to three.
> > (CONTINUED:)

56   CONTINUED:

CAMERA MOVES AROUND from Ziporyn's worried expression to
HOLD on the beautiful face of Marilyn as we:

                                        MATCH—CUT TO:

57   INT. MOTEL ROOM — NIGHT

MATCH—CUT ON FACE OF LYLE SIMON as he brings a very
expensive-looking reflex camera up to his eye and snaps
a shot. CAMERA PULLS BACK to show us this is clearly a
middle-quality motel room, with a couple of photographer's
lights on stands casting hard white brilliance around
the room. Shot after shot is taken as Lyle moves, weaves,
and CAMERA GOES WITH HIM, managing to show us only the
barest suggestions of a nude female body that he's
photographing. He keeps up a running line of patter as
he takes the shots.

                    LYLE
          That's it, baby. That's good, hold that.
          Now another one...terrific...you've got it,
          little mama...now wet your lips...okay,
          turn that way, give me some of that...right
          ...right...now a little backside...look
          over your shoulder...sensational...dynamite
          ...what a fantastic set this'll be...we'll
          both be running money like we never knew
          what it was...super, super...now arch your
          back...

CAMERA WHIPS AND DIPS to show us Lyle moving, moving,
and tantalizing bits of the girl, long hair, long legs,
and by incidento tolally naked.

                    LYLE
          Okay, now just sit on the bed and get
          your sensational little face happy. I'm
          gonna take a coupla dozen closeups of
          that mouth.

He moves in and CAMERA COMES AROUND so his head blocks
our view of the girl's face, as he snaps, snaps, snaps.
Then he stops, lets the camera drop to his side.

                    LYLE
          That's all of it, baby.
                    (beat)
          Marlene, you and me are gonna do real
          well together, mama.

                                        (CONTINUED:)

57   CONTINUED:

And CAMERA COMES IN FULL on MARLENE'S FACE. And we see
she is the girl from the opening scenes in act one, the
scenes Ziporyn showed us of Lyle Simon killing a girl.
It is the same girl. HOLD THAT FACE so we recognize it
and then:

                                        SMASH-INTERCUT:

58   SERIES OF RAPID INTERCUTS — 40 FRAMES PER SECOND

REPLAY of the ~~murdered~~ scenes from shots 2 thru 15, just
to kick us in the head and remind us this is the girl
Lyle Simon will murder at the end of the show.

                                        CUT BACK TO:

59   CLOSE ON MARLENE

as she smiles ~~suggestively~~ at Lyle, wetting her lips.

                         MARLENE
          You know, you're superneat, Lyle.

HOLD THAT FACE as we:

                                        FADE TO BLACK:

                                        and

                                        FADE OUT.

                   END ACT THREE

ACT FOUR

FADE IN:

60   INT. MAXIMUM SECURITY BLDG. - OAK MEADOWS FACILITY - DAY

EXTREME CLOSEUP ON A RED, FLICKERING BLUR - RIGHT INTO CAMERA

we are SHOOTING BETWEEN BARS toward the red glow as something
heavy hits the bars, shaking the CAMERA. As CAMERA FOCUSES
to show us a two-man cell with bunks, sink, toilet, usual
prison trappings we perceive that what hit the bars was a
3-legged wooden stool being held by a young prisoner, who
swings it again, bashing it against the enclosure as the
CAMERA CONTINUES PULLING BACK and we recognize the red
blur behind the prisoner as fire, leaping high in a far
corner of the corridor behind him. We HEAR the deafening
uproar of a prison riot and realize that the prisoners have
piled all their mattresses in a heap at the far end of the
max enclosure, and have set fire to them. They feed the
fire by throwing anything combustible on the mound. The
walls are covered with scrawled writing, filth, wads of
wet toilet paper. The PRISONER WITH THE STOOL wears only
jockey shorts. There is water on the floor, from someone
having hosed the corridor down.

As CAMERA PULLS BACK and BACK SLOWLY, the entire corridor
of the small building that serves as maximum is revealed.
Cells down both sides, giving onto a communal "tank" used
for exercise; gray floor and walls; one barred and wired
window at the far end; a long rectangular box, nothing
more. Standing in the corridor between the cells are half
a dozen prisoners--all young boys, black and white--clad
only in undershorts. One has wrenched a leg off the bunk
in his cell and is clanging it against the bars; a second
has a bucket filled with water and toilet paper and from
moment to moment throws wads of the sloppy mass at the
walls, at the camera, at the window; a third is wrestling
with a prisoner for his mattress, punches the kid and
takes the mattress and throws it on the already leaping
flames, which reach to the low ceiling, lath it and wash
out in a "topping" maneuver. Other prisoners are engaged
in similar shenanigans. All are shouting, howling...

(CONTINUED:)

60   CONTINUED:

PULL BACK all the way through the barred gate at the end
of the box, so we are SHOOTING PAST a fat man chewing a
soggy stub of cigar, hands on his hips. This is SGT.
SHUGGIE, who runs the max building. He looks like the
stereotype of the fat-gut, redneck yard bull we've seen
a million times in B flicks, but he's actually a nice
guy with a wild sense of humor. He has to be, to stay
sane in this lockup with the hardcases he runs. Beside
him, staring in through the bars is Elizabeth De Marco.
They watch the riot. One of the kids throws a wad of
dripping paper at them; it hits the bars and wraps around
--they jump aside and it just misses spattering them.

                    SHUGGIE
               (yells at them)
          I'm gonna come in there and bust
          your butts, you buncha animals!

                    DE MARCO
          If they throw it all at us, what'll
          they use when they need it?

                    SHUGGIE
               (angrily)
          Whaddaya askin' me for, I don't
          keep check on their potty habits!
               (to kids)
          You're gonna clean it up!

61   REVERSE ANGLE – THROUGH BARS – MEDIUM SHOT

as the door to the building, beyond Shuggie and De Marco
and the bars, opens and Ziporyn comes in. He stands behind
them watching for a minute; they are unaware he's there.
As Ziporyn moves up to them and they look back to see him
(with De Marco registering broadly, indicating there is
something going down between them), the CAMERA TRUCKS IN
TO CLOSE 3-SHOT.

                    SHUGGIE
          Hey, Sigmund Frood, you gonna stop
          this rev-uh-lootion?

                    ZIPORYN
                    (smiles)
          Ah don't know f'r sure, Gen'rl
          Custer, but I think them Injuns is
          too cranky to pow-wow.

                    SHUGGIE
          You're a lotta help.

                    ZIPORYN
          Well, howzabout I ease your pain some?
          Can you pull Richie Otis out of there
          for me?

                    SHUGGIE
          Me? Hell no, Doc. You want him out
          of that honey-pot, you get him out.
          I ain't ruining my shoes.

62   WITH ZIPORYN - CLOSE - SHOOTING PAST

as he gets up near the bars, being careful not to touch
them. He yells in to the inmates.

> ZIPORYN
>
> Hey!

> PRISONER #1
>
> Hey yose'f, ~~frustrated~~ *stupid*!

> ZIPORYN
>
> Richie Otis in there?

> PRISONER #2
>
> Naw, he went out walkin' his dawg, dummy!

> ZIPORYN
> (smiling)
> Don't shuck me, Rafael. Richie hasn't
> got a dog. Call him for me, will you?

> PRISONER #2
>
> Come on, Doc Zip, we havin' a riot! I
> ain't gonna do no messenger ~~errand~~ *jobs*!

> ZIPORYN
>
> C'mon, Rafe, I'll give you a Tootsie
> Pop when you come in for an interview.

Prisoner #2, Rafael, laughs, turns around, calls into one
of the cells.

> PRISONER #2
>
> Hey, Richie, the shrink wantsta talk to
> ya.

> RICHIE'S VOICE O.S.
>
> Tell him to go ~~fuck himself~~ *stick it in his ear!*

> PRISONER #2
> (to Ziporyn)
> Hey, Doc, he says you should go...

> ZIPORYN
>
> I heard him. Tell him to haul his tail
> out here if he wants off maximum this
> year.

Prisoner #2 goes walking into the cell.

63   2-SHOT — ZIPORYN & DE MARCO

as De Marco draws Ziporyn away from the barred door. (She)
indicates he should follow him outside.

                    ZIPORYN
                  (to Shuggie)
        Hey, Shuggie; when Richie decides to
        come out, put him in the office, will
        you?

                    SHUGGIE
                (biting his cigar stub)
        Before or after I hose him down?

Ziporyn, smiling, follows De Marco out the door of the max
building.

64   EXT. MAXIMUM SECURITY BUILDING — DAY

a clear, bright day in Fall, with the sky light and the
entire ~~Sky Combines~~ OAK MEADOWS facility spread out around them. Now
Ziporyn isn't smiling. He pulls out his pipe, starts to
fill it from a pouch, has trouble with the kitchen matches
he uses to get it lit. De Marco is troubled.

                    DE MARCO
        It's been a week, Marvin. Don't you
        think we'd better hack this out between
        us?

                    ZIPORYN (42)
        I'd just as soon not, ~~Frank~~. I'm still
        feeling a little ~~cranky~~ OUT OF SORTS about it.

                    DE MARCO
        Come on! You know damned well if ~~you'd~~ YOU'D LEFT A NOTE TO
        transcribe that dictation belt, and I'd
        seen the "hold" on Lyle Simon, I'd never
        have sent him out on furlough.
                  (beat)
        Live with it, ~~Marv~~ MARVIN. It was your mistake.

                    ZIPORYN
        That's why I'm cranky.

                    DE MARCO
        So why ~~the hell~~ are you taking it out
        on me? We have to work together, Marv;
        we may not agree, but at least give me
        credit for being as well-intentioned as
        you.

                                        (CONTINUED:)

133

64   CONTINUED:

Ziporyn has half-turned away. Now he turns back on ~~him~~ (her),
angrily.

> ZIPORYN (LIZ)
> That's what grinds me, ~~chum~~. You're
> well-intentioned. You'll give anybody
> the benefit of the doubt. Have you
> read the work-up on Lyle Simon? It came
> in from ~~Donnyville~~ [VALPARAISO] yesterday. You'll
> find it on my desk. Go take a look at
> it.

> DE MARCO
> I read it before you did.

> ZIPORYN
> That kid's a time bomb, ready to go off
> in someone's face.

> DE MARCO
> I don't see it.

> ZIPORYN
> (with sarcasm)
> Oh, really? Well, ~~hot damn~~ [hotcha], you don't
> see it. I see it, chum.

> DE MARCO
> He's in for swiping a car, Marvin, not
> for machine-gunning a kindergarten!

> ZIPORYN
> Car theft and assault.

> DE MARCO
> So he slugged the girl whose car he was
> trying to steal, he defended himself...
> his record doesn't...

> ZIPORYN
> His record shows he had school problems all
> the way back to the second grade; it shows
> he attacked a female teacher, went into
> wild rages, attacked the foster mother in
> a home he was sent to at nine, and he was
> back in trouble at 13...again for attacking
> a teacher, a female teacher, dammit!

> DE MARCO
> That's pretty thin to postulate...

(CONTINUED:)

64   CONTINUED: - 2

                    ZIPORYN
    I don't postulate a thing. I <u>know</u>
    that kid's going to get in trouble,
    a lot worse trouble than busting some
    girl's nose, which is bad enough!

                    DE MARCO
    ~~For Christopher's sake~~, You can't read
    the future, you aren't God. You can't
    keep someone in when they're due for a
    leave. <u>He</u> <u>was</u> <u>up</u> <u>for</u> <u>it</u>!

                    ZIPORYN (LIZ)
    How many kids you got, ~~Sam~~?

                    DE MARCO
    What?

                    ZIPORYN
                  (impatiently)
    How many kids; come on, how many kids
    do you and ~~Betty~~ have?

                    DE MARCO
    Three, ~~Liz~~ as you well know. Why?

                    ZIPORYN
    Planning any more?

                    DE MARCO
    What ~~business~~ has this to do--

                    ZIPORYN
                  (loud, pressing)
    Are you gonna have any more?

                    DE MARCO
    Not if we can help it. ~~I'm going anyway this way way was doing what month what best thank~~

                    ZIPORYN
    Okay, sweetheart, let's say you ~~and Betsy~~
    ~~get married before you go all your wife all this~~
    ~~any you are. And now way say~~ gets pregnant,
    and ~~she's~~ in ~~her~~ eighth month, carrying as
    big as the Houston Astrodome, and you go
    to a party, and some ~~clown walks~~ up to ~~her~~
    and belts ~~her~~ in the stomach for no special
    reason. Are you going to stop and think to
    yourself, "Gee, I bet his mommy used to
    lock him in the closet when he was a tot,
    he can't help himself, " or ~~are you~~ going to
    haul off and break the ~~son of a bitch's~~ jaw?
                                    <u>Klown's</u>
                            (CONTINUED:)

[handwritten margin notes: MARVIN, ARNOLD, you, you're, you, guy, you, "is Arnold as mild as he is — is he"]

64   CONTINUED: - 3

[handwritten: her]

De Marco is stopped by the ferocity of Ziporyn's tirade.
Ziporyn starts walking away from ~~him~~, back toward the max
building. The rest of the conversation is played over
an increasing distance between them, as they shout at one
another.

> DE MARCO
> You were wrong about Constantine, Marvin!
> You'd have kept him in another two years.
> He's out and he's okay. You were wrong
> that time!

> ZIPORYN
> And I was right about Sherman and I was
> right about Gus Logan; and I'm right
> this time!

> DE MARCO
> How do you know, how do you KNOW!?!

Ziporyn is at the door to the max building now. De Marco
stands fifty feet away across the road. Ziporyn turns to
look at ~~him~~, even as he holds open the door to enter.

[handwritten: her]

> ZIPORYN
> (levelly) *[handwritten: LIZ]*
> I don't have to know, ~~Marv~~. I only have
> to suspect. That's enough to want to
> protect ~~somebody's pregnant wife!~~ *[handwritten: somebody's pregnant wife!]*
> (beat)
> But how about this, chum:
> (beat)
> Lyle Simon was supposed to ~~check in with~~ *[handwritten: return from furlough]*
> ~~the company machine shop~~ two days ago.
> They haven't heard from him. That's why
> I'm talking to Richie Otis. Nobody knows
> where your innocent little nose-buster
> is, ~~Marv~~. Chew that one down for a while!

[handwritten: Liz]   *[handwritten: she]*

[handwritten: Elizabeth]
[handwritten: her]

He turns and goes inside the building as CAMERA COMES IN
FAST on ~~Marv~~ De Marco's face, and the dawning realization
in ~~his~~ expression that ~~he~~ may, just possibly may have
blown a big one. HOLD ON HER for several beats then:

> HARD CUT TO:

65   INT. SOUND STAGE - GARAGE - NIGHT

[handwritten: party]

This is a huge bus garage that has been turned into a
movie set for a porn flick. Under the lights there is
a dummy living room set-up with an ~~orgy going on~~, but
outside the lighted circle it's a grubby truck garage
with grease racks and oil pits and tool benches. But big.
The DIRECTOR is moving the ~~~~

[handwritten: bored men and women]

> (CONT'D.)

> (CONTINUED:)

65 CONTINUED:

(CONT'D.)
around for placement for a shot. The equipment is all
pretty shoddy, and the people, though in a state of
deshabille are blocked by kliegs, booms, furniture, and
other impedimenta so we cannot see anything revealing.
CAMERA MOVES AROUND from this scene to a far corner where
Lyle Simon leans against a portable counter with a coffee
urn and a box of doughnuts on it. He sips coffee as
Marlene--the girl he was photographing in scenes 57-59--
walks across from the lighted circle, wearing a wrapper.
Lyle looks cool. Italian shirt open almost to the waist,
revealing an expensive-looking Amerind silver pendant on
a chain, studded with turquoise jewelry. He has several
expensive cameras hanging around his neck and one sitting
beside the doughnuts. His hair is styled and blown, his
boots are shined and high-fashion, with platform heels.
Marlene comes to him as CAMERA CLOSES ON THEM, and gives
him a kiss.

There is no nudity.

                    MARLENE
          Isn't this a better gig than taking
          pictures in some old motel room?

                    LYLE
          You're a doll.

                    MARLENE
          I told you I could get you on this
          flick as still photographer.

                    LYLE
          Just like Hollywood.

                    MARLENE
          Oh, come on, now! Don't be a grouch.
          This director has a deal to do a
          spaghetti western in Rome. Maybe he'll
          take us with him if he gets to know you.

                    LYLE
          Baby, all that dude's interested in is
          wrapping this skin job by Thursday.

                    MARLENE
          It isn't a very good picture, is it?

                    LYLE
          They're going to have to bribe somebody
          to <u>get</u> an X rating.

                    MARLENE
          Well, don't pout. Just take some good
          shots you can sell to the magazines,
          and after work we'll go home and get
          loaded. ~~and I'll rub you all over.~~

                              (CONTINUED:)

65   CONTINUED: - 2

> LYLE
> After watching all these dogs, I'm
> liable to be turned off to sex for
> the next month.

At that moment the ASSISTANT DIRECTOR yells toward them.

> ASST. DIRECTOR
> Marlene! For crine out loud, will you
> get in here for your closeup, Freddy's
> waiting!

> MARLENE
> (yells back)
> Tell him to hang on to it, I'll be
> right there.

She kisses Lyle again, and dashes back, as another girl
passes her on the way to Lyle and the coffee. We can't
see her face because of the shadows in the garage.

66   REVERSE ANGLE - TOWARD LYLE ON GIRL'S BACK

as she comes to the counter and draws off a cup of coffee.
Lyle studies her. We still can't see her face, only her
long hair. She's wearing scant garb, and has a good body.

> LYLE
> Hi.

> SHERRI
> Hi.

> LYLE
> Haven't seen you on this movie before.

> SHERRI
> Haven't been here before.

> LYLE
> Just one day for the orgy, huh?

She nods, sips her coffee, starts to walk away. Lyle
grabs her by the arm.

> LYLE
> My name's Lyle Simon. I'm the still
> photographer. I'd like to shoot a
> set on you, maybe move it ~~in maybe~~ with Hefner
> or ~~Penthouse~~ one of the other slick magazines.

(CONTINUED:)

66   CONTINUED:

SHERRI
(caustic, she's
heard it all
before)
Gee, I'd just love to have you shoot ten
or twelve hours of back-breaking ~~beaver~~
shots for fifty bucks and let you peddle
the sets till I'm forty years old, but
I'm under contract to ~~Revlon~~ and they
simply for<u>bid</u> me to show bare butt.
(beat, hard)
Get your hand off, creep.

the milk-growers association as their all-American poster girl

She starts to walk away. Lyle's face gets ugly, a vision
of what's to come later.

LYLE _away from me, smartmouth!_
Don't you walk ~~mmmmmmmmmmmmmmmm~~
I'll rap you in the ~~mouth~~--

She spins on him and we can barely make her out in the
dim light as CAMERA MOVES IN STEADILY.

SHERRI
And I'll have my boy friend, who's a
button man for the mob, come and take
you off at the hips, you little wimp!

CAMERA now close enough to reveal that the girl is SHERRI,
the hooker from Ziporyn's encounter group whom we met in
scenes 38-44. HOLD HER FACE for a long beat so we know
her, then:

67   ON LYLE

SHERRI'S VOICE O.S.
Anything else you want to say, loser?

He says nothing. We HEAR her footsteps going away into
the garage, and HOLD ON Lyle's twisted hateful expression
as he crumples the coffee cup, spilling coffee on his
light-colored slacks.

DISSOLVE TO:

68   INT. KITCHEN - _(OAK MEADOWS)_ ~~SYCAMORES~~ - NIGHT

The clean-up crew is working on the last of the mess from
a co-op dinner. One white kid, MUEHLER, is working over
an enormous grease-trap sink, cleaning out a huge tureen
with steel wool as Ziporyn comes through the door, stops
to ask a question of the TRUSTY running things, gets
Muehler pointed out to him, and walks to the kid in f.g.

(CONTINUED:)

68   CONTINUED:

Steam rises up INTO CAMERA and Muehler is large in f.g.
as Ziporyn comes to him. As they talk, he continues the
scouring of the gigantic tureen.

                    ZIPORYN
          Hello, Jimmy.

Muehler has seen Ziporyn coming, is aware of him, gets very
laid-back and cool.

                    MUEHLER
          Hello, Doc.

                    ZIPORYN
          Scungy job.

                    MUEHLER
          It ain't so bad.

                    ZIPORYN
          When I was in the Army, a long time ago,
          I pulled K.P. and they stuck me in the
          sinks. Steam got so hot I damn near
          fainted, went face-first into the water.
          Took two guys to haul me out.

                    MUEHLER
          That right...?

                    ZIPORYN
          Worse than that's the grease trap. They
          ever set you to clean the grease trap?
          Smells like decaying bodies; really putrid.

                    MUEHLER
                    (impatient)
          What's up, Doc?

                    ZIPORYN
          If I hear that one more time, Jimmy, I
          swear I'll give the guy a carrot.

He stands there a while longer, just watching, getting
Muehler very nervous. Finally, Muehler stops, slumps
against the sink, wipes his sweating forehead, looks at
Ziporyn.

                    MUEHLER
          You didn't come down here just to talk
          over your Army stuff, Doc. You got a
          nice home in ~~Manhattan~~ so what're you the city,
          doin' here in the co-op?

69   ANOTHER ANGLE

> ZIPORYN
> I've just spent about three hours talking
> to Richie Otis.

> MUEHLER
> He ain't much of a talker.

> ZIPORYN
> That's why it took me three hours.

They look at each other. Muehler waits him out.

> ZIPORYN
> Richie tells me you knew Lyle Simon.

> MUEHLER
> Who?

> ZIPORYN *(VALPARAISO)*
> White kid, down from ~~Warravian~~. In for
> a car boost and assault.

> MUEHLER
> (thinks, shakes head)
> Don't know him.

> ZIPORYN
> I understand you're going up before the
> disciplinary court on Monday, Jimmy;
> they tell me you're real con-wise.

> MUEHLER
> That's a ~~bullshit~~ rap. They caught me
> with a jar of jelly in my locker.

(turkey)

> ZIPORYN
> And I hear you've got five peanut butter
> priors.

> MUEHLER
> Man, you're just like all the other screws
> in here. You want something from me, so
> you're gonna put it to me, right?

> ZIPORYN   *a screw*
> Jimmy, you make me ~~whatsman~~ so I'll act
> the part. I get the wind you're the
> candy man these days.

> MUEHLER
> I ain't dealt nothing since I got here.

(CONTINUED:)

69   CONTINUED:

                         ZIPORYN
          Uppers, sopers, grass, coke, skag,
          peyote buttons, glue, mesc, acid...
          I hear you could provide eye of newt
          and toe of frog for a black mass if
          someone could boom the price.

                         MUEHLER   *creep*
                         (angry)
          That what that ~~somebody~~ Otis said?
          I'm gonna...

                         ZIPORYN
                         (hard)
          You're not going to do squat, Jimmy.
          Anything happens to Richie Otis...he
          comes down with a bad cold or a
          hangnail, I come and fry your bad toosh.
          You got that?

                         MUEHLER
                         (surly)
          Yeah.

                         ZIPORYN
          No, I mean: you got that solid!?!

                         MUEHLER
          Yeah, yeah, I understand. What you
          want to know, just leave me alone.

                         ZIPORYN
          What was Lyle Simon doing?

                         MUEHLER
          What's in this for me?

                         ZIPORYN
          Disciplinary won't bother you. As
          long as Richie Otis stays fat.

     Muehler thinks on it for a minute, then nods.

                         MUEHLER
          Okay. He was into angel dust and DMT.
          And some Colombian grass.

                         ZIPORYN
          Where would he connect on the street?
          ~~scratched out text~~
          South side, maybe?

70   CLOSE ON MUEHLER

He gets a look of panic combined with stonewalling. He
shakes his head wildly.

                    MUEHLER
            Uh-uh. No way. No sir. No way.
            Forget it. No no no.

Ziporyn is impressed by his outburst. He stands there
staring at him. Then shrugs.

                    ZIPORYN
            I haven't got anything to scare you
            with, nothing that big anyhow. And
            I don't think I can bluff you like
            I did a minute ago with the court.
            So I guess that's it.

                    MUEHLER
            You bet your life that's it. Cause
            if I tell you that, you're bettin'
            my life. No way I'm gonna tell you;
            that's gettin' me set up for murder.

                    ZIPORYN
            Jimmy, you're nineteen years old.
            What the ~~hell have~~ you done to yourself?

heck have

                    MUEHLER
            Don't give me no lecture, Doc, just
            let me be. I told you a few things,
            that ought to be enough for you.

                    ZIPORYN
            Nothing would happen to you if you
            told me.

                    MUEHLER
            Oh, sure, sure. Right. Gotcha, chief.

                    ZIPORYN
            Nothing's going to happen to Richie Otis
            and he talked to me about you.
                    (beat)
            That's right, isn't it?

                    MUEHLER
                    (reluctantly)
            Yeah, I guess.

                              (CONTINUED:)

70   CONTINUED:

> _stone righteous_

                    ZIPORYN
        That's right for ~~certain~~ dead __certain__,
        Jimmy. So what's the difference if you
        give me a name for the street? I'm
        going out there, nobody's going to even
        know who I am, or that I spoke to you.

Muehler won't budge. Ziporyn sighs with resignation.

                    ZIPORYN (CONT'D.)
        Well, I guess that's it. Let's see, your
        parole hearing's coming up, and the board's
        waiting for me to see you and give you a
        psychiatric clearance, right? I've got this
        ugly feeling I'm going to be so busy looking
        for Lyle Simon I won't get a chance to talk
        to you for the __longest__ time...six months,
        nine months...who knows...?

He starts to walk away as Muehler realizes what Ziporyn
is hinting. He gets paniced.

                    MUEHLER
        __Hey__, man!

Ziporyn stops, turns around. Muehler throws up his hands.

                    MUEHLER (CONT'D.)
        You don't use my name.

                    ZIPORYN
        I don't even __know__ you.

                    MUEHLER
        It don't get back to me any which way.

                    ZIPORYN
        It stops with me.

                    MUEHLER
                (finally; whipped)
        Dude from Trinidad, someplace like that.
        Calls himself Amos the Prince. He lives
        over Back-of-the-Yards. He's mean, but
        he deals straight, never burns nobody.
        But he's mean.

                    ZIPORYN
        I'll watch myself. Thanks, Jimmy.

As he starts to walk away, Jimmy flips ~~him the finger~~ _a full flat hand in an imitation Mafia gesture._
Ziporyn sees it, and flips one back.

                            DISSOLVE TO:

71   SAME AS 65 — MOVIE SET IN GARAGE — ESTABLISHING

Most of the cast stand around now fully-dressed, watching
a final couple ~~~~~~~~~~~ Equipment conceals their ~~~~~~~~ activity
and what they're engaged in; As CAMERA MOVES AROUND we
get MED. CLOSE on Director, an occasional actor, Sherri,
Marlene, and then Lyle, busily snapping pictures. This
goes on for a few beats, then:

simulating a love scene.

what action goes on is obscured and in b.g.

                    DIRECTOR
          Okay, cut. That's a wrap!

Everyone sighs and starts to relax. Much ad lib about how
glad everyone is the picture is finished for the day.

                    DIRECTOR (CONT'D.)
          Listen, everyone...because you were all
          so good today, and worked so hard, and
          grunted and groaned so well, I'm having
          a little get-together at my house about
          midnight. You're all invited!

Much enthusiasm, even through the weariness. CAMERA COMES
TO MEDIUM CLOSE SHOT on Lyle as Marlene comes to him.

                    MARLENE
          Want to get something to eat and go up
          to Craig's party?

Lyle is watching Sherri as she walks past talking very
animatedly to one of the KING STUD actors, a very good-
looking muscle-type. There is hate in his face.

                    LYLE
               (indicating Sherri)
          She going to be there?

                    MARLENE
               (bothered)
          I guess. Why?

                    LYLE
          Well, is she!?!

                    MARLENE
          I think so, it looks like it.

                    LYLE
               (ruminatively)
          Yeah, let's go to a party...

He follows Sherri with his eyes as we:
                    RAPID MATCH-DISSOLVE TO:

145

72   INT. JU-JU SHOP – NIGHT

[handwritten: the city.]

MATCH–DISSOLVE TO EXT. CLOSEUP of the head of a Haitian
cicatrice (a demon-figure in wood bark of a tree) that
OVERLAYS the FADING IMAGE of Lyle Simon's face. HOLD
the CU till Lyle fades out, then PULL CAMERA BACK to show
us the dark, incense-laden interior of a voodoo shop in
the black ghetto of ~~Chicago~~. Icons and talismans from
Jamaica, Haiti, Africa, New Orleans fill the shop. (NOTE:
authenticity is important here. Consult author for the
proper set decorations.)

CAMERA PANS ACROSS the room slowly, encountering first
one hideous magic visage, then another. The alligator-
beaked head of a makundi sculpture from Mozambique, a
holy ceremonial mask from the Ivory Coast, a Trinidadian
devil-doll, a Haitian sculpture of Dambala, a Dahomean
cult-figure of Dâgbé, and then we realize we are looking
at the face of a human being: an old woman. Incredibly
old and withered and evil, the face of MAMAN CELESTINE.
Her face is in line with the others and only when we
hold on it and the eyes move do we realize she is alive.
She is watching something. CAMERA COMES AROUND HER to
show us she is watching Ziporyn, who moves slowly through
the shop in the semi-darkness. He stops, as though he
senses he's being watched.

                    ZIPORYN
               (to room at large)
          Bon nuit, Maman Celestine.

She continues watching, in silence, but we can see a tiny,
dangerous smile on her lips.

                    ZIPORYN (CONT'D.)   [handwritten: the city's]
          I've come to ask help of ~~Chicago's~~ most
          powerful mamaloi.

73   ON ZIPORYN – MOVING AROUND TO HOLD HIM IN F.G. – HIS POV

as he looks into the strange darkness, the flickering
lights of candles in strange bowls and votive dishes,
even a Greek kylix, which is virtually the only occult
piece in the room that isn't from a black society. The
VOICE of Celestine comes out of that darkness.

                    MAMAN CELESTINE
          Does Doctor wish to place a vódu ouanga
          on an awful enemy?

                    ZIPORYN
          No, Maman, I only wish to locate a man.
          He has things to say I need to hear.

                              (CONTINUED:)

73   CONTINUED:

She moves out of the darkness. A tiny, withered old black
woman in head-scarf and shapeless gown, beads, long finger-
nails. But the eyes are incredibly alive, alert, filled
with dark wisdom. She comes to him and brings with her a
candle in a votive dish. She places it so she can see
Ziporyn's eyes very clearly.

                MAMAN CELESTINE
        Why do you come to an old hougan? Why
        not go to the NAACP, the Black Caucus,
        the white police?

                ZIPORYN
        How is your grandson, Emil, Maman? Does
        he go sweetly these days?

                MAMAN CELESTINE
        He stays softly, Doctor. Do you ask a
        favor for a favor, is that it?

                ZIPORYN
        The man I seek pours killing drugs into
        the black community, Maman; that is why
        I come to ask you.

                MAMAN CELESTINE
        Who is this man?

                ZIPORYN
        He calls himself Amos the Prince. He is
        from Trinidad.

                MAMAN CELESTINE
        No. He up from Yard.

                ZIPORYN
        Yard?

                MAMAN CELESTINE
        Jamaica.

                ZIPORYN
        You know this man?

                MAMAN CELESTINE
        I know of him. I have no love for him
        or what he do to others.

                ZIPORYN
        Can you tell me where to find him?

                            (CONTINUED:)

73   CONTINUED: - 2

MAMAN CELESTINE
Yes...a favor to serve me as well as you.
(beat)
He was a Trenchtown toughie down Yard. Now
he's be up here. De Rastas forward him so
he cannot sell de herbs to children.
(beat)
You know the reggae music? (Pronounced rag-gay)

ZIPORYN
Jamaican rock steady?

MAMAN CELESTINE
Dats it. Find the reggae shop of Gregory
Barrett; dey call him Big Stoot. Dis Amos
always dere listn'in de rhythm. Here de
place...

She gets paper and pencil, laboriously writes out the
address. Gives it to Ziporyn.

ZIPORYN
You have a ouanga to protect me?

MAMAN CELESTINE
(smiles wide)
You g'wan! You doan b'lieve!

He smiles back, turns to leave. He goes out the door.
Maman Celestine stares after him, then speaks to the silence.

MAMAN CELESTINE (CONT'D.)
Even so, Doctor, I put up ouanga for
you. For my grandson. Small piece of
gold, small piece of silver, small piece
of lead, small piece of bronze, small
piece of thunder-stone, an eye without
an eye, a tail without a tail...

All of this diminishes in intensity and as her voice fades
away, the picture itself begins to fade out like an old
photograph until we have almost a ghost-image of the
ju-ju shop, all misty and washed out as if seen through
morning haze and we CONTINUE FADING till we:

FADE TO BLACK:

and

FADE OUT.

END ACT FOUR

ACT FIVE

FADE IN:

CITY
74   EXT. ~~CITY~~ STREET - NIGHT - ESTABLISHING

One of the busy, throbbing commercial streets in the South
Side ghetto. Very black. Storefronts open even at night.
A sprawling, vibrant street community. Everybody duded up
and on parade. The stroll. Little shops open to the
sidewalk serving food--souvlaki, pizza, hot dogs, ribs,
papaya drinks, sub sandwiches, soul food in cardboard
plates. CAMERA IN FROM LONG TO CLOSE on a record shop
about eight feet wide, a big sign that says (exactly)

BIG STOOT RASTAFARI

REGGAE!

And overriding this scene is the big SKA sound of the
Jamaican reggae music. (NOTE: for unhips who haven't
heard it, this'll be next year's white rage, already
the thing to listen to in the black community, way past
the O'Jays and The Spinners and Bobby Womack. Singers
like Alton Ellis, Jimmy Cliff, Don Drummond and The Wailers.
There is no mickeymouse substitute for it, so get the
right sound in this scene.)

CAMERA IN on the shop as we see people in the street
turning to look at something coming down the sidewalk.
CAMERA BOOMS DOWN to SIDEWALK LEVEL and PANS RIGHT to
get a shoe-level angle on Ziporyn coming through the
crowds toward the shop. Virtually the only white face
in that fine Friday night crowd of macks and pros and
ladies&gentlemen of fashion, kids and ~~young toughs.~~ [bopping street gang toughs.]
Just Ziporyn coming on, minding his own business. He
COMES TO CAMERA, passes OVER CAMERA as CAMERA WHIPS WITH
HIM to show him entering the store, pressing politely
through a crowd standing outside listening to the reggae
being piped out over a big speaker.

CUT TO:

75   INT. BIG STOOT'S RECORD SHOP - NIGHT

EXT. CLOSEUP on a poster of Haile Selassie. CAMERA BACK
to show a crowded record shop with bins and racks and an
old-fashioned trio of listening booths at the rear, near
an exit door with a curtain half-pulled across it. The
young men of the community, with their women, fill the
shop, clearly a gathering-place. Each listening-booth
has three or four people spilling out of it, the music
up to full gain, matching for decibel-count the reggae
being piped through the shop itself. The customers are
the very height of current black fashion, their hair done
in the ringlets of the rastas, corn-rows, afros, very
few conked or teased the way the uptown blacks do it.
The clothes are superfine and one outdoes the next for
elegance of material and color. Behind the counter at
the cash register is BIG STOOT. Two hundred and sixty
pounds, and all of it muscle. But a kind face. And a
huge sign on the wall behind him:

                POISON YOURSELF IF YOU
                WANT, DREADIE, BUT DON'T
                POISON ME! NO SMOKING!

Nobody is smoking. But it's as if the eye of the hurricane
passed through that maelstrom as Ziporyn enters. Every
head turns, every voice stops, only the music goes on, but
it's a sound of silence. CAMERA COMES THROUGH THE ROOM
FAST to HOLD Big Stoot and Ziporyn as the psychiatrist
reaches the counter.

76   2-SHOT

                        ZIPORYN
        Evening.

Big Stoot says nothing.

                        ZIPORYN
            I'm looking for a couple of things
            that're pretty hard to find. I was
            told your stock's the best in town.

                        BIG STOOT
                      (very aloof)
            Whot you site up for, mon?

He speaks a broad Jamaican dialect, but very bass, very
rich, and his face--though kind--is full of smarts.

                        ZIPORYN
            Two things. You got Bob Marley's new
            single, "Knotty Dread"?

                        BIG STOOT
            Yeah, wot else you got to have?

                                    (CONTINUED:)

76   CONTINUED:

                         ZIPORYN
               Amos the Prince.

Everybody near moves off. Fast. Big Stoot's eyes narrow
down. Now his voice changes; he doesn't speak the accent
patois any more, but a very upper-class British tongue.

                         BIG STOOT
               You're not the heat. Who are you?

                         ZIPORYN
               Would you believe a guy who means you
               no trouble?

                         BIG STOOT
               That's no answer, man.

                         ZIPORYN
               Wouldn't you rather know as little as
               possible?

                         BIG STOOT
               I don't want any aggravation. Things are
               quiet down here.

                         ZIPORYN
               I like quiet.

                         BIG STOOT
               You must be very brave or very anxious to
               get cut, coming down here with that white
               face of yours.

                         ZIPORYN
               Just passing through. A little talk with
               Amos the Prince and I'm gone and you get
               no waves behind me.
                    (he holds up his hands)
               Open hands, Mr. Barrett. Nothing in them.

The use of Big Stoot's real name gives Big Stoot pause.
He looks at Ziporyn a minute, then indicates the door
at the rear.
                         BIG STOOT
               Go on out through there. Back alley.
               I'll send him along when he comes in.

                         ZIPORYN
                    (nodding)
               Thank you. And how much is the Bob
               Marley 45?

                                        (CONTINUED:)

76   CONTINUED: - 2

Big Stoot reaches into a series of bins for 45's behind
him, pulls one out, puts it in a bag, hands it over.

                    BIG STOOT
        On the house. Don't come back.

Ziporyn nods again, takes the record and walks through
the shop as the crowd parts for him. He notes every face
as best he can, and reaches the curtained doorway, goes
through as CAMERA FOLLOWS. He goes out and the sounds in
the shop start up again, quickly reaching crescendo level.

                                    CUT TO:

77   EXT. ALLEY - NIGHT

as Ziporyn comes out among the garbage cans, the stacked
wooden crates, the broken-down flats of record boxes. He
puts the record down on one of the cans carefully, and
looks around, sizing up the terrain. It's dark, just a
few shaded bulbs on the rear faces of the buildings
casting dim glows here and there. He stands for a long
time, looking around, hearing the reggae faintly. Then
he stiffens, slowly turns, as CAMERA BACKS AWAY FROM HIM.

CAMERA PULLS BACK away from Ziporyn, showing him alone
in the alley, watching CAMERA until the frame includes the
dark, shadowed form of a man, back to us, filling the
right side of the FRAME, staring at Ziporyn.

                    AMOS
        You been lookin' for Amos, mon?

                    ZIPORYN
        Is that you?

                    AMOS
        I don't check for questions from some
        dreadie just come in off street, mon.
        Wot you want wit dis Amos?

                    ZIPORYN
        I want to ask him for some information
        and trade him some valuable information
        in payment.

Amos moves toward him. There is a smooth movement from
the side, as Amos--who we now see is all duded up in
red crushed velvet, mack skimmer, platforms, lavolliers
--gets a gravity shake-knife out in the free, and open
with an ominous, chitinous click. CAMERA SLOWLY MOVES
IN WITH AMOS a la Hitchcock as Ziporyn grows larger in
frame.

78   PAST ZIPORYN

TO AMOS who is tall, very good-looking, but very mean.

                    AMOS
          More time I check for you and I, mon.
          I and I think you best cohm wi' me
          some odder place, we do our jestering
          by-n-by, chuckie.

                    ZIPORYN
          Stoot might not like a dead whitey in
          the alley back of his shop.

                    AMOS
          I know dat, mon. Das why I sujjest
          we buff some bottom elsewhere.

Ziporyn moves into a stance that, for the first time,
gives us the idea he may not be entirely a social animal,
that he may be on speaking terms with some form of the
martial arts. It's subtle, but he's positioning himself.
~~as the knife knife moves toward him~~

                              BEHIND AMOS
79   CAMERA ANGLE FROM ~~POINT OF KNIFE~~

LIGHT CATCHES THE BLADE as though it were being shot through
a crosstar lens. Sense of movement ~~of the point of the~~
~~knife~~ toward Ziporyn who looks more and more like a target.

                    ZIPORYN
                   (reasonably)
          You wouldn't like to just do some
          talking and I'd go on my way, huh?

                    AMOS
                   (mildly)
          No, mon, I dohn think that serve.

                  - ZIPORYN
                   (resignedly)
          Okay, whatever you say.

80   ACTION SEQUENCE - ARRIFLEX SHOTS
thru
85   WITH THE MOVEMENT

as Ziporyn makes a sharp movement sidewise, toward the
empty face of the alley, away from the back of Stoot's
shop. Amos goes for the feint, takes the move toward
Ziporyn. As he goes to his left, Zipoporyn arrests his
movement, moves in behind the knife, lifts and throws
Amos against the garage door of the buildings on the
other side of the alley. Amos comes up against the
door, shaken but still holding onto the knife. He
                    (CONT'D.)
                                        (CONTINUED:)

80   CONTINUED:
thru
85
                         (CONT'D.)
      shakes his head, looks at Ziporyn, can't believe he's
      been dumped.
                         AMOS
                   Who de hell are you, mon?

                         ZIPORYN
                   Just a quiet country doctor trying to
                   find his patient.

                         AMOS
                   You wild crazy, mon. I gone cut on you.

                         ZIPORYN
                         (wearily)
                   You're going to wreck hell with that
                   suit, Amos. Crushed velvet can't take
                   this kind of knocking around.

      Amos comes up, circles, feints with the knife, dropping
      it from one hand to the other, moving in. Marvin Ziporyn
      sees it all, spins as Amos makes a thrust, half-turns
      and kicks him smartly in the chest with a jeet kune do
      maneuver. Amos windmills backward, tries to regain his
      balance, Ziporyn follows, gives him a shot in the face,
      the hand with the knife comes over, Ziporyn chops it,
      the knife flies up, arcs and comes down sticking in the
      slat of a wooden crate. Amos is half-lying against the
      rear of Stoot's shop. He's semi-coherent, but amazed.

                         AMOS
                   Dat's it, chuckie. You hail dis! I
                   gone ruin you. Where my blade, dammit!

      Ziporyn looks concerned. He moves away, indicates the
      knife.
                         ZIPORYN
                   Oh, that's over here.

      Amos staggers up, ~~scrambles to the knife, gets it in his
      hand~~ just as Ziporyn moves in, fast...a lot faster than
      a man his age should be able to move. He ~~grabs the wire
      off a garbage can and whaps Amos across the face with
      it. The knife slides off into the piles of crates and
      baskets.~~ Amos is flat on his back, spread-eagled.
      Ziporyn, humming to himself, sits down on Amos's chest,
      waits for him to come back to life.

      [handwritten note:] hits Amos. Amos goes down.

86   CLOSE 2-SHOT - FACES OF ZIPORYN & AMOS

      as Ziporyn puts his face right down near Amos's. He
      talks softly, earnestly.
                                        (CONTINUED:)

86   CONTINUED:

                    ZIPORYN
                 (pleasantly)
        I'm really a terrific fellah if you get
        to know me. Snappy dresser, good dancer,
        really a credit to my race.

                    AMOS
                 (bleary)
        What you want from I, mon?

                    ZIPORYN
        Kid named Lyle Simon. White boy, 20 years
        old, good-looking like a Via Veneto pimp.
        He's been in ~~Sam Charles and New York~~ for
        a while; he's on the street now.

        > OAK MEADOWS
        > AND VALPARAISO

                    AMOS
        So?

                    ZIPORYN
        You tell me where, and I tell you a thing
        you need to know real bad.

                    AMOS
        What dat?

                    ZIPORYN
        No fair. You tell first.

                    AMOS
        I got no tie wit him, dat screw-face
        get some buncha me frens in trouble.
                 (beat)
        Howzabout you let me up?

87   MEDIUM SHOT

     as Ziporyn lets Amos up. He helps dust him off.

                    AMOS (CONT'D.)
        You sure you not the man? Gawd, you hit
        lahk some kinda truck. Where you learn
        all dat stuff?

                    ZIPORYN
        You were saying about Lyle Simon...?

                    AMOS
        He come to see me t'ru frens, wanted to
        score some herbs. But he din have no
        moh-nee, so I put him onto a piece'a work
        he could do.

                                    (CONTINUED:)

87   CONTINUED:

> ZIPORYN
> You want to tell me about that?

> AMOS
> No.

> ZIPORYN
> I didn't think so. Okay, so you got
> him booked on a job and he messed it
> up for your people.

> AMOS
> He jus' s'posed to stan' there, look
> dreadie an' then go away with some
> stuff. Stead, he start stealin'
> cameras.

> ZIPORYN
> Cameras?

> AMOS
> I dohn know why. I don' check dat.
>   (beat)
> He took dat little bit moh-nee he have
> left after herbs, he took dem cameras,
> he leave us.

> ZIPORYN
> But he'll be back.

> AMOS
> Why you figger dat?

> ZIPORYN
> So he can score again.

> AMOS
> I dohn wanna see dat screw-face no more.

> ZIPORYN
> But I do. So I'll tell you what...
>   (he fishes in his
>   pocket, pulls out a
>   card, gives it to
>   Amos)
> ...here's a number. He shows up again,
> you call me.

> AMOS
> Why should I do a ting like dat?

                              (CONTINUED:)

87   CONTINUED: — 2

ZIPORYN
Because if you don't, I'll make sure
the immigration authorities send your
~~ass~~ back down the Yard, where I hear
there are some Trenchtown toughies
looking to burn you. And because he
doesn't mean a damn thing to you, so
why should you take risks for him?

AMOS
I think you gone make big trouble for
me, mon.

ZIPORYN
No, I'll tell you what: I'll throw that
into the deal. I don't hassle you, I
don't tell the ~~Cook~~ County authorities
—for whom I work, did I mention that,
no? I really should have mentioned that
—I don't tell them a thing about Amos
the Prince.

Amos takes the card. He nods okay. Ziporyn goes to the
crates, searches around for a moment, comes up with the
knife; Amos looks worried. Ziporyn puts the open blade
under his foot and snaps it off against the cement. He
hands back the broken weapon. Then he takes his record
and starts to go. Amos stops him.

AMOS
Hey, wait a minute, mon. What that
thing you gone tell me I need to know so
damn bad?

Ziporyn, as though remembering (but it's feigned), comes
back to him. He stops close and looks him dead on.

ZIPORYN
If I find out any more dope is coming
into ~~Cottonville~~ [OAK MEADOWS] by way of you—mon—
I'm going to come back down here and
wipe up the street with your ~~ass~~ [crushed velvet butt.] And
there's enough people right down here
I know who'll cover for me. Mon. So
what you need to know is that the route
is closed into ~~Cottonville.~~ [OAK MEADOWS.]
            (beat)
You check dat, mon?

Amos nods, unhappily. Ziporyn smiles and pulls the record
out of the paper bag. He slips it over the broken knife
that Amos still holds up like a useless magic wand.

(CONTINUED:)

87   CONTINUED: - 3

ZIPORYN
Go home and think about good thoughts,
Amos. Go hail Bob Marley. It's real
skeng-ay.

And, smiling, he turns and walks away down the alley as
Amos the Prince looks on after him, and we:

DISSOLVE THRU TO:

88   INT. HUGHIE'S HOME - LAKE SHORE DRIVE ~~WATERACE~~ — CITY - NIGHT

PARTY - ESTABLISHING

It's a hastily thrown-together affair, but all the people
from the porn flick are there, including Lyle and Marlene,
and Sherri and the Mr. Muscle she was talking to in scene
71. King Stud, that is. Also the Assistant Director and
HUGHIE, the Director. After the reggae sound of the past
scenes, the cocktail piano makeout music playing seems
very sterile and silly. People in small groups, talking,
dancing, making out. There are also a fine handful of
sleek, Playboy-style men and women, semi-out-of-place,
but obviously friends of Hughie...who scampers from one
to the other, making sycophantic sounds, trying to cop a
good impression with people on the next rung up. CAMERA
PANS THE PARTY and goes through the room to the terrace,
where we see Lyle talking to a pretty young girl, KATE.
Marlene also sees it, and moves in on them.

89   SHOT THROUGH TERRACE DOORS - FAVORING LYLE & KATE

as Marlene comes toward them.

LYLE
(in progress)
...I'd really like to shoot a glamour
set on you. Maybe move it at Play---

KATE
(spots Marlene)
Here comes your girl friend.

Marlene comes out on the terrace, obviously pissed-off
but trying to be cool. Her tone betrays her.

MARLENE
Hi, there, troops. Nice out here, isn't
it?

KATE
I need some ice.

She exits.

90   ANOTHER ANGLE ON LYLE & MARLENE

> LYLE
> That was terrific. I almost had her
> ready to do a shooting.

> MARLENE
> I'll bet you did.

> LYLE
> What's that all about?

> MARLENE
> (angry)
> I've been standing in there over a half
> hour getting hustled by some freak from
> the film distributor's office; he's got
> more hands than a bridge tournament; and
> you're out here hustling where everyone
> can see you.

> LYLE
> (angry right back)
> Where the hell you coming from?

> MARLENE
> You're with me, remember? You're living
> off me, hotshot, so pay some attention!

> LYLE
> (vicious)
> I'm about to pay you more attention than
> you can handle. You say one more word
> to me, I'll break your fat face!

Marlene crumbles. From her expression and her words we
now realize she is one of the ready victims of predators
like Lyle Simon. Instead of turning and walking out on
him, or slugging him, she gets all sad-faced and whining.

> MARLENE
> C'mon, honey, don't dump on me like that.
> I don't want to tie you down, I just want
> you to pay some attention to me, that's
> all...

> LYLE
> (cunning, feigns
> an attitude)
> Listen, baby, I understand. It's just
> I am living off you, and it makes me
> twitchy. I want to get my act together
> so I can make some money and contribute
> my share. That means I've got to work
> up some contacts. You know.

91 CLOSEUP – SHOOTING BETWEEN LYLE & MARLENE

as their FACES MOVE TOGETHER IN EXT. F.G. with Marlene
whispering to him, and Lyle husking his voice, whispering
back, doing a number on her.

                    MARLENE
          Baby, let's go home. I'm lonely here.

                    LYLE
                  (softly)
          In a little bit, love. I think I've
          got a couple of good things moving
          here.   (he kisses her, then
                  their faces move apart)
          See that guy over there?

As he nods away from CAMERA, their faces separate and
CAMERA SHOOTS BETWEEN THEM as it REFOCUSES to bring into
FOCUS a man standing in the living room, drinking and
talking to another man and two women. He is about forty-
five or –six, dressed in calculatedly hip gear, but it's
clearly a pose. If it were a woman trying to dress down
from her age, they'd call her a Shirley Temple; since it's
a man, he's just an aging phoney. This is STARBUCK.
CAMERA UNFOCUSES Starbuck after a beat and REFOCUSES on
Lyle & Marlene in f.g. as their faces move together again.

                    LYLE (CONT'D.)
          Listen, baby. That's Bill Starbuck. He's
          with some convention bureau or other,
          y'know? I met him a while ago. He books
          all these big conventions in town. He
          could do me a lot of good.
                  (beat)
          I want you to go over there and whip a
          little of that super-bod on him; get him
          wired up and maybe I can do some business
          with him.

CAMERA PULLS BACK as Marlene does the same.

                    MARLENE

          Lyle!

                    LYLE
          Come on, baby...I'm not asking you to go
          away for the weekend with him, just talk
          to him for a while and take a bunch of
          deep breaths while you do the talking.

                    MARLENE
                  (victimized)
          That's crummy, Lyle. I bet you'd
          send your mother out hustling if you
          needed...
                            (CONTINUED:)

91   CONTINUED:

CAMERA BACK MORE as Lyle moves very suddenly. He reaches
up with the speed of a striking adder and grabs her face
in one hand, squeezing her cheeks and chin painfully,
scrunching up her mouth into a moue. Her eyes widen.

                         LYLE
                      (fire, pain)
          That never comes out of your mouth
          again! You understand me? <u>Not</u> <u>ever</u>!

She tries to nod wildly. But he isn't even listening. He
is off somewhere on his own, on a very bad trip. Then, as
suddenly as it came, it stops. He shoves her away.

                     LYLE (CONT'D.)
          Now go do what I told you to do, *broad*!

Rubbing her face, Marlene moves off quickly toward Starbuck
as Lyle turns around, stares off the terrace toward the
lights of the city. Is he crying? We can't tell.

                                        CUT TO:

92   INT. ZIPORYN'S APARTMENT - BEDROOM - NIGHT

FRAME BLACK

SOUND of a telephone LOUD. Again. A third time. In the
darkness we HEAR the SOUND of someone trying to get out of
bed, struggling, something falling. Fumbling. Phone
rings again. Out of darkness we HEAR Ziporyn's VOICE.

                       ZIPORYN
          Coming, dammit! Coming!

Light goes on. The light is a bedside lamp that has been
knocked to the floor. Ziporyn is hanging half-in-half out
of a Murphy bed--one of those inner-door affairs that goes
up into the wall. It's trying to fold back up into the
woodwork and Ziporyn is struggling to keep it down as he
reaches across for the phone, which is on the floor. He
grabs the cord and pulls it to him, gets the receiver up
to his ear as the bed continues its inexorable retreat
into the wall.
                     ZIPORYN (CONT'D.)
          Yeah?
                      (he listens)
          Yeah. I'm on my way. Maybe an hour.

                                        CONTINUED:

92 CONTINUED:

He racks the receiver, slides the rest of the way out of
the bed and it vanishes into the wall. He ~~gingerly~~
~~crawling~~ stumbles into the bathroom to run water on his
face as we

DISSOLVE THRU:

93 TRAVELING SHOT - STOCK

Ziporyn's car on the ~~Bullnook~~ *interstate* freeway system, night, going
away from us and we

CONTINUE DISSOLVE THRU:

94 CLOSE ON ZIPORYN - IN CAR - DASH LIGHTS HIGHLIGHTING

as he bends to the wheel and the roadway whips past we

DISSOLVE THRU TO:

OAK MEADOWS

95 ANGLE ON ~~BROADMOOR~~ ROADWAY - NIGHT

leading into the complex of buildings. CAMERA picks up
his headlights coming, loses them for a moment as car
is obscured by a building or trees, picks them up again
as car comes TO CAMERA CLOSE ON HEADLIGHT and stops. The
lights go off as CAMERA HOLDS LOW ANGLE and we see his
legs getting out of the car, going PAST CAMERA. CAMERA
WHIPS WITH HIM to follow him as he enters the medical
building where his office is located.

96 INT. ZIPORYN'S OFFICE BUILDING - HALLWAY

as Ziporyn comes through the door, starts toward his own
office. De Marco pops out of ~~his~~ cubicle. [HER]

DE MARCO

Here.

Ziporyn comes to the office, enters.

97 INT. DE MARCO'S OFFICE   [ONE]   [ANOTHER.]
[LIZ]
In the office are De Marco, DR. JOE HENSLEY and the WARDEN
of ~~BROADMOOR~~, PHIL BONNARD. One gooseneck lamp is all
the illumination in the room, casting a strained, eerie
look to the room and its occupants. Ziporyn steps inside
and waits. He looks from ~~one~~ to ~~another~~. They look back at
him, and their expressions aren't happy.

[OAK MEADOWS]

WARDEN
What are you up to, Marvin?

Ziporyn looks at him hard. He doesn't like the tone. He
pulls a chair over with one foot, and sits down. He goes
for his pipe.

98   MEDIUM SHOT — FAVORING ZIPORYN

whose face is cut in half by shadows. It looks as though
his words are coming out of a nothing place; only the upper
part of his face is lit. Then the pipe match lights and
we see him.

                    ZIPORYN
          I'm up to about twelve hours dead sleep,
          Phil. You're the one got me out of bed,
          remember? Get your tail over here,
          remember?

                    DE MARCO
          Marv, for God's sake, stop playing word
          games. We've got a gang war on our hands
          and it looks like you started it!

                (42) WARDEN
          Okay, ~~Marv~~. I'm the Warden here, I'll
          clear it with Marvin.
                    (beat)
          Tell me what you've been into the last
          couple of days, Marvin.

                    ZIPORYN
          I get the feeling there's some things I
          don't know. Two in the morning, yanked
          out of town by the Warden, come in and
          Doc Hensley sits there looking grim...
Liz gets ~~then everybody~~ on my case...
                    (beat)
          How did I suddenly become the enemy?

Hensley is a man in his early sixties, but in good shape.
A trifle overweight, a chain-smoker, a great bush of white
hair, a very low bullshit threshhold. He stands up,
spilling ashes down his front. He's wearing a 3-piece suit.

                    HENSLEY
          I'm going home. Gwen's arthritis is
          acting up. She doesn't like to be alone.

                    WARDEN
          Tell him, Joe.

pete's   HENSLEY
          Oh, for ~~Marv's~~ sake, Phil! Tell him
          yourself; don't be such a political
          animal. Tell him and let him say what
          he has to say...oh, for ~~Marv's~~ sake...
                    (CONT'D.)
                         pete's   (CONTINUED:)

163

98   CONTINUED:

                        HENSLEY (CONT'D.)
                        (to Ziporyn)
Marvin. Somebody got to Richie Otis
in max. They used a shard of glass.
He's going to lose the left eye.

                        DE MARCO
He says it's your fault.

Ziporyn bites down on the stem of the pipe, then turns
away. He wants to move, there's nowhere to go. He gets
up, walks around the little room, comes back, standing
in the darkness.

                        ZIPORYN
Jimmy Muehler did it. Get him.

                        HENSLEY
                        (quietly)
Not possible, Marvin.
                        (beat)
Otis's gang stuck a knife in him
after lights out. He's dead.

                        ZIPORYN
Oh, ~~Jeezuss~~ my God...

                        WARDEN
Now do you feel like telling us what
you're into, Marvin?

HOLD on all four of them, silent, waiting, as we:

                                        CUT TO:

99   SAME AS 88 - THE PARTY

CAMERA IN FAST on Lyle and Starbuck, talking.

                        LYLE
Sure, she won't mind.

                        STARBUCK
She seems pretty heavy behind you,
kiddo.

                        LYLE
Marlene's a good chick. She won't
mind ~~putting out~~ being friendly... for a friend.

                                        (CONTINUED:)

99   CONTINUED:

                    STARBUCK
          Listen, I'll tell you what. Maybe here,   *grass*
          like this, she might feel a little bit
          hustled. Now, you understand, I really
          like this girl of yours...so maybe we   *and a good*
          ought to get some good ~~dope~~ and take   *bottle of*
          along two or three other nice people   *Scotch*
          and go back to, uh, your place and sort
          of all get to know each other...

Lyle catches the drift immediately. He smiles.

                    LYLE
          Great idea. I know just where to score
          some fine herb. You got some bread on
          you?

Starbuck fishes in his pocket, comes up with a wad.

                    STARBUCK
          How much you figure?

                    LYLE
          Lay about fifty on me, that ought to do
          it.

He peels off two twenties and a ten. Lyle takes out a felt-
tip pen, reaches for another bill. Starbuck lets him take
it. Lyle writes on the bill, then hands Starbuck a key.

                    LYLE (CONT'D.)
          Here's the address and the key. You go on
          ahead, I'll bring Marlene, we'll meet you
          at the apartment.
                    (beat)
          Just one thing...

Starbuck looks at him expectantly.

                    LYLE (CONT'D.)
          See that chick over there? Sherri?
          Get her to come. Don't mention me, just
          get her to come along. Minus King Stud.

Starbuck checks Sherri out, notes the muscle man she's
been with, smiles knowingly at Lyle.

                    STARBUCK
          What I mean, an interesting evening!

                              (CONTINUED:)

99   CONTINUED: - 2

He walks away from Lyle, goes straight to Sherri and King
Stud. Animated conversation. Lyle turns away and sees
Marlene. He signals her, and she comes to him.

> LYLE
> Let's cut out. We gotta go score
> some stuff for Starbuck.

> MARLENE
> He gives me the creeps.

> LYLE
> Terrific guy once you get to know him.

> MARLENE
> I don't _want_ to get to know him.

> LYLE
> Right.

They move toward the door together as we:

CUT TO:

100   INT. DE MARCO'S OFFICE - ANGLE ON ZIPORYN

> ZIPORYN
> So I've got to find Lyle Simon before
> somebody gets killed.

> WARDEN
> Somebody's _already_ been killed!

> ZIPORYN
> I've got to do it, Phil. It was my
> mistake.

> DE MARCO
> You're playing God again, Marvin.
> The kid hasn't ~~been with him the~~ leave
> ~~community~~, turn it over to the city
> police. Let them round him up.

~~yet~~   *returned from*

> ZIPORYN
> I can't just do that. I've got some
> leads...

> WARDEN
> You're a psychiatrist, Marvin, not
> Captain Wonderful. Leave this to the
> proper authorities, dammit! We've got
> a situation here that you're responsible
> for creating, that comes first.

101   FROM WARDEN TO ZIPORYN

                         ZIPORYN
            I thought I had Muehler boxed in.

                         DE MARCO
            You're wrong on this one, Marvin.
            I told you you were wrong; sometimes
            we're wrong...don't compound it.

                         ZIPORYN
                         (wearily)
            I'm right, ~~Phil~~. I know it, I feel it.
            Lyle Simon is out there and I feel him
            moving toward something. I feel it...
                         (beat)
            I can do both. Here and out there.

                         WARDEN
                         (with meaning)
            Maybe neither one, Marvin. If you don't
            give me your word you'll let the ~~████~~
            authorities handle Simon, I'm going to
            have to make a complaint.

                         ZIPORYN
                         (back up)
            Then do it, Phil. Get off your appointed
            ~~████~~, stop reading Skinner on behavior mod
            and just bloody well do it!

            He gets up and walks out, leaving them there staring
            after him as we:

                                        FADE TO BLACK:

                                        and

                                        FADE OUT.

                    END ACT FIVE

ACT SIX

FADE IN:

102   EXT. (SOUTH SIDE SLUM) ~~PHILADELPH~~ TENEMENT – NIGHT

EXT. CLOSEUP on two pairs of feet climbing a rickety flight
of stairs painted gunmetal gray. Sharp shoes, but one pair
of feet are a man's, the other a woman's. CAMERA ANGLE
TILTS UP and CAMERA PULLS BACK as the people climb and we
see it's Lyle and Marlene. They're climbing up the back
stairs of a tacky ghetto tenement, toward a back door.
CAMERA HOLDS A BEAT as they reach the top and then BOOMS
IN on them as Lyle rings a doorbell. They wait.

                    LYLE
          You hear it ring in there?

                    MARLENE
          No, maybe it's broke.

Lyle knocks. They wait. He knocks again. A light goes
on inside. CAMERA TO THEM and SHOOTS PAST THEM to the
door. The curtained window in the door shows a dim
figure moving inside, then the curtain is pulled back
and Amos the Prince looks out. His eyes widen a bit but
he opens the door.

                    AMOS
          Hey, what the hell you do here, mon?

                    LYLE
          Wanted to do a little business.

                    AMOS
          You done me all the bus'ness you gone
          do, chuckie. You g'wan now.

He tries to close the door; Lyle puts his foot in the
door. Amos opens it again, looking mean.

                    AMOS
          You doan wan' scuffle me, screw-face!

                    LYLE
          Listen, Amos, I got lots of bread and
          I want to score some stuff. We need
          it for a party...

                                        (CONTINUED:)

102   CONTINUED:

Amos looks out, up and down the bit of street that can be
seen around the buildings, then steps back to let them in.

103   INT. AMOS'S KITCHEN - FULL SHOT

HIGH ANGLE SHOOTING DOWN on the trio and the slovenly mess
that a bachelor dude like Amos would live in. Cats all
over the damned place. Boxes of kitty litter. Dishes
growing moss in the sink. And apothecary jars, big ones,
filled with beans and condiments prominently displayed on
one wall. We now see Amos has his face pretty well banged
up--from Ziporyn. He's holding an ice-bag to his jaw.

                    LYLE
          What happened to you?

                    AMOS
          Remember, you de one ast to be let in.
                    (indicates Marlene)
          Who dis?

                    LYLE
          One of my models.

                    AMOS
          Whot de hell you puttin' out, models?

                    LYLE
                    (bragging)
          I shoot glamour sets for the men's magazines.

                    AMOS
          (Trampie stuff)(derides)
          ~~Entertainment~~, you check.

                    MARLENE
          Hey, watch that!

                    LYLE
          Shut up, Marlene.
                    (to Amos)
          Hey, man, why'd you think I copped those
          cameras? You got burned at me because I
          messed up the job, but them cameras are
          more important to my career than all the
          dope you could ever bring in.

                    AMOS
                    (sarcastic)
          Dat right?

104   ANGLE ON LYLE & AMOS

He's baiting Lyle. Later, we will understand Amos is
doing it on purpose, for a trade with Ziporyn.

                    LYLE
               (pissed off)
          Yeah, that's right! Listen, man, I
          sold a set of Marlene here, that I
          shot last week in about three hours,
          and I got a hundred and fifty bucks
          for it.

                    AMOS
          To where, mon? I wanna see pick-churs
          this little lady in de altogether.

                    LYLE
          To Filigree Magazine.

                    AMOS
          I and I never check that book.

                    LYLE
          It's one of the smaller men's magazines.
          I'll bring you one when they publish the
          shots I took.
               (beat)
          What the hell happened to your face?

                    AMOS
          I hurt meself. Dohn ask bout dat no more,
          because de more I tink on it, de madder I
          get; an' you dohn wanna me mad at you, you
          best believe, chuckie.

                    LYLE
               (placates)
          Okay, okay, take it easy. I just came to
          get some dope for a party a big wheel is
          throwing.

                    AMOS
          Whot kinda herb you want, mon?

                    LYLE
          Here's fifty. Do the best you can with it.
          Mix it up. Some of all the goodies in the
          candy store, but include some of that fine
          Colombian home-run hitter you laid on me
          last time...

Amos takes down a small brown paper bag from a shelf and
goes to the apothecary jars filled with beans. He opens
one after the other, reaches down into the middle of the
beans, etc. and brings up plastic bags of dope.

105   CLOSE ON AMOS

as he scrabbles through the beans and sunflower seeds and
other loose items--raisins, short macaroni, spaetzle,
crunchy granola--and pulls out the tightly-bound plastic
bags. He starts opening them and putting what seems to
be too much of the goodies in the paper bag for a mere
fifty bucks. LYLE MOVES INTO FRAME BEHIND HIM.

                    LYLE
          Isn't that a little easy for the heat
          to find if they come looking, right up
          there on the wall? In plain sight?

                    AMOS
          I don't keep it there alla time. Now you
          seen it, I gone have to change it again.
                    (beat, as he works)
          You ever read de book "De Poor-loined
          Letter" by Edgah Allin Poe?

                    LYLE
                    (confused)
          No. What's that got to do with it?

Amos laughs, shakes his head at Lyle's stupidity. He keeps
giving him caps and packets and grass.

                    LYLE (CONT'D.)
          Hey, I don't mind, but isn't that an
          awful lot of stuff for just fifty bucks?

                    AMOS
          It my bargain day special.
                    (beat)
          You cause me too much grief awreddy, mon.
          I gone give you li'l bit reward for you
          to stay way from me.

He turns around, hands him the paper bag, takes the fifty.
But when Lyle's hand closes on it, Amos's hand is still
there, holding on. Amos looks at him closely.

                    AMOS
                    (deadly)
          You got dat rhythm, slouchin' chuckie?
          You know whot I say? You doan come
          back here no more. Not tomorro', not
          a week from Wezday, not forever...or I
          and I make you cry some a lot.

Lyle looks at him. Amos has seemed a little weak before
this, perhaps because of the beating Ziporyn gave him; but
now there is no doubt he will kill if Lyle doesn't answer
the right way. Lyle just swallows and nods fervently.
Amos lets go of the bag. Lyle and Marlene start to the
door hurriedly.

                              (CONTINUED:)

105   CONTINUED:

                          AMOS
                     (calls after them)
              Miss Marlene, I gone make effort to
              check you in dat Filigree; I and I
              sad you gone go way. You know de
              meanin' of "dubbin' a daughter"?

She seems to get the meaning, gets a horrified look on her
face and Lyle pulls her through the door as Amos breaks out
in wild Jamaican laughter. The door slams and we HEAR their
footsteps receding down the stairs, fast. Amos keeps laughing
wildly until suddenly he stops and holds his jaw, goes "ouch!"
and puts the ice pack up to his face again.

106   ANOTHER ANGLE ON AMOS — TRAVELING SHOT

WITH HIM as he goes through the kitchen, down a hall, into
a dimly-lit bedroom where a water bed on the floor holds
the shape of a woman, sleeping. He finds the telephone,
finds the card Ziporyn gave him in his jacket hanging in
the closet, dials the number, waits.

                          AMOS
              Lemme talk to dis Doctor Zip-or-un.
                     (beat)
              What's dat? Oh. Den you tak a message
              for him, okay? You tell him Amos de
              Prince call. You give him dis numbah...
              [insert appropriate blocked number in
              urban ~~exchange~~ exchange]...tell him he Simon
              dreadie come on here...

He hangs up. He's sitting there on the edge of the bed,
as the shape behind him moves.

                          BED WOMAN
              Come on to bed, sugar.

                          AMOS
              Go on back sleep, woman. I hurt too
              much to go foolin' round, an' dat hurt
              wors'n de odder hurt!

                                             CUT TO:

                                    (OAK MEADOWS)
107   INT. HOSPITAL — ~~PSYCHIATRIC~~ CORRECTIONAL — NIGHT

A DARK CORRIDOR WITH CEILING LIGHTS every ten or fifteen
feet. The corridor dark and empty, sterile white, the
lights throwing small pools of illumination almost directly
below. ZIPORYN WALKS INTO FRAME as his footsteps echo
very loud. He walks away FROM CAMERA toward a room at the
end of the corridor. CAMERA HOLDS POSITION as Ziporyn
reaches the end of his lonely walk and enters the room.

108   BLACK FRAME — INT. HOSPITAL ROOM

as the darkness is suddenly split by the opening door.
Ziporyn pushes the door all the way open and it stays
that way. Now a shaft of light slices the room in half,
and in the beam there is a slab table, with a sheet-
covered figure. Ziporyn goes to it, and pulls the sheet
back. Jimmy Muehler lies there. Ziporyn stares down at
him for a long time, in silence, then drops the sheet
back. He goes to the door, pulls it loose, lets it slide
shut behind him and we go to

                              BLACK FRAME

                              and

                              CUT TO:

109   ANOTHER ROOM IN THE HOSPITAL — ANGLE PAST BED

in which Richie Otis lies with his head swathed in white
bandages. Almost like a mummy. The door opens and
Ziporyn is standing there. He comes in silently, but
Richie isn't asleep.
                    RICHIE
          Who's that?

Ziporyn says nothing.

                         RICHIE (CONT'D.)
the love of God!   If you come to finish me off, man, do it
          quick, for ~~Chrissakes~~ The pain's killin'
          me now.

Ziporyn says nothing, but the CAMERA COMES IN SLOWLY on
him and we can see that he is crying.

                         RICHIE (CONT'D.)
care   I don't ~~give a damn~~ if you kill me now.
          I'm only gonna have one eye is what they
          said, so do it, ~~goddammit~~, do it
          and let me out of here!

CAMERA HOLDS ON ZIPORYN and the anguish in his face for
several beats as we:

                              LAP—DISSOLVE TO:

                    (OAK MEADOWS)
110   EXT. ~~SPRINGFIELD~~ LAKE — NIGHT

MATCH ON ZIPORYN'S FACE as he stares out at the small
lake. The SOUND of crickets and frogs and the night
wind. CAMERA PULLS BACK as he turns to face two young
boys, one black, the other white. They watch him warily.

                              (CONTINUED:)

110 CONTINUED:

The white boy is chunky, very solid, like a good tackle.
Thick features, but with a native intelligence in his face.
He is ENZO, head of a prison gang called The Minute Men.
The black boy is perhaps sixteen, tall, his hair in corn
rows, his expression cool and waiting, almost languid. He
is MOJO HAND, leader of the rival black gang, Brotherhood.

                    ENZO
          Why'd you pull me out of bed at a time
          like this, man? I was sleeping.
                    (beat)
          I gotta stand here with this dumb ~~whore~~ _spook?_

Mojo Hand gets a look of murder in his face. He trembles
as if he'd slice Enzo in a second if Ziporyn weren't there
watching them.

                    ZIPORYN
          I need your help.

                    ENZO
          You don't get no help from me, you creep.

                    ZIPORYN
          I need help from you both.

                    MOJO HAND
                    (deadly polite)
          I'd like to go back to my dorm. Sir.

                    ZIPORYN
          Listen to me, for just a minute.
                    (beat)
          Enzo, you run the white gang here. Mojo,
          you tell the black kids what to do. Don't
          bother saying you don't know what I'm
          talking about. What we say here doesn't
          go any further.

                    MOJO HAND
          Like it didn't go no further with Richie
          Otis?

That hurts. Ziporyn moves uncomfortably under the pain.

                    ZIPORYN
          I did a dumb thing. I needed to know
          something, to try and stop a boy who's
          on the street...

                    ENZO
          From doing what?

                                        (CONTINUED:)

110   CONTINUED: - 2

                          ZIPORYN
                         (helplessly)
        I don't know what. Just something very
        bad. I feel it...

                          MOJO HAND
        You feel it!?! And for that you got
        Richie Otis turned into a snitch and
        let this ~~mother~~ cut him up? Man, you
        some kind of terrible ~~motherfucker~~ eggsucker!
                         (beat)
        Sir.

                          ZIPORYN
        And your people killed Jimmy Muehler.

Mojo Hand sneers, half turns away. Ziporyn grabs him, turns
him.

111   CLOSE 2-SHOT - MOJO HAND & ZIPORYN

There is a wild fire in Ziporyn's face. He speaks very
low but with enormous power and emotion. Mojo Hand is
frozen in his grip.
                          ZIPORYN
        I went in and looked at Muehler. They
        put the knife into his stomach, and they
        ripped up with it, and then they did it
        again. He's all open down the front.
        There's nothing in there but sewage.
                         (beat)
        Richie's lost an eye. He's in a dark
        room with his head covered by bandages.
        He's only going to see half the world
        from today on. When I came in, he thought
        I was going to finish the job. He's
        sixteen years old! It's my fault, and I've
        got to stop both of you before it goes any
        further.

                          ENZO
        They killed Muehler, man! We don't take
        that. It's a matter of honor!

Ziporyn turns on him. CAMERA ANGLE WIDENS TO INCLUDE ENZO.

                          ZIPORYN
        What do you want that I can give you?
        Name it, both of you. Name what you
        want and I'll get it for you! I started
        this, I want it to end here, now, tonight!

112   FULL SHOT – THE THREE OF THEM

Enzo looks at Mojo Hand. The black kid looks back. Their
faces register interest.

                    MOJO HAND
          Can I talk to this honk alone? Sir.

Ziporyn nods, turns away from them, wanders toward the lake.
Mojo Hand and Enzo talk heatedly, then the conversation
quiets and they are obviously dickering, planning, running
ideas out and agreeing. Then they stand and look at Ziporyn,
who--through all this in the f.g.--has been chucking pebbles
in the lake, hunkered down on his haunches, staring into
the night.
                    ENZO
                (calling across)
          Hey, Doc!

Ziporyn gets up, brushes off his hands and looks across at
them.
                    MOJO HAND
          You want to cool the war?

                    ZIPORYN
          Yes.

                    MOJO HAND
          Okay. We tell you what we want. You
          get it and there's a truce. You don't,
          there's gonna be heavy blood. Sir.

Ziporyn starts walking toward them as we:

                                        SLOW DISSOLVE TO:
                                     (OAK MEADOWS)
113   INT. WARDEN'S OFFICE – MAIN BUILDING OF ~~OAK MEADOWS~~ – NIGHT

Ziporyn can still be seen walking toward the boys as the
DISSOLVE FADES and superimposed over it is a HIGH ANGLE
SHOT FROM CEILING HEIGHT in the Warden's office, on Phil
Bonnard, the Warden, and Ziporyn as Ziporyn walks to a
chair and sits down. Bonnard circles the room.

                    WARDEN
          What do they want?

                    ZIPORYN
          You understand this means an end to
          the gangs themselves. They break up
          the cliques. Of their own accord.

                                        (CONTINUED:)

113 CONTINUED:

> WARDEN
> You don't believe that, do you? This
> is a prison, Marvin. It's got bridal
> paths and schools and a machine shop,
> but this is a <u>slam</u>. They know it, I
> know it, and you'd damned well <u>better</u>
> know it after all these years.
>> (beat)
> Gangs come with the territory. They can
> no more do away with gangs than I can
> give them all some kind of a release.

> ZIPORYN
> If they get what they want, they won't
> need gangs. Enzo and Mojo Hand both
> understood that. It was <u>their</u> idea.

> WARDEN
> The only way they'll bust their clubs is
> if I empty this place and turn them all
> onto the street. Yeah, in <u>that</u> way they
> don't need gangs.

> ZIPORYN
> It's easier than that, Phil. And it stops
> the war right now.

> WARDEN
> Okay. Thrill me.

> ZIPORYN
> You ever hear a kid say, "You're bumping
> my head"?

> WARDEN
> Maybe a million times.

> ZIPORYN
> You know what it means.

> WARDEN
> Of <u>course</u> I know. It means the kid   ⟨petty harassment⟩
> thinks a guard is running some ~~chickenshit~~
> on him. Giving him a write-up for a minor.
>> (he laughs)
> How many times you heard a kid tell a guard,
> "Okay, man, you got the pencil, not me"?

> ZIPORYN
> Maybe a million times.
>> (beat)
> So that's it. No more bumping. And an inmate
> review board to make sure, to handle all that.

                                (CONTINUED:)

113   CONTINUED: - 2

Bonnard gets furious. He stalks around Ziporyn, who sits
quietly.

                    WARDEN
          More respect, that's what they want, right?
          I know this fable by heart. They don't like
          us reminding them we're on top and they're
          on bottom.

                    ZIPORYN
          That's it, Phil.

                    WARDEN
          Well, let me tell you a couple of things,
          Doctor. You and I have butted heads on
          this kind of thing before. You've got it
          easy, you just have to plough their heads.
          I've got to keep them in line.
                    (beat)
          This facility was projected to accomodate
          a population of eight hundred wards. At
          the moment we're servicing over eleven
          hundred and fifty. You tell me how I
          supervise a plant this size with an overrun
          like that, without strict correctional
          procedures?

                    ZIPORYN
          You know, Phil, there are times when I'd
          like to wash your mouth out with soap.
                    (beat)
          Facility. Projected. Population. Wards.
          Correctional procedures!   ~~procedures~~ yeechhhhw!
                    (beat)
          Does it make it any easier for you to think
          of this joint as if it were a singles
          condominium? You've got more euphemisms
          than a Thesaurus.
                    (beat)
          It's a slam, Phil! A prison. Guards
          aren't correctional officers, they're screws.
          Maximum isn't segregation, dammit, the kids
          call it the hole! If one of them goes out
          to dig a ditch you call it a "correctional
          industry"...he calls it the ~~shit~~ detail.   scum

                    WARDEN
          They've got to be taught to stay in line.
          Reward and punishment, that's all they
          understand. The contract. The deal. Or
          the hole!

Now they are both shouting, and Ziporyn is up, nose-to-
nose with Bonnard.

114 ANOTHER ANGLE -- FAVORING ZIPORYN

                    ZIPORYN
          You and that damned Skinnerian behavior
          modification. People aren't animals,
          you can't get right with God by making a
          fifteen year old black slum kid to say
          yessir nosir and wear pressed clothes
          by treating him like a pigeon you've
          trained to peck a green lever so he'll
          get a mouthful of birdseed!
                    (beat)
          You and all those behaviorists at Western
          Michigan University, you don't think
          there's any person underneath all that.
          Just Clockwork Orange them and they'll
          shape up fine. Sure, for a prison
          environment, which isn't a normal situation!
          But what the hell happens to them on the
          street?

                    WARDEN
          That isn't fair. Just because I took a
          few courses at WMU to better facilitate--

                    ZIPORYN
          Stuff it, Phil! Just stuff it in your
          ear, man! They changed the name of the Chester
          Hospital for the Criminally Insane to the
          Chester Mental Health Center, but it's still
          a nuthouse full of miserable slobs who aren't
          getting what they need to make them whole.
                    (beat)
          You call the dorms "cottages" and that schlub
          Congreve who runs it the "Supervisor of
          Cottage Life," but the kids know he's just
          a white collar screw!

Ziporyn runs out. He is sweating. Bonnard stares at him,
almost afraid Ziporyn will come for him. Bonnard goes to
his desk and sits down. He nods acquiescence.

                    WARDEN
          Okay. Okay. Just sit down and take it
          easy. I've known you too many years for
          us to go at each other like this. Just
          tell me what they want, and we'll see what
          I can do. I've got people over me, too,
          you know.

Ziporyn sits.

                    ZIPORYN
          Then they've got to be told, made to
          understand. Pushing buttons for a
          cookie isn't going to make these kids
          decent human beings.

115 FROM ZIPORYN TO BONNARD – 3/4 ANGLE CATCHING DESK LIGHT

Ziporyn speaks slower now, reasonably. Bonnard listens.

> ZIPORYN (CONT'D.)
> No more bumping. No six days in the hole
> for talking in line or listening to the
> radio after lights out. No seven days
> loss of cigarette or movie privileges for
> passing a kite to a kid in the next roost.

> WARDEN
> They just do what they want, right? They
> get to wander into unauthorized areas
> without a pass, they get to look like
> slobs...?

> ZIPORYN
> They don't mind authority, Phil. They <u>know</u>
> that's part of the gig. But they want <u>some</u>
> respect.

> WARDEN
> Nobody <u>gets</u> respect; everybody's got to <u>earn</u>
> it!

> ZIPORYN
> (shoots it down)
> Super, Phil, just super. I bet that worked
> real keen when your daddy said it to you
> forty years ago. But it's just another
> easy shot of mouth-to-mouth resucitation,
> one of those cornball slogans we use in
> place of real intelligence.

> WARDEN
> (angrily)
> Don't forget <u>you</u> work for <u>me</u>, Marvin!
> When you've been in this system as long
> as I have, <u>then</u> you can tell me about
> respect...

> ZIPORYN
> Back off, Phil; I'm not some ghetto kid you
> can browbeat. Even the worst of them
> has something going for him, something that
> deserves respect. But if he's always told
> he's an idiot, always told he's rotten,
> always punched in the mouth when he screws
> up, he gets to know he's inferior, some kind
> of social bug you want to stomp, a moron––
> nothing to gain if he's good, nothing to
> lose if he's bad.

(CONTINUED:)

115   CONTINUED:

                    WARDEN
          What is all this mealy-mouth guff?
          I'm a warden of a jail...a <u>jail</u> dammit!
          I haven't got time to coddle--

                    ZIPORYN
                 (loud; intense)
          <u>Not coddle, Phil</u>!
                 (softer)
          Encourage. Is that so hard to grasp?
          Encourage! Find a man's ability, the
          thing he's got that's worthy of respect,
          and nurture it, praise it, develop it
          until he's got some pride, some self-
          respect, till he's not a bug any more.
                 (beat)
          We're always correcting the negatives.
          Would it kill us to push the positives?
                 (beat, weary)
          The world's always ready to tell you
          what a bum you are...why the hell is
          it so miserly about handing out a
          few words of praise?

They sit silently for a moment. Apparently Ziporyn's
lengthy diatribe has sunk in. Bonnard nods wearily, says:

                    WARDEN
          What about the rules, Marvin? What
          do I do about them?

                    ZIPORYN
          An inmate review board can handle all
          that niggling chicken stuff. It'll
          take work off our hands and give them
          a feeling they have a voice in their
          own lives.

Bonnard sits silently.

                    WARDEN
          I'll have to think about it.

                    ZIPORYN
          You haven't got time for that. They
          want the word announced at breakfast
          tomorrow morning.

                    WARDEN
          Too soon, too soon. I have to go over
          this...

                                (CONTINUED:)

115 CONTINUED: - 2

>   ZIPORYN
> Phil, I made a bad move and I started
> World War III in here. One kid's dead,
> another one's got half his face cut off.
> If you waffle on this, tomorrow will get
> it going faster...we may not be able to
> put an end to it this easily.

Bonnard thinks. Finally, he sighs and nods.

>   WARDEN
> Okay. Tell them they've got it. We'll
> work out the machinery tomorrow.

(CONTINUED:)

100.

115 CONTINUED: -3

Ziporyn looks at him for a long time, to make sure he won't go back on his word. Then he nods agreement. Gets up.

ZIPORYN
It's been a bad day. I'm going home to bed. I won't be here for your breakfast announcement, but the "population" will fill me in when I get here.

He starts for the door, stops, turns around.

ZIPORYN (CONT'D.)
I'm sorry about all this, Phil. Maybe it'll do some good. That doesn't let me off the hook for Otis and Muehler, but...well...
(beat)
Good night.

He goes. Bonnard stares after him, then clicks off the desk lamp and sits in darkness, silhouetted by the window as we:

CUT TO:

116 thru 125 INT. LYLE SIMON'S APARTMENT - ESTABLISHING

Lyle and Marlene, Starbuck and Sherri are in the room. Lights low. Everyone looks wasted. Empty bottles OF LIQUOR and incense, remains of the joint-rolling works~~[illegible]~~ EVERYTHING IN SHADOW SO WE GET NO SPECIFICS. The music is slow and understated. This entire scene should be played without dialogue, if possible, to give it an increasing sense of ominousness and betrayal, NOTHING HAPPY.

Lyle rolls a joint, takes it to Sherri, who has been lying back half-dreaming. As he moves away, Starbuck gets up from the chair where he's been waiting, and moves in on Marlene. He slides down beside her, WITH A GLASS OF SCOTCH IN HIS HAND, on some overstuffed pillows and starts talking to her very low, so we cannot make out what he's saying, but it's clearly suggestive; ~~[illegible]~~ HE TRIES TO GET HER TO TAKE A DRINK FROM HIS GLASS BUT SHE shakes her head, tries to get up, he pulls her back, talks some more.

Lyle, meanwhile, has put the joint between Sherri's lips and is having her toke deeply. She isn't really aware of who's doing it, but when he slides down beside her she looks up at him, reconciles herself to the fact that it's a guy she doesn't much care for. ~~[illegible]~~ THERE IS A STRONG SENSE OF DISSIPATION, DOWN VIBES.

(CONTINUED:)

116   CONTINUED:
thru
125   Suggest this entire sequence be shot in SOFT FOCUS.

Now Starbuck looks meaningfully across at Lyle, nodding
his head as if to ask where the bedroom is. Lyle makes
a motion with his head that indicates through the alcove.
Starbuck smiles a nasty smile, and gets to his feet,
pulling Marlene up with him. She doesn't quite know
what's happening, but as Starbuck moves toward the bedroom
she catches on fast and tries to pull away. He holds her
in an arm-behind-back maneuver and keeps her moving. She
looks at Lyle and makes a noise. He looks up, and as if
she and Starbuck were two sweet tots on a picnic, waves
them on. She looks pleadingly at Lyle, but he signals
her to be a good girl and simply put out, and shut up.

SHE'S SO LOADED, LOOKS SICK, SOPORIFIC, LOST;

Starbuck half-drags, half-pushes Marlene into the bedroom.
Sherri looks up, sees them gone, starts to get up. Lyle
stares down at her with some of the venomous ugliness we
saw in scene 67. She looks worried, but able to take
care of herself. She thinks. Lyle starts to strip off
his shirt. She moves. He shoves her back...hard!

                         LYLE
            That just leaves us left to play
            in the grass, baby...

CAMERA IN on Sherri's frightened face as we:

                              FADE TO BLACK

                              and

                              FADE OUT.

                    END ACT SIX

ACT SEVEN

FADE IN:

126   INT. ZIPORYN'S APARTMENT - BEDROOM - DAY

SAME AS SCENE 92 except we can now see what a hideous
tangle of bedclothes Ziporyn lies in. But as we come
to the scene, he is dialing his service. He lets it
ring twice, then speaks.

                    ZIPORYN
          Good morning, this is Dr. Ziporyn.
                    (beat, as he listens)
          Okay. Good afternoon, this is Dr.
          Ziporyn.
                    (rueful expression;
                      beat)
          Got any calls for me?

He listens. Suddenly he sits up, flings the bedclothes
off himself, grabs for a pencil and pad on the floor.

                    ZIPORYN
          Hold it, hold it. Okay, give me that
          address again.
                    (he writes)
          Thanks. No, save the rest of them.

He racks the receiver hurriedly, and dashes for the
shower as we

                                        CUT TO:

127   EXT. AUTO-CRUSHING LOT - DAY

LONG SHOT WITH TELESCOPIC LENS toward the high wall
surrounding the crushing machine that cubes derelict
cars. We HEAR the SOUND of metal being rent and smashed
as the last car dumped down the trough is pressed into
a neat cube by the closing walls of the cubicle.

                                        (CONTINUED:)

127   CONTINUED:

CAMERA TELESCOPES IN to MEDIUM SHOT as we realize Amos
the Prince and Ziporyn are up there talking. How they're
talking is another matter, because Ziporyn is holding his
hands over his ears to shut out the ungodly cacophony. He
motions Amos to follow him and they begin to climb down
as CAMERA FOLLOWS THEIR PROGRESS.

DISSOLVE TO:

128   AUTO CARCASS STORAGE AREA - MEDIUM SHOT MOVING IN

on Amos and Ziporyn sitting in a wrecked, wheelless car.
Something spiffy like a 1951 Packard, maybe. Amos behind
what's left of the wheel, CLOSE TO CAMERA as it threads
its way through the rows of dead vehicles. CAMERA COMES
TO LEFT SIDE and STOPS as Amos and Ziporyn talk.

                    AMOS
          He come to visit me las' night.

                    ZIPORYN
          Where is he now, do you know?

                    AMOS
          I doan check dat current address.
                    (beat)
          But I know how you gone fine out.

                    ZIPORYN
          And as a responsible citizen of the
          community you've come to tell me what
          I need to know to find him.

                    AMOS
          Das not quite what I had in de mine.
                    (beat)
          I had de trade in mine.

                    ZIPORYN
          What do you want in trade?

                    AMOS
          You give your word. You strike I and I
          lahk de big man who word good.

                    ZIPORYN
          Yeah, but what do you want?

                              (CONTINUED:)

128 CONTINUED:

AMOS
I not gone tell raht now. Not too big
de ting. But I want your word. First
I tell you ever'ting, den I ask me ting.

ZIPORYN
I've got to be nuts, but okay, I give my
word. Now...

CUT TO:

129 EXT. SMALL OFFICE BUILDING & PRINTING PLANT - DAY

(NOTE: Location shooting for exteriors and interior of
these scenes is available in North Hollywood, at the
offices and plant of Parliament Publishing Company,
printers of more porn magazines than any other house in
the United States. Ask the author. He has friends in
low places.)

ESTABLISHING SHOT as Ziporyn's car comes tooling into
the lot. CAMERA DOWN to the car as Ziporyn gets out,
runs around the other side and practically drags a
resisting Amos from the front seat.

AMOS
(frantic)
Mon, you crazy wild! How I got mix up
with you? You gone get me kilt I certain.

ZIPORYN
Look: you know what the girl looks like.
We'll just go through the recent photos
they've bought, you spot her, we get an
address on the photographer, and I take
you home.

AMOS
And fulfill you promise.

ZIPORYN
Right, right. But first you cooperate.

AMOS
(bewildered)
How I done adopted you, mon, I dunno!

NOTE: even though these scenes deal with men's magazines, we will see no nude shots, either in photos or on magazine covers.

CUT TO:

130 INT. PUBLISHER'S OFFICE - FILIGREE MAGAZINE

Covers of a half a hundred different men's magazines on
the wall, with notations on them. Stacks of magazines
everywhere. Behind the desk is LAURENCE BERGEN, publisher.

(CONTINUED:)

130   CONTINUED:

The office is large, but every available sofa, chair,
table and drawing board is littered with layouts, color
transparencies, artwork, cover dummies, etc. The walls
~~which where we don't need remove~~ are foursquare filled
with time schedules, printing run order forms, clipboards
filled with data. Bergen is a great toad of a man. Very
expensive suit, sincere tie, white shirt, all of it
surrounding a mass of salamander flesh that sweats easy.
He chews on a cigarette surrogate, one of those filter
things. Amos stands looking at the nekkid females on the
walls. Bergen eyes him suspiciously every once in a
while. Ziporyn sits across from Bergen, talking.

clothed pin-up shots of women, no nudes,

            BERGEN
So you really have no, uh, official
standing for this visit, is that right,
Doctor, uh...

            ZIPORYN
Ziporyn. That's right, Mr. Bergen. But
all I want to do is take a look at the
recent photo sets you've bought from
free-lancers. I'm trying to locate a
young man who's on absentee leave from
the ~~Fort Charles~~ Correctional Facility.

OAK MEADOWS

            BERGEN
Well, I don't know...

            ZIPORYN
You've seen my credentials, Mr. Bergen.
This is, quite literally, a matter of
extreme urgency. One boy is already
dead and another will be blind in one
eye for the rest of his life because of
this person.

            BERGEN
Well, uh, you know we, uh, we've had
quite a lot of trouble from the various
authorities. Censorship. The ugly
stain of repression, the ominous specter
of blue-nosed...

He seems intent on launching into a Fifth Amendment diatribe.
Ziporyn cuts him off. He stands up.

            ZIPORYN
Nothing like that this time. I just
want to go over the photo sets you've
bought in, say, the last three weeks.

            BERGEN
Well...

                              CUT TO:

131   PHOTO STORAGE ROOM

The walls, from floor to ceiling, all four sides, are
filled with unpainted wood bins, narrow shelves that
contain photo sets. There are in-baskets on the desk
filled with sets. Stacks on the chairs. On the tops
of the eight filing cabinets that dominate the middle
of the room. Ziporyn is looking around in bewilderment.
Amos is riffling through a set. Bergen is eyeing Amos
suspiciously.

                    ZIPORYN
          But...but...these were purchased for
          Filigree Magazine.

                    BERGEN
          Listen, Doctor, uh...listen to me. We
          publish two hundred and sixty-five titles
          the last time I checked. All photos are
          bought on Filigree's account. That's our
          leader. But we buy all rights, and we
          can use those photos in any of our books,
          maybe all of them if we hit a number who
          gets some mail.

                    ZIPORYN
          So I'd have to go through all these?

                    BERGEN
          If you want to find the model release with
          the name and address of the photographer
          on it. That's how we pay.

Ziporyn removes his jacket, tosses it over a chair.

                    ZIPORYN
          Okay, Amos, let's get started.

                    BERGEN
                 (eyeing Amos)
          Who, uh, who's he?

                    ZIPORYN
          My director of esthetic judgments. All
          state correctional facilities have them.

Bergen looks nonplused, nods, and edges out the door.
As he goes, Amos is sitting down at the desk, and
Ziporyn is bringing over stacks of photos to be looked
at. Amos checks one, shakes his head, puts it on one
side, takes another folder from the "in" stack as we

                              DISSOLVE THRU:

132   ANOTHER ANGLE ON SCENE 131

Amos and Ziporyn going through the photo folders, with
the "in" stack getting first lower then higher and the
"out" stack only getting higher as we

DISSOLVE THRU TO:

133   A THIRD ANGLE ON SCENE 131

as Amos opens a folder, takes out an 8x10 contact sheet
and gives a whoop. Ziporyn sits up, he's been almost
asleep.

AMOS
Dis de one! Mmmm, ain't she superfine!

Ziporyn grabs the folder, rummages through it to find the
model release form. He gets it out. Reads it.

ZIPORYN
What'd you say her name was?

AMOS
Dat screw-face call her Mar-lene.

(model release form)   ZIPORYN
This ~~form advising~~ says her name is Candice
Storer.

He sits there, chewing his lip a moment, then gets up and
goes out. Amos sits there and continues looking at the
women, apparently never tiring of the sight of naked butts.
In a moment Ziporyn returns with Bergen. Bergen holds the
model release form.

BERGEN
These model release forms are strictly
a con. The girls don't want their real
names in the magazines, usually. Too
many chances of bananas calling them on
the phone if they're listed...or their
mothers in Des Moines finding out about
it.

ZIPORYN
And the photographer's name isn't there
at all.

AMOS
Hey, mon, I tole you dat de one. I doan
care what name it say dere.

BERGEN
Well, if you want to trace it further,
the address we sent the check to is in
the file. Here's the voucher number.
Give me a minute and I'll have it for
you.

134   ON ZIPORYN

As Bergen starts out, Ziporyn joins him.

                    ZIPORYN
          We'll go with you. If you've got
          an address, we'll be leaving.

                    AMOS
          I could sit here an' look dese fine
          ladies all week, mon.

                    BERGEN
          Say, who, uh, who ~~the hell~~ is he?

                    ZIPORYN
                (confidentially)
          The Dauphin of France. Been lost for
          years. If De Gaulle hadn't stolen
          power, he'd be the King today.

Bergen looks at him as though he's grown another head.

                    BERGEN
          Are you sure you're the psychiatrist
          out there?

Ziporyn smiles enigmatically, and follows Bergen, with
Amos slipping a folder under his jacket and following
the psychiatrist. HOLD ANGLE on their departure as we:

                                              CUT TO:

135   (CITY) STREET - CAR WRECKING LOT - DAY

as Ziporyn's car pulls into FRAME and stops in front of
the gate to the car-crushing lot of scenes 126-127. Amos
gets out, slams the door and walks around to Ziporyn's
side as CAMERA COMES IN on them.

                    AMOS
          You tink dat address do it?

                    ZIPORYN
          I don't know. Maybe it's a drop for
          Lyle Simon or the girl. Check was made
          out to him; it's a lead, whatever.
                (beat)
          Now we come to your request, right?

                    AMOS
          Dat right. You give de word, mon.

                                      (CONTINUED:)

135   CONTINUED:

                    ZIPORYN
          Okay, let's have it.

Amos's attitude changes. Now he is no longer the amused
celebrant at a silly honkie game. He is more the man we
saw in the alley behind Big Stoot's. His face gets hard.

                    AMOS
          You know, mon, I sense you laugh a lot
          at Amos de Prince. I want you to know
          I and I not de clown you might s'pose.

                    ZIPORYN
          I never for a moment thought that charming
          facade was the real you. I remember the
          knife.

Amos feels his face where it's still raw from having
grazed the concrete in the alley.

                    AMOS
          I remember also, mon. So here my request.
          You promise to do it, dat true.
                    (beat)   (OAK MEADOWS)
          I and I doan want be cut outta ~~Han Ohamtos~~
          lahk you say. I want my route back.

                    ZIPORYN
          You want to be able to send dope into ~~Ban~~ OAK
  [MEADOWS] ~~Chamtas~~ through Muehler, without me blowing
          the whistle on you?

                    AMOS
          Dat's de trut'.

                    ZIPORYN
          Okay. You've got my word. You can run
          your route through Muehler and I won't
          make a sound.

                    AMOS
          Dat's a promise?
                    (amazed)
          Dat simple?

                    ZIPORYN
          That simple, Amos. You and Muehler are
          still partners. And may you prosper.

He throws it into drive and takes off, leaving Amos
standing there smiling. For a moment. Then Amos starts
to look worried as we:

                              DISSOLVE TO:

136 INT. LYLE & MARLENE'S APARTMENT - DAY

Lyle, naked to the waist and barefoot, has just pulled on
his pants. Save for him, the room is empty, with the
remnants of the previous night's debauch around him in
ugly profusion. He wanders around, as if looking for
something, he doesn't know what; running his hands through
his thick hair, finding ~~a cigarette butt~~ *a cigarette butt* and getting
it lit ~~~~ with considerable difficulty. Then,
he looks toward the alcove leading to the bedroom and yells.

> LYLE
> Hey! Marlene! Rise and shine!

There is no sound for a moment. He waits. There is faint
movement from the dark interior of the bedroom. Then
Marlene comes out, wrapped in a sheet, looking very badly
used. Her face is puffy, eyes red, and she has the look
of a whipped dog. She stands there and stares at him,
saying nothing.

> LYLE
> (as if oblivious)
> What's for breakfast?

She stares at him.

> LYLE
> You'd better make something. It's
> late. I've got an appointment...
> (beat)
> What ~~~~ are you looking at me
> like that for?

She settles slowly to the floor, gathering the sheet
around her as if she were cold. She talks as much to
herself as to him.

> MARLENE
> I used to think I was just dumb unlucky.
> Every time I got hooked up with some guy
> he'd turn out to be a ~~louse~~ *louse* and dump
> all over me, so I'd say well, he was just
> a stinker and it'll be better next time.

> LYLE
> (getting angry)
> Get your butt into the kitchen and make
> me something to eat. Do it now!

> MARLENE
> (dreamily)
> But I guess I'm just a loser.
> (beat)
> That's an awful thing to find out.

137 ARRIFLEX SHOT - WITH THE ACTION

(shoves) (down)

as Lyle comes across the room and ~~slams~~ her /where she
sits. Marlene goes over, tries to crawl away, and Lyle
grabs her, ~~████████~~, yanks her erect. She is now
screaming at him:

> MARLENE
> You <u>gave</u> me to him, that pig, you just
> gave me to him...you planned it all
> evening...what he did to me and you
> didn't even come when I called you...

(shaking)

He is also shouting, ~~slapping~~ her. ~~████~~

(just)

> LYLE
> Shut up, /shut ~~the hell~~ up; you're no
> damn good, none of you are any ~~████~~
> good, always trying to cut some guy
> to pieces, trying to make me feel
> lousy...

he subsides.

Finally, ~~████████████████~~ He looks down on her.

138 CLOSE ANGLE ON LYLE'S FACE AS HE LOOKS DOWN AT HER

There is now a viciousness in his face, a total lack of
humanity that tells us just what it was lurking in his
manner that has driven Ziporyn all these days.

> LYLE
> Listen, you dumb broad. Starbuck came
> up with a fine idea last night. He
> figures with his connections at the
> conventions, and my connections with
> the right kind of girls, I can make
> some good moves running a string of
> action like you.

(pushes)

He pulls her up, ~~shoves~~ her toward the telephone.

> LYLE (CONT'D.)
> It's going to be a lot cushier for me
> starting right now. You get your face
> on that phone and start calling all the
> chicks you know in the business. You
> tell them there's a new man here who's
> going to need some heavies, and I'll
> take good care of them, not like those
> ripoff macks who run some chick's tail
> ragged.

(CONTINUED:)

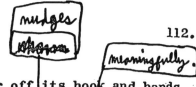

112.

138   CONTINUED:

He bends down, pulls the receiver off its hook and hands
it to her. She won't take it. He ~~slaps~~ her. She takes
it.

                    LYLE (CONT'D.)
          I've got an errand to run now. When I
          get back I want half a dozen live ones.
          And if you mess me around, baby, I'm going
          to make what Starbuck did to you look like
          good clean fun.

He slips into his shoes, grabs a shirt, and takes a big
manila envelope stuffed full of something or other off
the bookcase television set. He gives her a long look.

                    LYLE (CONT'D.)
          You got it straight?

No answer.

                    LYLE (CONT'D.)
          You going to do what I say?

No answer. She looks at the floor, silently crying.

                    LYLE (CONT'D.)
                      (smiling)
          Yeah, you'll do what I say.
                      (beat)
          Because you're a loser, baby.

He goes, leaving her there on the floor. Beat, beat,
beat...then she slowly starts dialing as we:

                                        CUT TO:

139   INT. MARLENE'S PARENTS' HOME - DAY

A very lower-middle-class home. All the appurtances
of restricted, simple living. A Garden Grove sort of
home. An Evanston sort of home. A Bronx sort of home.
Cheap furniture with a few old pieces, a tv prominent
in the living room, comfortable chairs and a view out
onto a street of small homes. Marlene's MOTHER and
FATHER are gray little people. Quiet, reserved, very
polite. Nice people. Solid. Married thirty years.
Never asked for much, never got very much. They survive.
CAMERA PULLS BACK from VIEW OUT WINDOW to PAN THE ROOM
and give us all the above, finally settling casually on
a MEDIUM CLOSE SHOT of the Mother's face as she speaks:

                                        (CONTINUED:)

139   CONTINUED:

> MOTHER
> Yes, the check came here. Marlene
> stopped by to pick it up.

CAMERA PULLS BACK to show the Father sitting beside the
Mother on the sofa, Ziporyn in an easy chair, leaning
forward to speak.

> ZIPORYN
> Do you know where she's staying?

> FATHER
> (a little bitterly)
> Why should we know where she's living,
> sir? We're only her parents.

> MOTHER
> Walt, shhh!

> FATHER
> We haven't known where she's been living
> for almost two years.

> MOTHER
> (hastily)
> Marlene likes to lead her own life.
> She's very self-sufficient. She
> calls almost every week. She called
> about the check; then she came to get
> it.

> ZIPORYN
> Was there a young man with her?

> MOTHER
> Why, no. She came alone. We had a
> very nice afternoon together...

> FATHER
> She came and went in fifteen minutes.

> ZIPORYN
> Did she say anything about where she
> might be, or what she was doing?

> FATHER
> Listen, Doctor Ziporyn, I'm still not
> sure I understand what this is all
> about. I mean, you say she's in no
> trouble, but you ask like she is.

> MOTHER
> Marlene would never do anything wrong,
> Walt. You know that.

(CONTINUED:)

139 CONTINUED: - 2

                           ZIPORYN
Let me assure you both, Marlene hasn't
done a single thing wrong. But I think
she's gotten herself involved with a
young man who might be very dangerous...
no, I think he is very dangerous.
                    (beat)
I want to find him before...

                           MOTHER
                    (worried now)
Oh. I see. Well, let me think.
                    (beat)
Walt, didn't she say something about
working on some motion picture?

                           FATHER
                    (reluctantly)
I think so. She said she was a script
girl or a production secretary, whatever
that is.

                           ZIPORYN
Can you remember the name of the film,
or even better, the company making it?

                           MOTHER
                    (slowly)
No...I don't...yes, yes, I do. It was
a very musical name, I thought at the
time. A dance? No, it was...oh, Walt,
don't you remember she said it was a
big movie and the company was one of those
foreign dances...

                           FATHER
Flamenco.

                           MOTHER
                    (brightly)
Yes, that's right. That's it. Flamenco
Films in ~~the~~ the downtown mall.
                    (beat)
I've never heard of them before, have
you, Doctor? I asked her who the stars
were, and she said no one I'd know.
                    (beat)
Isn't that a peculiar thing to say. Walt
and I watch all the films on television.
And we can name almost everyone.

                                   (CONTINUED:)

139   CONTINUED: - 3

Ziporyn rises, preparatory to leaving.

                    ZIPORYN
          Well, I'd better get going. I want
          to locate Flamenco Films and see if
          they can help me find Marlene.

                    MOTHER
          Wouldn't you like a nice cool drink,
          perhaps? It seems such a shame to have
          to run off after just getting here.

                    ZIPORYN
          No, I'd better...

                    FATHER
          Let him go, Joyce.

                    MOTHER
          Walt! Please!

                    ZIPORYN
          No, that's all right. I understand.

                    FATHER
                    (rising)
          Do you? Do you really? Do you have
          any kids?

                    ZIPORYN
          No, I--

                    FATHER
          Then you don't know what it is to be
          cut off like something useless.
                    (beat)
          Her room upstairs. My wife keeps it
          the way it was when Marlene graduated
          from high school. Waiting for her to
          come back. To come home one day and
          tell us this nice fellah with her is
          going to be her husband...

                    MOTHER
                    (apologizing)
          Since they laid so many off at the plant,
          my husband has been a little nervous; he
          doesn't mean any of this--

                    FATHER
          Let it go, Joyce. Just let it go.

                              (CONTINUED:)

139   CONTINUED: - 4

Ziporyn moves toward the door. He's very polite, but
really wants out of there.

                    ZIPORYN
          Thank you, thank you very much. I'll
          tell her you'd like to hear from her
          when I see her.

                    MOTHER
               (suddenly tougher)
          We don't want to pry into her life.
          Just tell her we said hello and sent
          our love.

Ziporyn nods hastily and gets out of there. CAMERA HOLDS
on this American Gothic couple, living with their sadness
as the Father says one last thing:

                    FATHER
               (softly)
          Let it go, Joyce...please let it go...

He says this as we slowly

                                        DISSOLVE TO:
                              (CITY MALL)
140   EXT. OFFICE BUILDING - DOWNTOWN ~~CHICAGO~~ - DAY - STOCK

      ESTABLISHING

      CAMERA MOVING IN ON THIRD FLOOR WINDOWS.

141   CAMERA IN ON WINDOW

      with the legend in flaking paint on it: FLAMINGO FILMS
                                              FLAMENCO FILMS
                                              FLARE FILMS

      CAMERA INTO WINDOW as we   -
                                        DISSOLVE THRU TO:

142   INT. WAITING ROOM - FLAMENCO FILMS

      A RECEPTIONIST standing behind a swinging gate in a
      ratty, burn-the-lot operation. Fleabag city. Ziporyn
      stands before her INTO CAMERA.

                    RECEPTIONIST
          You won't have to go looking, mister;
          we're expecting him in here any time
          with stills from last week's shooting.
          I don't know when, but you can wait if
          you like, I don't care.

Ziporyn nods thanks, looks around, takes a beat-up chair
behind the door as it would open.

143   CAMERA ANGLE TIGHT ON ZIPORYN
thru
146   as he sits there, thinking. We HEAR VOICE OVER as he
       thinks.

                        ZIPORYN'S VOICE OVER
                            (Filter)
              There was a boy, nineteen years old. John
              Butterman. His time for parole came. They
              said he needed more treatment. I said let
              him go, the situation that brought him in
              would never come up again, one in a million.
                              (beat)
              So he went out.
                              (beat)
              Four days after he hit the street he bought
              a target pistol and a length of rope, went
              into ~~Emanuel~~ Park, found a seven-year-old
              girl and tied her to a tree near the lagoon
              and pumped twenty-eight shots into her.
                              (beat)
              Come with your pictures, Lyle Simon. Come
              now while I'm here. I'll wait.

Through this DIALOGUE OVER we CONTINUE TO LAP-DISSOLVE
while the day wanes in the window, so we can tell much
time has passed. And as the DIALOGUE ENDS, the CAMERA
ANGLE TILTS UP as we see Lyle Simon coming out of the
elevator down the hall, walking toward the office. But
Ziporyn is slumped down in the chair, half-asleep from
the efforts of the past night and the days preceding.
He doesn't see Simon come to the door, start to open
it and then suddenly recognize Ziporyn in the chair.

BISHOP

147   CLOSE ON ZIPORYN

as a movement or a sound--something small--causes him to
look up and over his shoulder at Lyle Simon, frozen at
the door. He jumps to his feet. Lyle shoves the door
with all his might. It catches Ziporyn on the side of
the face, right at the angle of door's-edge, and Ziporyn
can only get his hand through to barely grasp Lyle by
his hand holding the envelope. Lyle tries to wrest free
but Ziporyn holds on tightly. He can't get through the
door to get at Lyle, but he won't let go. Lyle pulls and
strains, and Ziporyn pulls and strains. It's a tug-of-war.
Ziporyn begins to win, pulling Lyle toward the sliver of
open door. Lyle pulls the door back an instant, just as
Ziporyn's hand is in the jamb, then slams it hard against
Ziporyn's hand, then again. He squeezes Ziporyn's hand
in the door. Ziporyn moans with pain and tries to hold
on. Lyle drops the envelope, which spills open, showering
its contents of still photos all over the hall. CAMERA
DOWN to CLOSE on Ziporyn's grip being loosened, loosened
as Lyle crushes the hand in the door, painfully, and we:

FLASH-INTERCUT:

148   INTERCUT

The parallel scene we saw at the outset of the story,
the last image of shots 2-15, of Ziporyn's bandage-
wrapped hand grasping for Lyle as the young man slips
off the roof of the building to which he has jumped.
The bandage and brutalized condition of Ziporyn's hand
should be made clear, to pre-establish the irony of what
is to come later in scenes 172, 181 & 182.

OVER this SHOT we should HEAR Ziporyn moaning in pain,
to accentuate the drubbing his hand is taking. It will
inform our observations later.

CUT BACK TO:

149   SAME AS 147

as Lyle Simon pulls loose, shoves the door open into
Ziporyn again, throwing him off-balance. By the time
Ziporyn has regained his balance, Lyle is down the hall,
down the stairs, and gone.

150   WITH ZIPORYN – ARRIFLEX TILT-ACTION

as Ziporyn races after him. He gets to the stairwell,
sees Lyle Simon is gone and resignedly slumps back to
the office. He sees the photos lying there as CAMERA
GOES WITH HIM and SHOOTS DOWN AND PAST HIM. He stoops
to pick up the photos and put them back in the envelope, *using mostly his good hand,*
but suddenly stops. CAMERA HAS COME AROUND TO REGISTER
HIS FACE but now it TILTS DOWN to give us a FULL CLOSEUP
of the 8x10 glossy he's looking at.

massaging his chewed-up hand with obvious pain.

A clear, unmistakable photograph of Sherri, the girl from
his encounter group. HOLD ON THE PHOTO as we

                                        FADE TO BLACK:

                                        and

                                        FADE OUT.

                        END ACT SEVEN

ACT EIGHT

FADE IN:

151   FRAME BLACK

SOUND of APARTMENT DOOR BUZZER. Then silence. FRAME
remains BLACK. SOUND of BUZZER again. Then a CIRCLE
OF LIGHT suddenly appears in the middle of the FRAME.
We may not recognize it at once, but it's the peephole
security window in an apartment door. An eye appears
in the peephole. We HEAR the VOICE of SHERRI O.S.

                    SHERRI'S VOICE O.S.
        Who is it?
                    (beat)
        Oh. What are you doing here?

The SOUNDS of multiple LOCKS being OPENED and the peep-
hole closes as FRAME GOES TO BLACK AGAIN and then,
SYNCHRONIZED with the SOUND of a final door LOCK being
OPENED we

                                        CUT TO:

152   INT. HALLWAY - POSH CONDOMINIUM - DAY

CLOSE ON THE DOOR as it swings open. We are looking at
Sherri in EXTREME CLOSEUP. She speaks INTO CAMERA.

                    SHERRI
        Come on in. Big surprise. Thought I'd
        had all the big surprises I could handle
        for one week.

She steps back to permit Ziporyn to MOVE INTO FRAME
and into the apartment. As she CLOSES DOOR and FRAME
TO BLACK again and as we HEAR LOCKS being thrown we

Ziporyn's hand has been hurriedly bandaged with a hankie.

                                        CUT TO:

153   INT. SHERRI'S APARTMENT - LIVING ROOM - DAY

The money must come from somewhere. We can assume Sherri
does well as a hooker, or we can assume she gets a stipend
from her parents in Grosse Point. Or we can draw other
conclusions. Whatever, her taste is impeccable, the
apartment is light, cheery, sybaritic and commands an   *tasteful*
awesome view across ~~Chicago the house~~. Sherri is in a baby
doll nightie. ~~Again we can assume she's waiting for a
john to show up, or we can assume she's recovering from
the night before, or we can take it as all play.~~

the heart of the city and the lake.

                    SHERRI
          You haven't said anything yet, Doc.
          Are you here offering your services
          as a professional, looking for the
          services of a professional, or just
          doing some amateur slumming?

                    ZIPORYN
          I'm not here for laughs, Sherri, if
          that's what you mean.

He pulls out the stills from the porn flick. Sherri's
eyes widen. She slaps them out of his hand. She's
ashamed. How peculiar. Brazen, unflinching in the
encounter group when her profession comes up, yet here
in her apartment she is ashamed.

                    SHERRI   — (almost hysterical)
          Why'd you bring those here? None of
          that ever gets in here!! I'm someone
          else here!

                    ZIPORYN
          I didn't bring them to shame you or
          even to pass a value judgment.

                    SHERRI   — (spiraling up)
          It's a lousy stunt, Doc. I may be a
hooker ~~whore~~, but in this building I'm just
          another tenant.

                    ZIPORYN
          Sherri, stop pillorying me for a
          moment and I'll explain.

She quiets down. Stares at him for a second, then seems
to realize she's half-dressed. She gets skittish.

                              (CONTINUED:)

153   CONTINUED:

                         SHERRI
          Excuse me a second. I was just going
          to bed. I was out all night. Let me
          put on a robe.

She goes through a doorway, apparently into the bedroom.
Ziporyn looks around the apartment. It's pretty impressive.
When she returns, she finds him examining a piece of glazed
pottery. He doesn't see her. She stands in the doorway.

                         SHERRI (CONT'D.)
          T'ang dynasty. Glaziers have been trying
          for five hundred years to match the chroma
          of that blue. They can't do it. One of
          the lost wonders.

                         ZIPORYN
          You live well, Sherri.

                         SHERRI
                         (pointedly)
          In here, I do. Out there...
                         (beat)
          ...well, you have the pictures.

This brings Ziporyn back to his purpose. He goes to the
glossies still lying on the rug and picks one from the
mess. It's the photo of Marlene. He brings it to her.

153A   CLOSE ON ZIPORYN'S HAND

          as he hands out the photo, she notices the bloody hankie
          wrapped around his hand. As CAMERA ANGLE WIDENS she
          takes his hand.

                         SHERRI
          What happened to you?

                         ZIPORYN
          It's okay.

                         SHERRI
          Yeah, but what happened?

                         ZIPORYN
          I got it looking for a girl named
          Marlene Storer. The girl in this
          photo. Do you know her?

                                        (CONTINUED:)

153A CONTINUED:

                              SHERRI
Let me put some iodine on it; it
looks mean.

                              ZIPORYN
                            (frustrated)
<u>Forget</u> <u>it</u>! Take a look at this photo.
Do you <u>know</u> this girl?

She stares at his face for a long moment, realizing he's
into something very nasty and very heavy, and slowly
removes her gaze from the hand and his expression, and
looks at the photo in his other hand. Her face crumbles.

                              SHERRI
                           (sick at heart)
I know her.

                              ZIPORYN
She's hanging out with a kid named
Lyle Simon. How about him, do you
know him?

Sherri trembles. She turns away, goes to the window
and stares out. Then, after a long moment, she speaks
very softly.
                              SHERRI
He's no kid.

Ziporyn goes to her. She's really shaken. Her body
is trembling. He turns her slowly. She's crying.

154   2-SHOT - CLOSE - AGAINST WINDOW

She looks up at him and tries to smile. But it's too
hard.
> SHERRI (CONT'D.)
> I know him. I was with him last night.
> (beat)
> But not by choice...

Half-turning, she pulls the robe away from her neck
slightly. Dark marks are on her pale flesh, upper chest.

> SHERRI (CONT'D.)
> He wanted me to play some pretty nasty
> games. When I said I'd rather not...
> he used me for an ash tray.

Ziporyn is sickened. He examines the wounds.

> ZIPORYN
> How's your medicine cabinet? Let me
> tend to these.

155   ANGLE FROM BEDROOM - ON THEM

as he leads her into the bedroom CAMERA GOES WITH THEM
and they enter the bathroom. CAMERA GOES TO DOOR of
BATHROOM and SHOOTS THRU as Ziporyn opens the medicine
cabinet and takes out cotton, petroleum jelly, swabs,
whatever is handy to repair her.

> ZIPORYN
> (as he works)
> Listen, Sherri: I want you to tell
> me where he is. He's broken his
> furlough from ~~Stony Prairie~~ [OAK MEADOWS]; I ran
> into him earlier today and I think
> he's pretty dangerous.

> SHERRI
> Marlene's still with him.

> ZIPORYN
> Well, I'll figure a way to get him
> away from her before I have the cops
> grab him.

She's been watching him with interest deeper than that
of a patient for a doctor. Her hand lightly rests on
his shoulder. He doesn't pay any attention.

(CONTINUED:)

155   CONTINUED:

> SHERRI
> I could get her out of there. Keep
> him thinking about other things
> while you moved in on him.

> ZIPORYN
> Thanks for the offer, but that isn't
> necessary. Once near him seems to
> have been enough for you.

> SHERRI
> What if he's got a gun?

> ZIPORYN
> (considering)
> It's unlikely. Not his kind of thing.

> SHERRI
> You don't know what his kind of thing
> is. I do. He might even use her for
> protection.

Ziporyn leans back against the wall of the bathroom.
He looks at her, considering.

> ZIPORYN
> Why the sudden heroics?

> SHERRI
> (chuckles)
> Well, you wouldn't think I'd be so turned
> off by a guy, not after all the elevators
> I've been in...but Lyle Simon is a twisto.
> A real twisto. I'd like to see him get
> put away. I'd like that a lot.

> ZIPORYN
> (makes up his mind)
> Okay. But we'll do it with the police,
> and we'll do it slow and easy.

> SHERRI
> Now that I ve got you sold, there's one
> condition.

He looks at her inquiringly, not yet catching on. But
her naked invitation, expressed in a long, lingering
look, quickly hips him to her "condition."

> ZIPORYN
> Hold it, hold it.

156   ANGLE ON ZIPORYN FROM BEDROOM

as he backs out of the bathroom. He's not shy or silly
about it, but he's not about to go to bed with one of
his patients. Sherri follows him out of the bathroom.

>   SHERRI
>   What's the matter, Doc? Afraid
>   you'll catch a social disease,
>   like empathy?

>   ZIPORYN   (seduce)
>   Doctors who ~~bed~~ their patients
>   give the profession a bad name.
>   Just thinking of my reputation.

>   SHERRI
>   I've been watching you, Doc.

>   ZIPORYN
>   (suddenly serious)
>   Okay, knock it off, Sherri.

His tone is so forceful, she stops her half-playful moves.

>   ZIPORYN (CONT'D.)
>   Don't make me start acting like a
>   shrink. We've got an ugly situation
>   I have to deal with, you're burned
>   and in considerable pain...and you
>   are <u>still</u> a member of my encounter
>   group. And that's all the reasons
>   I'll give you.
>   (beat)
>   Now, do you still want to help?

She smiles with resignation, shrugs.

>   SHERRI
>   Sure. I was just curious ~~anyway~~
>   what you looked like without your
>   clothes.

>   ZIPORYN
>   When I have more leisure, we'll
>   talk about it.
>   (beat)
>   Right now, I'd like to make a
>   phone call.

She points to the phone in the living room.

>   SHERRI
>   I'll get dressed. Be with you,
>   in a couple of minutes. *Now that you've
>   doctored me, wouldn't you let me tend to your hand?*

He leaves the bedroom, pulls the door shut behind him.

157 WITH ZIPORYN

as he goes to the phone, dials a number, waits.

ZIPORYN
Give me the Warden, please.
(beat, beat)
Phil? Marvin. I've found Simon. I want to bring him in, but I'll need you to run interference with the cops. I think we can pull an end-run around publicity on this. I know you were worried.
(listens)
Right. Have a 'tac squad meet us there.
(listens)
Where? Oh.
(calls in to Sherri)
Sherri! Pick up the extension, will you?
(listens)
Phil, this is Sherri. She's a friend of mine. Sherri, Phil Bonnard, Warden out at the facility. Will you give him the address, please...

As CAMERA HOLDS Ziporyn listening, we begin to

DISSOLVE TO:

158 INT. LYLE & MARLENE'S APARTMENT - DAY

as Lyle bursts in from outside. Marlene is still sitting where he left her, the phone receiver in her hand. We can HEAR the HIGH WHINE of the warning tone tracer placed on the line when it has been off-the-hook too long.

LYLE
(frantic)
That [redacted] [shrink] from [redacted] [OAK MEADOWS] was waiting for me when I got to the movie distributor. It was close. He...
(beat, he looks at her in a new way)
Did you call him? Did you call him and tell him I was going there? [Nobody else knew I was going over there today... just you!]
(spiraling up)
Is that what happened, you crummy...

[redacted]

(CONTINUED:)

158 CONTINUED:

He starts toward her; she clutches the blanket around her
as she scuttles backward, getting a coffee table between
her and his bull rush. With a wild swipe of his hand he
throws the table out of the way, sending all the bottles
and glasses and refuse of the previous night's party
flying toward the CAMERA which is a signal for CAMERA TO
GO SLIGHTLY OUT OF FOCUS.

158A THE ACTION - ARRIFLEX

NOTE: through the use of judicious cutting, editing, out
      of focus shooting, wild angles and coverage reaction
shots, we will <u>totally</u> <u>avoid</u> the actual show of violence,
while maintaining a feeling of desperation and menace. At
no <u>time</u> will we see the murder that is about to take place.
The use of the blanket and the dimness of the ~~apartment~~ *apartment*
because of drawn drapes will insure the direction of this
pivotal scene as tasteful and within the bounds of accept-
ability even for a mature audience.

158B REACTION SHOT - LYLE

as the latent hostilities Ziporyn has deduced in him are
freed. His face tells us the depth of his anger and
frenzy.

158C REACTION SHOTS - MARLENE

at first in a dreamlike state of sorrow and loneliness,
then as Lyle reaches her and we see her rough-housed out
of the FRAME, panic, fear, desperation, a passion to flee.

NOTE: these reaction shots will lend important tone to
      the misdirected angles and cutaways and allow us the
interior tension of the scenes without showing violence.
They should be INTERCUT FREELY and OFTEN.

158D ANOTHER SERIES OF WILD ANGLES - ARRIFLEX
thru
158J of the action in bits and pieces, with closeups on hands,
      feet, bodies in movement. As Lyle grabs her and we HEAR
      Marlene crying, the MUTED SOUNDS of Lyle striking her.

158K WITH MARLENE - OUT OF FOCUS - ARRIFLEX

Now freed of her dreamlike state entirely, on her feet
but tangled in the blue blanket she tries to hold up,
                    (CONT'D.)

                                        (CONTINUED:)

158K CONTINUED:

> (CONT'D.)

and, sobbing pitifully, mumbling curses and self-loathing, she starts slapping him back, windmilling wildly. He takes a few slaps on the forearms, backing away from her, but she keeps coming, and he ~~punches~~ *shoves* her. She goes down. But gets up, grabs a bookend and comes for him. She grazes his cheek with it, and he knocks it from her hand. ~~And~~ ~~begins beating her across the room with it.~~ NOTE: now we begin to see snips of scene that were intercut in the opening of the story, from scenes 2-15, except now they're wholly in context. ~~and their appearance should match~~

Suggest these shots that were FLASH-FORWARDS in scenes 2-15 be SHOT AS IF THEY WERE DOUBLE-IMAGE. Not the entire action, just the snippets that happened at the beginning.

He proceeds to ~~beat her into the floor~~ *STRUGGLE WITH HER,* done in such a way *that we* and shot through the furniture and obscuring angles so *do not* we don't have the actual view of violence, but get its *see actual* impact. *mayhem,*

He grabs a table lamp and, as *[hit]* CAMERA PANS AWAY AND AROUND THE ROOM, we HEAR him ~~bludgeon~~ her ~~to death~~ with it. The action goes on for an unbearable time and then Lyle staggers erect and into the frame, wiping his mouth, still holding the shattered lamp.

> LYLE
> (mumbling)
> All alike...all of you...damn you...
> all try to make me feel small and
> stupid...but I'm not...I knew you
> called him...

He stumbles backward and hits the wall, slides down and sits there, with his limp hands over his drawn-up knees, staring at ~~whatever is across~~ *the blanket-covered mound* across the room, as we

> CUT TO:

159   EXT. ~~CHICAGO~~ *CITY* STREET - BOOM SHOT

LOOKING DOWN on a ~~Chicago~~ 'tac squad of cops drawn out in skirmish lines (to be checked for accuracy). BOOM DOWN to Ziporyn, De Marco, Warden Phil Bonnard and Sherri around the back of the 'tac squad van filled with riot equipment.) The 'TAC LIEUTENANT is buttoning up *from* the front of Sherri's bodice as CAMERA BOOMS DOWN to *which* MEDIUM SHOT on the group, favoring the Lt. & Sherri. *a bare leg extends,*

Ziporyn's hand is still bandaged ~~with~~ hurriedly with the hankie. He favors it, as if in pain.

> (CONTINUED:)

159   CONTINUED:

> 'TAC LT.
> Okay, Miss. The power-pack doesn't
> show, and this pin-mike right here
> under the collar will pick it all up.
> > (beat)
> If he so much as blinks weird, just
> give a howl and stay out of his way
> for three or four seconds and we'll
> be all over that place.

She nods, smiles at Ziporyn and starts to move out. She
stops, turns back to Ziporyn. *He is holding his wounded hand in his good one.*

> SHERRI
> Hey, Doc: does this get me a wholesale
> on future therapy with you?

> ZIPORYN
> Only if you get sicker than you are
> now.

> SHERRI
> You sweet-talking devil, you.

And she moves off across the street. As CAMERA FOLLOWS
we find it impossible to locate any of the cops we know
are all over the area.

160   MOVING SHOT — ARRIFLEX — WITH SHERRI

as she enters the building, takes the stairs quickly,
and comes to the door of the apartment. She stops,
draws a deep breath, and knocks. No answer. She knocks
again. Waits. There is the SOUND of MOVEMENT from
within. The door opens.

161   SHOT THROUGH APARTMENT DOOR

ZOOM in PAST LYLE standing at the door with the *(broken)* ~~smashed~~
lamp in his hand to the ~~xxxxxxxxxx xxxxxxxxx~~
~~xxxxxxxx~~ in the middle of the room.

blue blanket-covered mound

162   CLOSEUP OF SHERRI

as she screams, her face contorted in terror.

> SMASH-CUT TO:

163   EXT. STREET – CLOSE ON PORTABLE BROADCAST UNIT

ZOOM OUT to MEDIUM SHOT as her scream is translated over
the speaker system in the truck and the cops and Ziporyn
are galvanized into movement. He is off and running as
the 'tac Lt. tries to stop him.

                         'TAC LT.
              Hey! Not you! We can––

But Ziporyn is already heading the parade as we see
the convergence of cops when CAMERA MOVES AROUND TRUCK
to show us everybody spilling toward the building.

164   TILT-ANGLE ON BUILDING FRONT

as Ziporyn and the cops hit it at a dead run and start
to vanish inside.

                                        SMASH–CUT TO:

165   INT. APARTMENT – ON SHERRI & LYLE

ashen-faced, Sherri is being ~~strangled~~ (manhandled) by Lyle, who
is dragging her toward the corpse of Marlene. Sherri
is fighting him as best she can, kicking and trying to
punch. But Lyle is quite psychopathic now, cannot hear,
won't let go. She starts to go limp and we SHOOT IN
DOUBLE-IMAGE again to show this is a scene from the
beginning of the show, scenes 2-15.

                                        CUT TO:

166   SHOT DOWN STAIRWELL – ZIPORYN & COPS

Another DOUBLE-IMAGE SHOT for a brief moment, then the
single image asserts itself, of the 'tac cops with
Ziporyn fighting to get ahead of them, coming up from
below...all of it looking like a print by Escher.

                                        CUT TO:

167   CLOSE ON LYLE

as he hears the horde coming up the stairs. He flings
Sherri away from him and she staggers, ~~bounces off the
wall~~ slips to one knee, tries to crawl away. Lyle
looks around like a trapped thing, just as the cops
and Ziporyn burst in through the door one of the cops
has kicked in. Some of this in dramatic DOUBLE-IMAGE.

168   SHOT FROM DOORWAY TO LYLE

as the cops break through, and Lyle dashes into the
bathroom, slams and locks the door. Cops boil into the
room and start kicking the bathroom door, down as Ziporyn
howls at them. *He still favour the wounded hand.*
                          ZIPORYN
            Let me get to him...he's from ~~the~~ OAK
(MEADOWS) ~~Hospital~~...he'll know me...let me...

But the cops are intent on hammering through.

                                              CUT TO:

169   INT. BATHROOM - LYLE IN FISH-EYE LENS SHOT

He's crouched in the small bathroom window, guaging
the drop. It's a dizzying five-storey fall into a
passageway between buildings, narrow and dark. He
stares back into the fish-eye lens as we DOUBLE-IMAGE
and then turns back just as we

                                              CUT TO:

*We can
see a
dusty glass
skylight at
the bottom
of the passage,
apparently the
roof of a
one-story
building below.*

170   ANGLE ON ACTION

as a burly 'tac cop jacks up his foot with its heavy
boot and delivers a kick to the door just under the
lock that shatters the lock, springs the door, throws it
open with tremendous impact. A clear view through to
Lyle in the window as Ziporyn pushes past the two cops
in front of him. And Lyle jumps.

                                              CUT TO:

171   UP-TILT ANGLE - PASSAGEWAY

SHOOTING STRAIGHT UP to Lyle as he launches himself
into the emptiness. We see him go across and seem to
grab onto the ledge of the next building.

                                              CUT TO:

172   SHOT THROUGH WINDOW - CLOSE ON ZIPORYN IN F.G.

Shooting across to Lyle hanging on by his fingertips
as we saw him in scenes 2-15. DOUBLE-IMAGE as Lyle
starts to slip, turns back at the last moment, reaches
out with a flung hand--DOUBLE-IMAGE--touches Ziporyn's *bandaged*
fingers and we
                                         INTERCUT:

173   RAPID CUTS OF ASSORTED SCENES — 40 FRAMES PER SECOND
thru
180   of Lyle in Ziporyn's office at Oak Meadows when he first
met the psychiatrist; of Lyle in the motel with Marlene;
of Lyle at the movie shooting; of Lyle with Marlene at
the party; of Lyle menacing Sherri the night of the party;
of Lyle with Amos; of Lyle jamming Ziporyn's hand in the
office door (and FLASH THIS HALF A DOZEN TIMES FAST); of
Lyle killing Marlene; of Lyle dragging Sherri; of Ziporyn's
bandaged hand...all so fast we can barely register them
on our consciousness and

SMASH—CUT BACK TO:

181   EXTREME CLOSE — THEIR HANDS
&
182   as the fingertips barely touch and then grasp. Ziporyn's
bloody hankie-bandaged hand trying to hold on, writhing,
the pain obvious even though we see only hands and no
faces. Ziporyn's hand weakening, clearly because of the
pain inflicted by Lyle. And as the fingers slide away
from Lyle's, DOUBLE-IMAGE, and Ziporyn's hand falls back
out of FRAME, we have an unobstructed view as CAMERA
TILTS UP: Lyle's face in that instant when he realizes
his own viciousness and brutality have conspired to cause
his demise. Then he slips off the ledge to which he's
clinging and vanishes OUT OF FRAME as CAMERA WHIPS AROUND
to HOLD ZIPORYN as we HEAR the SOUND of Lyle falling and
then...a tremendous crash of glass...which we take to be
the sound of Lyle plunging through the skylight five floors
below/out of sight. And, just as in scenes 2-15, the
FRAME NARROWS DOWN to a SLIT OF WHITE LIGHT and HOLDS FOR
SEVERAL BEATS, as we

MATCH—CUT TO:

When sliver of white light expands, it is the white on
the side of a city ambulance, as two sheet-covered forms
on gurneys are loaded aboard.

183   ANGLE ON STREET SCENE — ZIPORYN IN F.G. — HIS POV

as he watches the dead Marlene and Lyle being driven
away, Sherri being helped into a second ambulance, the
'tac squad van and the cops packing it in. He holds
his bandaged hand painfully, clutching it as though it
were something evil and traitorous.

CAMERA PULLS BACK as Bonnard and Elizabeth De Marco come
to him. They stand silently, watching it all go away
until only the three of them are left alone in the street.
CAMERA MOVES IN to TIGHT 3-SHOT.

(CONTINUED:)

183 CONTINUED:

> DE MARCO
> This time you were right, Marvin.
> You could have been wrong, but <u>this</u>
> time you knew. <u>I</u> was wrong.

> ZIPORYN
> (wasted)
> Yeah. Terrific.

> WARDEN
> What a helluva waste. That girl.
> God!

> DE MARCO
> They're all victims.

(CONTINUED:)

183   CONTINUED: – 2

                          ZIPORYN
             Would either of you two like me to get
             a string background for this unseemly
             sanctimonious ~~bacancatant~~ *garbage*?

Both are affronted.

                          WARDEN
             We admitted you were right, Marvin.
             What ~~otherwise~~ else do you want?

                          ZIPORYN
                       (tightly)
             What I want is for you two philosophers
             to go somewhere else and let your hearts
             drip. The noise is making me want to
             vomit.

                          DE MARCO
             ~~Listen,~~ Ziporyn, you are the chillest,
             most insensitive, most calloused ~~sonofa——~~ *psy——*

                          ZIPORYN   *(De Marco)*
             Fade to black and credits, ~~pal~~. You're
             so full of the sweetness of human sorrow
             I'm getting diabetes just listening to
             you.
                       (he mimics him)
             "They're all victims." God!

Bonnard and De Marco look at him, then at each other, then
they walk away without a word. He stands there staring
after them as they get in Bonnard's car and drive off.
He starts walking away FROM CAMERA as we

                                   SLOW LAP-DISSOLVE TO:

184   EXT. ~~VINCENZO~~ *(SUBURBAN)* STREET – SAME AS SCENE 139

The street we saw through the window of Marlene's parents'
home. CAMERA HOLDS STREET till we recognize it, then
PANS SLOWLY LEFT to show us Ziporyn standing on the front
porch of the house. CAMERA MOVES IN STEADILY as Ziporyn
waits for the door to be opened, and while he stands
there, and throughout this shot, we HEAR his VOICE OVER.

                   ZIPORYN'S VOICE OVER
             There is a beast in each of us. And when
             that beast stirs, when it comes to full
             wakefulness, there is no place to run.
                       (beat)
             Speck, Manson, Starkweather, Whitman...
             Lyle Simon...you...me...
                       (CONT'D.)
                                      (CONTINUED:)

184 CONTINUED:

ZIPORYN'S VOICE OVER
(CONT'D.)

There is no place to run in the madhouses
of the cities. The real victims. You?
Me? Young people with dreams? Old people
with memories? The answers aren't here
yet. We simply don't know.
(beat)
More prisons? More "facilities"?

~~Did you know that 68% of the crimes committed by
women occur in the week before their
menstrual periods begin?~~
(beat)
No answers yet, and even fewer choices...
become a beast or die as a victim of the
beasts? Is that the choice?
(beat)
I don't have an answer for you. If you have
one, don't keep it to yourself...
(beat)
There are sounds in the darkness.
(beat)
The tigers are loose.

As this VOICE OVER DIALOGUE nears its end, the door to
the house is opened and Marlene's Father stands there.
Ziporyn says something to him we cannot hear, the old
man's face shrivels and he begins to cry. He stands
aside so Ziporyn can enter, the door is closed and the
last three lines of the dialogue are spoken as we begin to

FADE TO BLACK:

and

FADE OUT.

THE END

Rumble

Editor's Note: Beach Party Goes to Brooklyn

In 1963, shortly after arriving in Los Angeles and breaking into screenwriting with an episode of *Ripcord* (see BRAIN MOVIES, Volume Five), Ellison began adapting his first novel—the 1958 juvenile delinquent gang thriller WEB OF THE CITY—for American-International Pictures, where his contemporaries had been adapting their own work (as with Charles Beaumont's THE INTRUDER) or adapting the tales of Edgar Allan Poe for the screen (as Richard Matheson did with a string of successful Vincent Price vehicles).

The movie, titled *Rumble* (the title under which Pyramid had published the book after buying it from Lion; see Installment #2 of *Ask Uncle Harlan* in THE LAST PERSON TO MARRY A DUCK LIVED 300 YEARS AGO for more on this), was to have starred teen idols Frankie Avalon and Annette Funicello, then famous for such light-hearted fare as *Beach Party* and *Beach Blanket Bingo*.

In the screenplay, Ellison allows former gang leader Rusty Santoro to interact with the movie's unseen narrator, cleverly casting exposition as banter betwixt the with-it protagonist and the slightly square and not-so-omniscient narrator.

For reasons obscured by the passage of time, Ellison never completed the screenplay. The sixty extant pages appear here, as lagniappe for those who pre-ordered this volume.

RUMBLE

FADE IN:

1   EXT. LONG SHOT - ESTABLISHING - CITY STREETS - NIGHT

a 90-DEGREE ANGLE looking STRAIGHT DOWN into the complex
labyrinth made by alleys and streets. SILENCE. Then--
softly at first, then more clearly--the SOUND of RUNNING
FEET. Far down below, moving through the maze of streets
like a hamster in a reaction tunnel, someone is fleeing
in terror as THEME MUSIC UP. CAMERA HOLDS as the running
figure darts down one street, then another, then begins to
COME DOWN toward the streets. CAMERA COMES DOWN to WAIST
HEIGHT as the running figure flattens against a wall
directly opposite. CAMERA ZOOMS IN on the face of RUSTY
SANTORO. Eighteen years old, a subdued cruelty in his
face, lean, good-looking but more than anything, filled
with numbing terror. HOLD for several beats, then CAMERA
TRUCKS RAPIDLY WITH Rusty as he bolts away down the wall.
He turns suddenly, runs into an alley.

2   LONG SHOT - ESTABLISHING - THE ALLEY - NIGHT

CAMERA HOLDS at THIGH HEIGHT on Rusty, running down the
long, filthy alley. One side of the passageway is littered
with garbage cans, lids off, tipped over, scummy water and
refuse spilled out across the bricks. Rusty pounds down
the length of the alley and CAMERA HOLDS as he finds a
dead end brick wall, rising above him. CAMERA MOVES IN
SLOWLY as he tries to jump and catch the top. It is too
high. Abruptly, as THEME MUSIC RISES, jack-booted legs
MOVE INTO FRAME. Top of frame cuts them off at mid-thigh,
but through the line of dominating legs we can still see
RUSTY SANTORO. Back to the wall now, he faces his
attackers. The legs move forward as CAMERA DOLLIES IN on
Rusty. Suddenly, the legs run forward.

3   SERIES OF ANGLES
thru
5   on walls, garbage cans, brick pavement, hands holding tire
chains, booted feet. AEROFLEX ANGLES that tilt crazily as

(CONTINUED)

3
thru
5

CONTINUED:

SOUNDS of SCUFFLING mix with THEME MUSIC OVER. Camera does
not settle on actual combat as Rusty is beaten, but CAMERA
PANS down one wall, between two garbage cans, where a
drunken bum, bottle still clutched in one hand, watches
avidly, smiling sickly as the action progresses.

6   MED. CLOSEUP - ON RUSTY

as he pulls himself to hands and knees, head hanging down,
thoroughly beaten. The boy tries to crawl forward, slips
down onto one elbow against the wall, and looks across at
the bum. As he sees him, recognition dawns on his face.

7   CLOSEUP - THE BUM

smiling evilly; he nods amiably as though they had just
passed a civility. He feebly raises the bottle, the empty
bottle, mindlessly offering an incongruous drink to the
beaten boy.

8   CLOSEUP - ON RUSTY

as he tries to move toward the bum. He slumps back.

                    RUSTY
                  (faintly)
          Pop...Pop...help m-me...

9   ANOTHER SHOT - ON BUM

as he smiles again, vacantly, and the bottle slips from
his hand. POP SANTORO, the lines of years of dirt and
drunkenness in his ruined face.

                    POP
                 (dreamily)
          Y'got a half'a dollar...Rusty son...
          so your Pop c'n getta 'nother...bottle...

He falls asleep, still grinning. CAMERA PULLS BACK to
include Rusty, who pulls himself up the alley wall,
takes several steps toward us, then falls. CAMERA COMES
DOWN TIGHT on him, struggling on the pavement. His hand
stretches out before him as he tries to move, then slumps
down fully unconscious, his hand just finger-touching a
pool of dark water. The water ripples as his fingers
slip in, and from the ripples CAMERA HOLDS 100 FEET FOR
OPTICALLY SUPERIMPOSED

          RIPPLED MAIN CREDITS IN WATER

                              DISSOLVE TO BLACK.

10   MONTAGE
thru
13   THRU STREETS as NARRATION OVER.   PROGRESS SHOTS:

In an alley, three young boys and a girl, paying a man for sticks of marijuana; the man leaves furtively; the kids light up, cup their hands around the smoke, puff deeply.

Two boys prying hubcaps off a car, running away.

In a doorway, a boy and a girl making out, sharing a pint of cheap liquor, a flashlight beam suddenly spotlights them.

                     NARRATOR
                  (conversationally)
       This is the "turf".   It means the
       territory, the neighborhood, the area
       ruled by a bopping club.   A gang.   It
       stretches from that street down there,
       all the way past the Park, and the
       juvenile delinquents who own it are--

                   RUSTY'S VOICE
                 (cutting in hotly)
       Hey, fellah, watch that stuff.   The
       Barons aren't a bopping club...we're
       a, uh, "social group".

As scenes of delinquency flash.

                    NARRATOR
       That's quite a social calendar you've
       got there.   Say, who _are_ you?

                   RUSTY'S VOICE
       My name's Rusty Santoro.   I used to be
       President of the Barons.

                    NARRATOR
       Santoro.   Hmmm, is that Puerto Rican
       or Italian?

                   RUSTY'S VOICE
       What's it to ya?

                    NARRATOR
                  (hurriedly)
       Oh, nothing, nothing.   You say you live
       here, ny on the turf?

                               (CONTINUED)

10   CONTINUED:
thru
13   As an AERIAL SHOT shows us half a dozen kids running across
      rooftops, knocking over a forest of television antennas with
      baseball bats. They don't stop, merely swing wildly, knocking
      the metal stems flat as they dash from buildingtop to
      buildingtop.

      Two boys hold a third against a brick wall as a line of
      basketball-jacketed swingers step up one at a time and
      belt him in the mouth.

      A trio of girls breaking a car's wind-window, reaching in,
      opening the car door as a boy jumps the wires under the
      hood; they start the car, careen away from the curb. AS
      NARRATION CONTINUES.

                         RUSTY'S VOICE
            Yeah, I live here. If you call that
            living.

                         NARRATOR
            Rusty...hmmm, the name sounds familiar.
            Weren't you the boy who was beaten up
            in an alley...

                         RUSTY'S VOICE
            Drop it!

                         NARRATOR
            But weren't those members of The Barons?
            I thought you said you were the Prez of
            that club...

                         RUSTY'S VOICE
            I said drop it, man! I quit the club.
            I'm too old for that kinda jazz.

                         NARRATOR
            It looked like they had their doubts.
            And that bum in the alley...isn't that
            your fath--

                         RUSTY'S VOICE
                      (breaking in sharp)
            Hey, look, that's my school down there.

      CAMERA COMES IN on a bleak, brick building, more like a
      soot-covered prison than a school. CAMERA CLOSES TIGHT
      on a window and PASSES THRU as NARRATION CONTINUES.

14   INT. WOOD SHOP - DAY - ESTABLISHING

HIGH SHOT coming down on the room. Lathes and drill presses
roaring, teen-aged boys working at various projects. As
CAMERA COMES DOWN toward Rusty, working on a chair leg
between the points of a wood lathe, chisel sending a wedge
of sawdust flying back, NARRATION CONTINUES.

                    NARRATOR
          You mean you go to school too?

                    RUSTY'S VOICE
                    (outraged)
          Whaddaya mean, do I go to school. Of
          course, I go to school. What are
          you, man, some kinda smart aleck?
          You think I hang around the stoops
          like the rest of them bums?

                    NARRATOR
          No offense, Rusty. Is that you?

                    RUSTY'S VOICE
                    (proud)
          Yeah, that's me. Y'like that chair leg
          I'm workin' on? I use a special chisel,
          one I designed myself, man. I call it
          the Santoro Special.

CAMERA COMES DOWN to MED. CLOSEUP on Rusty, working at lathe.
Suddenly, a LOUD VOICE cuts through the sound of machinery
and dovetails, synchs in with Rusty's words X "Santoro Special".

                    CANDLE'S VOICE O.S.
                    (loudly, viciously)
          Santoro Spick!

15   ANGLE PAST RUSTY

to CANDLE, a good-looking, well-built boy of perhaps 19,
with carefully-pompadoured hair and several curls hanging
over his forehead casually. He is muscular and there is
a cold look in his eyes. He might be ferocious if there
wasn't an adolescent petulance in his face. He stalks
toward Rusty. As Rusty spins to look at him, Candle
shoves him roughly, and the chisel scrapes wood with a
SHRIEK, and splits the chair leg.

                    RUSTY
                    (flatly)
          Why you, stinkin'--

                                        (CONTINUED)

15   CONTINUED:

                         CANDLE
              What's the matter, **spick**? You got
              the shakes?

                         RUSTY
              Don't call me that, Candle.

                         CANDLE
              Whaddaya mean, **spick**? That beatin'
              last night must of scrambled your
              brains; I **spick** good English.

16   INTERCUT - RUSTY'S HAND

      as he shifts his grip on the wood chisel, now holding it
      underhand, like a knife.

                         RUSTY
              I **told** you, you lousy punk, don't
              call me that, or--

17   ANOTHER ANGLE - RUSTY & CANDLE

      as Candle realizes Rusty has dropped into a knife-fighting
      stance, and the chisel has become a weapon. He takes two
      small, cautious steps back, hands at his sides.

                         CANDLE
                       (softly, flat)
              Finally got you bugged, hey man?
              Now you know how **we** feel.

                         RUSTY
              I told you. I'm through with the
              club. I'm out.

                         CANDLE
              Nobody's out till **we** say so. That's
              the way it goes, man.

                         RUSTY
              Get away from me, Candle. I'm warnin'
              you.

                         CANDLE
              I always said you were chicken, Santoro.

      He makes a sharp, short movement, and a knife drops out
      of his sleeve into his hand. He holds the closed weapon up.

                              (CONTINUED)

17   CONTINUED:

Hold a beat on Rusty and Candle, unmoving, as the machines in
the shop are shut off, one by one, and the other boys form a
silent audience. As the last machine whines into silence,
there is a moment of soundlessness and then the SHARP CLICK
of Candle thumbing the button. The knife snaps open with a
VICIOUS SOUND. They circle each other.

Rusty lunges, Candle jumps back. Candle bobs sidewise,
tossing the knife from hand to hand so Rusty must follow it
with his eyes. Then Candle thrusts, misses Rusty by an inch.
Rusty kicks over a short stack of lumber, forcing Candle
back. Leaping the boards, Rusty wails in, forcing Candle
to toss over a heavy drill press. Rusty dances out of the
way and avoids being brained, but Candle is on him suddenly.

18   MED. CLOSEUP - RUSTY & CANDLE

clinching with weapons at each other's chests, bent halfway
over a wood lathe. Rusty manages to gain the upper hold,
swings wide as if about to skewer Candle, when the other
boy grabs up a handful of sawdust and throws it directly
into Rusty's face.

19   ANGLE ON RUSTY

stumbling back, clawing at his eyes, he stumbles over the
leg of a workstand, and tumbles on his back, his kutf chisel
clattering away across the floor. CAMERA GOES DOWN WITH
HIM and then MOVES AROUND to shoot past him to the chisel
lying just out of reach. Rusty turns and looks DIRECTLY
UP INTO CAMERA with fear on his face.

20   INTERCUT - ON CHISEL

and empty sawdusty floor as Rusty's hand comes into frame
reaching for it. A foot suddenly comes down on his hand.

21   UP-ANGLE - FROM RUSTY TO CANDLE

standing above him, his foot planted on Rusty's hand. The
knife looks huge in Candle's hand. Candle smiles gently.

                         CANDLE
              Don't sweat it, man. Nothin' serious.
              I'm just gonna recondition your face a
              little.

He starts to bend toward Rusty, when suddenly an arm goes
around his neck and he is jerked violently up and away.

22   MED. SHOT - THE SCENE

Candle half off the floor, his knife hand bent up and back
by MR. PANCOAST, an athletic redhead in his mid-thirties,
wearing a suit that has seen newer days, a vest, and glasses.
Pancoast has one arm locked around Candle's neck, the other
twisting the knife-arm. They struggle back away from Rusty,
as CAMERA CLOSES on them, to EXT. CLOSEUP of their faces,
twisted in tension, Pancoast behind Candle.

                    PANCOAST
          Drop...it...boy! Drop...it...or I snap
          ...your arm...like...a...wishbone...Drop
          it!

Candle's eyes roll up in his head as Pancoast twists harder.
There is the SOUND of the knife hitting the floor.

23   ANOTHER ANGLE

Pancoast kicks the knife away, and it skitters into a pile
of shavings, and is lost. He hurls the boy from him, up
against a drill press. He grabs Candle's shirt-front.

                    PANCOAST
          Get out of here. And don't come back or
          the next time I'll pack your tail down
          to the Principal.
                    (beat)
          And with your record, that means suspension.

Candle stares back at him, frightened. Pancoast manhandles
him across the room, bouncing him off workbenches and lathes.
He slams him against the wall next to the door, pulls it
open, and bodily hurls Candle out into the hall. The door
slams shut. Pancoast whirls to the room.

                    PANCOAST
          All right, the rest of you...get back to
          work!

24   REVERSE ANGLE - PANCOAST'S POV - WHAT HE SEES

The roomful of surly boys murmur back to their machines and
in a moment the pace of activity is picked up. Pancoast
moves back toward Rusty as CAMERA GOES WITH him. He stoops,
helps Rusty to his feet, and supporting him, they move
to the door. Pancoast opens it as Rusty is helped through,
shaking his head to clear it.

25   ESTABLISHING SHOT - THE BASEMENT HALLWAY

as Rusty and Pancoast emerge. A rickety stairway rises up,
wooden bannisters dominating the frame. They move toward us.

26   REVERSE ANGLE - ON STAIRS

helping Rusty to the steps, Pancoast settles him down.
The hall is dingy, plaster peeling from walls, barrels
filled with wood scrap and shavings line one wall, a small
wall-mounted drinking fountain. Pancoast leans up against
the bannister.

                    PANCOAST
                  (musingly)
          I'd like a smoke. Or do I have to sneak
          into the head for a cigarette, like the
          rest of you?

Rusty looks up, smiles faintly.

                    PANCOAST
                  (Continues)
          What was that all about, Rusty?

                    RUSTY
          Nothing.

                    PANCOAST
          The janitor would've had a helluva
          time cleaning that "nothing" off the
          floor.

                    RUSTY
          He wouldn't have sliced me.

                    PANCOAST
          I thought you and the Barons were done
          with each other?

                    RUSTY
          We are. It's just--

                    PANCOAST
          Just nothing, \Rusty. I bailed you out of
          that last scrape because I had faith in
          you. You've been remanded into my custody
          because I*m convinced the juvenile authorities
          I could keep you straight.
                  (beat)
          Look at me, boy, when I'm talking to you.

Rusty looks up, shamefacedly. He rubs a bruise on his
forehead. Two beatings in two days have left him pulpy.
And the shaking after-effects of the fight have set in.

27   CLOSEUP - ON RUSTY

> RUSTY
> I told them I was through, last night.

> PANCOAST
> You didn't get marked up like that
> shaving. They said you <u>weren't</u> through,
> right?

> RUSTY
> (softly)
> Yeah.

> PANCOAST
> How many of them?

> RUSTY
> More than I could handle.

> PANCOAST
> Nobody said it was going to be easy.

> RUSTY
> (bristling)
> I didn't ask for easy, man. I just
> asked for possible. They ain't gonna
> let me walk down the street. And one
> of these mornings the street cleaners
> gonna pick me up with the rest of the
> crap.

> PANCOAST
> (intently)
> When they caught you with the rest of
> those Barons trying to break into
> the liquor store, I went out for you,
> Rusty...

> RUSTY
> ...it'd of been easier if you'd let them
> send me to the farm.

> PANCOAST
> No farm, this time, Rusty. You have a
> record as a juvenile offender, you know
> that. No farm. You're on the edge of
> the big leagues. Next fall and
> they send you to the big boys playpen.

> (CONTINUED)

27   CONTINUED:

CAMERA MOVES AROUND THEM SLOWLY as they talk, catching every
expression as Pancoast tries to get through to the boy.

> RUSTY
> After last night that doesn't sound
> so bad. I'm gettin' tired of guys
> knocking on me like I was somebody's
> front door.

> PANCOAST
> Rusty, you've been as good as your word
> since I got you out of that mess. At
> first I thought you were like some of
> these jokers--like Candle and his bunch
> --a loser. But you've shown me you've
> got it on the ball. You've got real
> woodworking talent; you could be a
> designer or a master toolmaker with no
> sweat...

> RUSTY
> (embaressed)
> Yeah, so?

> PANCOAST
> So we're both going to have to go over
> to the Barons and get this pretzel
> straightened out...

Rusty is shaking his head firmly no.

> RUSTY
> You're kidding. Being in the Barons
> ain't like being a member of the Rotary
> or the PTA. It's like nothin' else in
> the world. Only way you get out is if
> you land in the slammer or you move
> away. That's what I tried to tell ya
> when you made me quit.

> PANCOAST
> You remember Tony Green?

The fear of a memory lives in Rusty's face for a moment.
He nods somberly.

> PANCOAST
> (continues)
> Remember him lying in that parking lot
> with a .22 slug from a zip gun through
> his face...because somebody danced with
>
> his girl? You can keep on with the
> Barons, Rusty, and wind up the same way.

28   ANOTHER ANGLE - UP-ANGLE FROM PANCOAST TO RUSTY

Rising, Rusty looks down at his teacher and friend.

                    RUSTY
         Okay, Mr. Pancoast. You made your
         point. I'll go over there tonight,
         it's meeting night. I'll have a
         talk with some of the guys.

                    PANCOAST
         Want some extra muscle?

                    RUSTY
         No thanks. I walk in with you and
         I'm bombed-out before I open my mouth.
         I think I can hack it alone.

He slams the bannister with his hand for emphasis. The entire
stairway trembles.

                    RUSTY
                 (continues)
         Lousy school. Gonna fall apart under
         us.

He turns and goes back into the woodshop, leaving Carl Pancoast
sitting on the stairs. XXXXXXX Pancoast gets up slowly, walks
to the drinking fountain and stoops for a drink. No water. He
slams it with the palm of his hand, and in the same movement
rakes his fingers along the wall, loosening a long line of
plaster bits. CAMERA COMES IN on his angry face.

                    PANCOAST
                 (to himself)
         One of these days I'm going to tell
         the PTA what causes delinquency.

He walks back into the woodshop as we

                              DISSOLVE TO:

29   HIGH SHOT - ESTABLISHING - SCHOOL CAFETERIA - DAY

Long tables with boys and girls eating from metal trays.
A steam table down one wall. High windows letting in light.
A few adults monitoring the room. A great CLASH of TRAYS
& SILVER. A line waiting to get food, another line dumping
trays and refuse and paying checks.

30   MED. SHOT - ON SWINGING DOORS

as Rusty comes through, moves toward the steam table.

31   MED. CLOSEUP - ON RUSTY

Enetering line at steam table, suddenly realizing line is
empty. He starts to get food. The hub-bub dies down behind
him gradually, and abruptly a HIGH VOICE breaks thru the din.

>   1st VOICE O.S.
>   (like calling a
>   chicken)
>   Chick-chick-chick-spick-spick-spick...

Rusty spins. Room goes silent suddenly.

32   LONG HIGH SHOT - THE CAFETERIA

as CAMERA PULLS BACK from Rusty, we see the entire room. He
stands alone down there by the steam table line, a wide empty
space between him and the crowded tables and benches. He
stands nakedly alone as another VOICE starts the "chicken
chant" from another corner.

>   2nd VOICE O.S.
>   Chick-chick-chick-chick-chick...

He spins to the voice. Another joins in, from the rear of
the cafeteria.

>   3rd VOICE O.S.
>   Chick-chick-chick-chick-chick-chick...

Then another. And another, till the room is a reverberating
wall of chanting. CAMERA COMES BACK DOWN TO CLOSEUP of Rusty.
Anguish, anger and--almost--tears as he stands helpless before
the vocal attack. He turns, grabs a cellophane wrapped
sandwich and a pint carton of milk. CAMERA FOLLOWS as he moves
down the line, pays his check and moves across the room.

33   MED. LONG SHOT - ON RUSTY

as he comes toward a table in F.G. The two boys and a girl
at the table get up, move to other seats as he approaches.
Rusty tenses, but sits down. Alone.

34   CLOSEUP - ON RUSTY

alone, eating, as the voices hammer at him. He eats as though
he is not even tasting the food. Fury begins to mount in him,
a desperation. We watch him get more and more tense, till he
suddenly stands up, slamming his chair back.

35   MED. CLOSE - PANNING - WITH RUSTY

moving to the refuse bins, the voices chick-chick-chick
following him, mounting in intensity. (Several adult
monitors can be seen scurrying around worriedly in B.G.)
Rusty dumps his food into one of the bins, and stands,
letting the chant drench him with sound. Then, with a
sharp movement he SLAMS the empty tray onto the stack of
empties and spins around. It is such a VIOLENT SOUND the
chant trickles off into SILENCE. As he turns the CAMERA
GOES PAST HIM to the room, to Candle and a group of boys
--with one girl in their midst--at two tables jammed together.

36   MED. CLOSEUP - ON CANDLE

watching. A touch of fear? Has he pushed Rusty too far?

37   REVERSE ANGLE - PAST CANDLE TO RUSTY

as Rusty walks across the room toward the group. POOCH, a
small, weasel-faced boy, sits next to Candle, eating a piece
of lemon meringue pie and milk. Rusty walks up to table,
leans close to Candle.

                    ~~CANDLE~~ RUSTY
          I want to talk to you, Candle.

                    CANDLE
                    (nods at Pooch)
          Talk to my agent.
                    (to Pooch)
          Hey, Pooch; find out what the spick wants.

                    POOCH
                    (insipidly)
          Candle wantsta know whatcha want.

                    RUSTY
                    (to Candle)
          You know I got trouble with the cops. I'm
          on probation. If I don't want The Man
          sending me to the farm, I gotta stay away
          from the club.

                    POOCH
          Sounds like the Cisco Kid is afraid of the
          fuzz, Candle.

                    RUSTY
                    (ignores Pooch)
          Get off my back, Candle. I don't want a
          bop with you.

                              (CONTINUED)

37   CONTINUED:

CAMERA MOVES TO 3-SHOT - RUSTY IN F.G.

                    POOCH
          Chick-chick-chick-ch...

He is cut off as Rusty smashes the pie into his face. Candle
jumps. Three boys grab Rusty's arms. Across the room, an
adult monitor starts toward them hurriedly as kids put their
chairs in the line of passage, anxious to see a brawl.

                    CANDLE
                    (flat)
          That tears it, chicken. You and me,
          we're gonna go 'round and 'round.

                    RUSTY
               (straining forward,
                 furious now)
          Anytime, anyplace, slob!

Candle sees teacher on the way, speaks hurriedly, punctuating
his speech with a finger in Rusty's chest, poking hard.

                    CANDLE
          You be at Cannon's joint. After school.

                    RUSTY
          I'll be there.

The SOUND of the PERIOD BELL RINGING sharp and loud. The room
suddenly erupts into a mad throng, streaming toward the doors.
The teacher is caught up in the maelstrom, the boys release
Rusty, and the group moves off, leaving him standing there.
CAMERA CLOSES on Rusty as we

                              DISSOLVE TO:

38   EXT. STREET - DAY

CLOSEUP on WEEZEE, a beautiful young girl of approximately
seventeen, wearing a cashmere sweater filled out a trifle
better than one would expect in a seventeen-year-old. She
stands beside a tree, her books clutched to her, and she
watches the long walk from the school. She might almost be
trying to keep out of sight by the tree. We follow her
POV to the clutches of kids emerging, laughing, walking
down the street, heading for cars, etc. CAMERA MOVES
AROUND HER as Rusty emerges from the building, starts
down the walk to the street. Alone. She watches silently.

39   MED. CLOSEUP – ON RUSTY

walking down the pavement. Abruptly, he stops, does not
turn, but pauses, as though he senses something. He turns
slowly and registers recognition of Weezee.

40   REVERSE ANGLE – PAST RUSTY – HIS POV

Weezee looks uncomfortable, as though she wishes she had
not been seen by Rusty. She makes a short move to go, then
holds as Rusty walks to her, CAMERA GOING WITH. He moves
to her and CAMERA MOVES INTO 2-SHOT.

> RUSTY
> Didn't see you all day.

> WEEZEE
> I was working on the dance arrangements
> with Miss Flynn, in her office.

> RUSTY
> (slowly)
> You been dodgin' me, Weezee?

> WEEZEE
> (covering)
> No, I told you, Rusty, I was--

> RUSTY
> You heard about the trouble.

> WEEZEE
> Well, yes, I heard, but I didn't think--

> RUSTY
> Listen, Weezee, I gotta know. It's
> gettin' warm for me, and there's only
> two kinds of people: their team, and
> my team.
> (beat)
> Which one're you on?

> WEEZEE
> (confused)
> Rusty...I don't like trouble...you know,
> my mom and dad've been making a lot of
> noise about us going around and...

> RUSTY
> In or out, Weezee, that's the way I am.
> It's gotta be one way or not at all.

She is torn. He'll walk if she says the wrong thing.
But she's frightened. Teen-aged, and not sharp enough
to handle real trouble. CAMERA HOLDS on her confusion.

41   ANOTHER SHOT - RUSTY & WEEZEE

He wants to help her, but he can't. Neither can articulate
what they need, what they fear. He is unable to ask her to
stick, and she is unable to make a decision.

                    WEEZEE
          I--I don't know, Rusty.

                    RUSTY
          You been my girl a long time now,
          Louise.

She doesn't answer, looks away, bites her lip.

                    RUSTY
                  (continues)
          Weezee...

                    WEEZEE
          I heard you're going to have a stand
          with Candle Shaster. Is that true?

Rusty nods.

                    WEEZEE
                  (continues)
          He's mean, Rusty. I never liked him,
          he always looked mean enough to do
          anything.

                    RUSTY
                  (shrugs)
          Gotta be. He didn't leave me any other
          way.

                    WEEZEE
          Mr. Pancoast is going to stop you.

                    RUSTY
          He won't know about it, till it's done.
          I'm going over to Cannon's. Want a
          Coke?

                    WEEZEE
          Are they going to be there?

He nods again. There is a moment of trembling between them
as he waits for her to say she won't go. Then, almost as
one, they turn backs to camera and walk away together, not
touching. CAMERA HOLDS as they walk down street. Together,
yet somehow apart.
                              SLOW DISSOLVE TO:

42   INT. CANNON'S MALT SHOP — ESTABLISHING — DAY

Built like a chianti bottle, the **same** shop opens onto a
narrow passage with the soda fountain and counter and
stools along the left wall, magazine racks bolted to the
righthand wall. The narrow passage runs thirty feet and
opens into a larger square area with booths around the
walls, Coke cases stacked near a service door, and a juke
box in the corner. Several boys and a girl sit at the
counter and several more groups in booths in back. LOUD
MUSIC blares through the shop. CAMERA PAST STOOL-SITTERS
with their backs to us, to CANNON, a short, feisty ex-pug
with a heavy Brooklyn accent. He is making an egg cream.
As he finishes an order, he pulls the string on an old
ring-bell mounted beside the backbar mirror.

                    CANNON
          Hey, you! Big spender, c'mon pick
          up your egg cream.
                    (to himself)
          Egg cream...phosphate...Cokes...I'm
          bein' nickel an' dimed to death.
          Some one of these days I'm gonna
          close up this squirrel cage and go
          back inna ring.

As the boy comes to pick up his drink, he shoulders between
customers, answering Cannon.

                    1st BOY
          Sure you're gonna go back inna ring.
          An' I'm Little Orphan Annie...only I
          left my blank eyeballs in my other
          suit.

He takes drink as Cannon swings at him with a backbar
towel, and misses.

                    CANNON
          G'wan, get outta here, ya busymouth.
          I'll blank your eyeballs for ya!

The SOUND of a bell tinkling as the front doors open, draws
his attention. CAMERA PANS LEFT to doors.

43   MED. SHOT — DOORWAY

Rusty and Weezee enter. Rusty looks around. They move
down the line toward the booths at the back.

                    CANNON
                    (continues)
          Here's another spendthrift. Ten,
          twenty, thirty cents means **nothin'**
          to him.

                              (CONTINUED)

43 CONTINUED:

CAMERA ON RUSTY & WEEZEE TO CANNON as they pass him.

                    RUSTY
          Coupla chocolate Cokes?

                    CANDLE
                 (to himself)
          Cokes, always Cokes. I useta think
          gettin' punchdrunk was a bad way to go.

He turns to his fountain to mix the drinks.

44 MED. SHOT - ON BOOTH

Coming down the passage toward the booth, Rusty notices the
other kids in the room whispering about him; they fall
silent as he passes. Rusty and Weezee slide into the booth,
opposite each other, Rusty facing the front door.

                    RUSTY
                 (pulling pack)
          Want a cigarette?

Weezee shakes her head no as Cannon comes up to the booth
and sets down their drinks.

                    CANNON
          Two chocolate Cokes, twenty cents, Diamond
          Jim.

Rusty pays him.

                    RUSTY
          Thanks, Cannon.

Cannon starts to walk away, stops, returns, leans in close.

                    CANNON
                 (confidential)
          Y'know, this block's peculiar...

                    RUSTY
          Got any other late flashes?

                    CANNON
                 (ignores remark)
          I mean: it knows when something's wrong.
          All the hacks go back to Manhattan to
          pick up the nine-to-fivers; the shopkeepers
          start puttin' up wire screens, their
          windows shouldn't get broke...

                              (CONTINUED)

44   CONTINUED:

                    RUSTY
                  (cuts in)
        Make your point, Cannon.

                    CANNON
        There's a trouble smell in the street.
        People are stayin' indoors. There's a hot
        rumble the gangs are gonna bop again.

                    RUSTY
        You sound like one of them old ladies that
        sits out on the stoops...forget it.

                    CANNON
        Rumble is you're in for some aggravation.

                    RUSTY
        Don't believe everything you hear.

                    CANNON
        When I was scufflin', and I'd get matched
        against some hot-dog who knew I could take
        him, I could tell he was scared, even at the
        weigh-in. Scared comes outta you like sweat,
        boy.

                    RUSTY
                  (bristling)
        I'm not scared of nobody!

                    CANNON
        That's a dummy remark, kid. Only time you're
        not scared is when they put you down the hole.
                  (beat)
        What I'm tryin' to tell you is, you're not
        a bad kid--even if all you ever order is
        Cokes--and if you ever need anything...some
        muscle, a place to duck into...I got a
        big basement under this joint.

Rusty is not used to kindness. He doesn't know quite how to
react. But in a casual sort of way, entirely transparent, he
manages to register understanding and gratitude.

                    RUSTY
        Thanks, Cannon. Thanks a lot.

                    CANNON
        F'get it. I took too many punches. I must
        be gettin' soft in the gourd.

45   ANOTHER ANGLE

PAST CANNON & BOOTH as the service door to the basement opens
and a huge, lumbering, somehow childlike young man in slovenly
clothes emerges, carrying four cases of empty bottles. It is
THE BEAST, a dull-witted, pathetic creature whose simple-
mindedness is so gentle, he rapidly fades into the woodwork.
Cannon turns at the sound of The Beast coming up the stairs
from the basement and the door opening.

                    CANNON
                  (continues)
          Hey, dummy! Stack them empties next
          to the juke box, with the others.

Cannon walks back to the fountain, the Beast puts the empties
where he has been told, and straightend up, brushing off his
hands on his sides the way a five-year-old would. He sees
Rusty, and shambles over. There is a soft-sweet smile on his
face, and despite his great hairy shape, it is impossible to
think of The Beast and violence in the same category.

                    BEAST
          H-hi, Rusty...

                    RUSTY
                  (absently)
          Hello, Beast, what's happenin'?

                    BEAST
                  (childlike)
          I made two dollars an' ten cents working
          for Mr. Cannon, an', an' pretty soon I'll
          have enough t'buy me a little wood wagon
          I c'n pull t'collect old cardboard, y'know,
          old cardboard, like flats, y'know--

                    RUSTY
          We know, Beast. Flats.

                    BEAST
          Uh-huh, uh-huh. Like that. I'll buy me a
          little wagon, an' pull it all around an'
          Mr. Hirschmann at the groc'ry'll give me
          a whole buncha flats, an' I'll make me a
          lotta money an' I'll buy me a dog an' get
          me a room with white nice sheets an'--

                    RUSTY
          You still sleepin' on roofs, Beast?

                    BEAST
          Uh-huh.

                              (CONTINUED)

45   CONTINUED:

The sudden RINGING of the BELL over the backbar mirror pulls
their attention. The Beast shuffles to look toward Cannon.

                    CANNON
          C'mon, c'mon, stop jivin' around.
          Load them empties out back!

                    BEAST
          S'long Rusty. Bye.

                    RUSTY
          So long, Beast.

Weezee and Rusty watch as The Beast shambles to the stack of
empties and lifts four cases without difficulty. CAMERA
HOLDS PAST THEM as he gets the rear alley door open and goes
out.

46   2-SHOT - ON WEEZEE   ,

She sips at her Coke, but looks uncomfortable.

                    WEEZEE
          He gives me the creeps.

                    RUSTY
          He's just a big dummy. He never grew
          up in the head. But he's okay...

                    WEEZEE
               (suddenly)
          Rusty, what're you gonna do?

                    RUSTY
          I don't know. But I got to get away
          from The Barons. Pancoast ain't kiddin'
          around with me. An' he's right, y'know.
          I been runnin' the streets with them
          for five years, and look at me. I'm
          eighteen an' I got a record. Nice thing
          t'know? Like hell it is! It's killin'
          my Mom...I been usin' my fists since I
          xxxxx was old enough to swing, and I'm
          just up to here with it, that's all I
          know!

                    WEEZEE
          They're going to make it rough on you,
          Rusty.

                              (CONTINUED)

46   CONTINUED:

CANDLE'S VOICE O.S.
Oh, we wouldn't do that to our old buddy,
Mr. Russell Santoro...

And the frame is BLACK as Candle slides into the booth very
close beside Weezee, who gives a start and slides in as far
as she can. Rusty makes a move, but there is a sharp CLICK
next to his ear and CAMERA PULLS BACK to show JOHNNY SLICE
--a thin, tall, assassin-style boy with cold eyes and hair
plastered straight back--holding a 12" Italian stiletto
almost to the flesh of Rusty's ear. CAMERA CONTINUES TO
PULL BACK and we see Pooch, several other boys, and FISH
--a good-looking boy with a sensitive face, wearing a
Bach sweatshirt and sneakers--lounging around the booth.
Rusty settles back. He's trapped.

47   ANOTHER SHOT - BETWEEN RUSTY & CANDLE OPPOSITE

Candle puts an arm around Weezee casually. She shivers, but
does not move away. Rusty starts to rise again, but Johnny
Slice's voice, soft near his ear, stops him.

JOHNNY SLICE
Eeeezeee, baby...

CANDLE
I didn't get called onna carpet by the
Principal. Pancoast sure watches out
for you, man. He din't report me, he
kept his mouth shut...

RUSTY
Sharp idea: why don't you try it?

Candle's hand comes up off the table so rapidly there is
no stopping him. He smacks Rusty full across the mouth.
Rusty is instantly grabbed from behind--from the next
booth--by two boys who pin his shoulders to the rear wall
of the booth. Rusty's eyes narrow and grow cold as the
red welt flames on his cheek.

Candle reaches across and grabs Rusty's hand in a vise-like
grip. Almost instinctively, they settle into arm-wrestling
position. A show of strength, as they taunt each other.

CANDLE
Last night was just a sample...an' that
bit this morning...it's nothin' to what
we're gonna give you...we don't like no
chickens running out on the Barons. Now
that I been elected Prez...

(CONTINUED)

47   CONTINUED:

Sweat stands out on their faces as they struggle, each to
put down the other man's hand.

>   RUSTY
>   What's it all about, big mouth? Just
>   what's your beef? You weren't _mud_ in
>   The Barons till 1 left, now you think
>   you're God or somethin'...

>   CANDLE
>   (hissing)
>   It ain't _my_ idea, you stinkin'--

>   RUSTY
>   Then why keep buggin' me?

>   CANDLE
>   There's some of 'em think you was a
>   good Prez. I think you was crap, but
>   I gotta...

>   RUSTY
>   (realizing)
>   You gotta try an' get me back, 'cause
>   the Barons ain't sure, an' you're
>   scared they'll dump you if I want back
>   in. An' that leaves _you_ standin' with
>   your finger up your nose!

Candle, furious, tries doubly hard to force Rusty's hand
down. Rusty makes a sudden violent move, but in the direction
Candle is pressing, allowing him to throw his hand down...
but as he does it CAMERA PULLS BACK to catch the action as
Rusty lunges sidewise, pulling Candle half out of the booth,
and at the same time cracking a shoulder into Johnny Slice.
As Candle fumbles to regain his seat, Rusty moves swiftly.
One flat, fingers-together hand slashes across Johnny Slice's
Adam's Apple. The boy falls back, drops the knife. Rusty
scoops it up and in one movement has his arm locked around
Candle's neck, the knife hidden from Cannon's sight, but
ready to drive into Candle's neck if he moves. Fear lives
in Candle's eyes. Rusty is panting as he speaks.

>   RUSTY
>   All right, you jokers. Now you're gonna
>   listen to _me_. I been takin' crap from
>   you, and listenin' to this creep get
>   salty with me...now it's my turn.

>   FISH
>   (reasonably)
>   Okay, Rusty, some of us want to hear.

48   PANNING SHOT - THE GROUP

Rusty realizes as CAMERA PANS ACROSS the members of the
gang, that there are two distinct camps: those who are
all the way with Candle, who hate and want to put-down
Rusty, and others who still feel a comradeship with their
ex-President, who want to be shown, who need a direction.
This is Rusty's chance. CAMERA COMES AROUND to CLOSEUP
ON RUSTY, knife still held at Candle's face.

> RUSTY
> (intent)
> I'm out, and that's the end of it.
> And the first one of you tries to
> box me in--I'll cut him, s'help me
> God!

One of Candle's lieutenants tries to make a move, but Candle's
frightened voice stops him.

> CANDLE
> No, cheez, stay away from him, or
> he'll open me.

> RUSTY
> Listen, how long you guys figure I gotta
> run with this crowd? How long you figure
> I gotta keep screwin'-up with the school,
> and the fuzz, and my old lady? You guys
> wanna do it, that's your business, but
> leave me be. I don't talk about what goes
> on in the club, and I don't bother you--
> so don't bother me!

> FISH
> You been fed too much of that good jazz
> by Pancoast. You ackchully believe that
> stuff, man?

> RUSTY
> He'd been tight with me. He says I got a
> good chance to be an industrial designer
> or toolmaker or somethin' if I work at it.

A snicker from Johnny Slice, now recovered, makes Rusty snap.

> RUSTY
> (continues)
> Listen, creep, I like the idea. I like
> it just fine. You think I wanna wind
> up like Pony, in the slammer...or Tony
> Green, six feet under? I gotta life,
> man, an' it ain't much, but it's mine,
> and I wanna live it!

49   ANOTHER SHOT - FISH & POOCH

Fish understands, but has not quite made a decision. Pooch
is too stupid to understand, and he laughs.

                    POOCH
                  (mocking)
            Life, liberty anna pursuit of--

                    FISH
                  (cuts him off)
            Shuddup!
                  (beat, to Rusty)
            You mean all that, doncha, man?

                    RUSTY
                  (nods)
            It feels good, Fish. Bein' able to
            do somethin with my hands, not haveta
            lay around the stoops or boost hubcaps
            for kicks. Maybe it's what Mr. Pancoast
            says: maybe I got me a future.

                    JOHNNY SLICE
            Some future! You'll wind up inna Army
            like the rest of us, man, and then it
            don't matter.

50   WIDER ANGLE - THE GROUP

                    RUSTY
                  (earnest)
            Whaddaya say, Fish? You guys? We call
            it square?

They look at each other. CAMERA CLOSES ON FISH as he must
make a decision. To a boy who has never known responsibility
it is a visual struggle. We see that struggle in his face.

                    FISH
            It sits okay with me, Rusty. I'm off
            your back.

                    RUSTY
                  (relieved)
            That go for the rest of ya?

One by one, reluctantly in some cases, they nod. Rusty
breaks the knife and tosses it back to Johnny Slice. He
moves away from Candle, takes two steps from the booth as
CAMERA HOLDS ON HIM.

51   CLOSE ON RUSTY

Suddenly Candle is on him, and in a wide-sweeping gesture
his hand snags the knife from Johnny Slice. He snaps it
open and with brute force slams Rusty into a wall. Cannon
yells, starts toward them. Three Barons move to stop him.
For a moment Cannon looks as though he'll go right through
them, but a word from Rusty stops him.

                    RUSTY
          Back, Cannon!

                    CANDLE
              (close to Rusty,
               intense, wild)
          I don't buy it, man. As long as you're
          still around, these creeps won't wanna
          take mxxxorders from me, and I'm the
          Prez, man, me, I'm the big honcho now.

                    RUSTY
          So be it, man, nobody's stoppin' ya.

                    CANDLE
          There's only one way. I challenge!

There is a hushed stillness. The way he has said it makes
it an official thing. Rusty wets his lips. A stand. He
has to oblige Candle.

                    RUSTY
          You want a stand? All the way to the
          finish?

                    FISH
          That's dumb, Candle! We got it straight,
          let it alone!

                    CANDLE
          Shut up, all of you.
              (to Rusty)
          Well, spick? You gonna stand or chicken
          out?

A long beat. Back into the sewer for Rusty...

                    RUSTY
          I'll stand. When?

                    CANDLE
          Tomorrow. In the morning. At the dumps.
              (beat; he backs off)
          And come heeled, baby, 'cause I'm gonna
          split you all the way down.

He turns, throws closed knife to Johnny Slice. They leave.

52   ANOTHER SHOT - ON RUSTY

walking slowly back to the booth and Weezee, whose fist is
in her mouth, a reflex action still held from the moments
of violence. Cannon comes to them.

> CANNON
> Lousy punks; I'd like to kick that
> dumb muthuh in his tail!

> RUSTY
> It's okay, Cannon. I suppose it's
> gotta be. But this's the end of it.

> CANNON
> Your end if he gets to you.

> WEEZEE
> Rusty...

> RUSTY
> Let's get outta here, Weezee.

She rises, and they move off down the passage to the front
door as Cannon watches. CAMERA HOLDS on his worried face,
watching them go.

53   EXT. STREET - DAY

as Rusty and Weezee emerge. Fish waits by the wall of the
building. He comes forward.

> FISH
> Hey, Rusty...listen, I, uh, I just want
> ya to know, I, well, I understand, and
> I'm sorry about...

> RUSTY
> Forget it, man.

Fish goes silent, nods, lopes away. Weezee stares at Rusty.

> WEEZEE
> I gotta go home, Rusty.

> RUSTY
> (with finality)
> Yeah, sure. Me too.

He turns away from her and she looks after him as, hands
sunk in pants pockets he goes in the opposite direction.
CAMERA HOLDS on her looking after him as we

                                        DISSOLVE TO BLACK.

54   BLACK FRAME

that becomes DOOR TO RUSTY'S APARTMENT as he opens it, goes thru.

55   INT. SANTORO APT. - ESTABLISHING - LATE DAY

Not-quite-enough, is the phrase that comes to mind. Not precisely poverty, but just not-quite-enough. The lamps have old-fashioned, fringed shades. The TV is a small-screen set. The sofa and overstuffed chairs look worn, tired. Tired. That's another word that comes to mind, as Rusty enters, throws his light jacket on the sofa. The SOUND of pans and kitchensounds distantly, from the rear of the apartment.

                    MOMS VOICE O.S.
          Russell...is that you?

                    RUSTY
          Me, Moms.

                    MOMS VOICE O.S.
          Wash up, dinner's almost ready.

CAMERA GOES WITH Rusty as he moves around the room absently, touching this piece of old furniture, then that, showing us by his random movements how depressing the room and the life lived in it must be. He calls to Moms without looking up.

                    RUSTY
          Hey, Moms, is Dolores home?

                    MOMS VOICE O.S.
          She's in the bathroom. You can wash in
          this sink.

56   TRUCKING SHOT - WITH RUSTY

walking through living room, down an equally dismal hallway with rooms branching off. Not quite a railroad flat, but the next thing to it. CAMERA ON HIS BACK as he goes down the hall to the kitchen. As he passes one door, he bangs absently, without passing. A voice comes back at him.

                    DOLORES VOICE O.S.
                      (impatiently)
          I'll be out, I'll be out! Can't I be
          in here for two minutes without someone
          banging the door down, for crine out loud!

                    MOMS VOICE O.S.
          Dolores! Don't use that kinda language!

57   INT. SANTORO KITCHEN - ESTABLISHING - LATE DAY

MOMS SANTORO standing by the sink, hands on hips, staring
down the hallway to Rusty, ambling toward her. She is a
pale, wan-looking woman with large hips and capacious
bosom. Like her home, she is tired-looking. CAMERA HOLDS
ON HER as Rusty comes into the kitchen.

                    MOMS
          Where have you been? School let out
          two hours ago. Have you been running
          with those rotten kids again?

He does not look at her, as though he has been through this
two hundred thousand times. He goes to the sink, begins to
wash his hands. He does it with great intensity, washing
over and over again, over the same area, as if by being clean
he can escape her questions.

                    RUSTY
          I stayed after; worked in the shop.

                    MOMS
          You telling me the truth? I don't know
          why you always lie lie lie to me all the
          time...it's just as easy to tell the
          truth.

                    RUSTY
          I'm not lying.

                    MOMS
          I don't know what it is about you, I try
          to bring you up right, God knows it
          isn't easy, your father always...

The SOUND of HER VOICE FADES as CAMERA COMES IN TIGHT on
CLOSEUP of Rusty, as he now frantically washes. And over
the undecipherable monotone of Moms talking, NARRATION.

                    NARRATOR
          They hit you from all sides, don't
          they, Rusty?

                    RUSTY'S VOICE O.S.
          She can't help it, man. She works all
          day, down inna garment center, she's a
          presser inna clothing place, man, and
          that's hot work. She just don't unnerstand.

                              (CONTINUED)

57   CONTINUED:

> NARRATOR
>
> where's your father, Rusty?

> RUSTY'S VOICE O.S.
>
> You saw him. The bum in the alley.

> NARRATOR
>
> Drunk.

> RUSTY'S VOICE O.S.
>
> Yeah, drunk. Muscatel, gin, rye if he
> can con Moms out of the money. And if he
> can't get musky, he'll drink wood alky
> he filters down through a loaf of bread
> into a ketchup bottle.

> NARRATOR
>
> And your sister, Dolores...?

> RUSTY'S VOICE O.S.
>   (quickly)
> She's okay. She's a good kid.
>   (beat)
> The only thing is...

> NARRATOR
>
> Yes, the only thing--

> RUSTY'S VOICE O.S.
>
> I shouldn't of gotten her into the Barons.
> But it's a rough turf; if she wasn't inna
> club, it'd be murder for her to walk the
> street to school...

> NARRATOR
>
> I thought the Barons was all boys, Rusty.

> RUSTY'S VOICE O.S.
>
> No, they got a girls' auxill'y'ry, the
> Baron Debs. And most of them chicks are
> worse than the guys...I'm worried about
> her.

MOMS VOICE FADES BACK IN as Rusty turns off the water tap.

> MOMS
>
> ...lying, always lying. You've been a
> liar all your life!

> RUSTY
>   (shouting)
> Yeah, yeah, yeah, for God's sake, I'm
> tellin' the truth!

                                   (CONTINUED)

57   CONTINUED: - 2

MOMS
Don't use the Lord's name in vain in
this house!

RUSTY
Wow! We're back on the holy kick!
What'd you do, find Pops' old bible?

Moms takes two steps to him and slaps him across the face.
Rusty falls back, holding his cheek. Again, there is the
frenzy and fury and helplessness that borders on tears.
He is stunned by her act. But silent.

MOMS
And where were you last night? You didn't
come home last night? Where were you?

RUSTY
I come in late.

MOMS
With your face all bruised and your lip
split? Fighting in the streets? I'm
telling your probation officer...

RUSTY
Moms, please! Lemme alone! What do you
want from me! I come home late and left
early, that's the truth.

Moms is as shaken by the fight as Rusty. She abruptly cuts
the conversation, roughly.

MOMS
Sit down at the table.

Rusty sits as the SOUND of the BATHROOM DOOR OPENING precedes
DOLORES SANTORO. She comes down the hall and into the
kitchen. She is a striking girl of perhaps sixteen, dark-
eyed, dark-haired, a direct opposite to Weezee's blonde
good looks. Dolores is obviously of Spanish (possibly
Italian) descent, and at the rate she is going, destined
to be a stunning woman. She sits down across from Rusty
as Moms serves them.

RUSTY
I didn't see you around today. Where
ya been?

58   CLOSEUP - ON DOLORES

eating.

>   DOLORES
          Around.

                     RUSTY
          1 know, around. I din't ask you around,
          I asked you where?

                     DOLORES
          Around, just around! I was with the kids.

                     RUSTY
          What kids?

                     DOLORES
                  (blows up)
          What is this around here...first her, now
          you! Can't a person lead a private life
          without everybody always asking where where
          where!

                     RUSTY
          Don't call her her, that's your mother.

     Dolores looks heavenward. She is a martyr.

                     MOMS
          Eat. No more. No more tonight. You're
          both home, that's what counts, so eat.

     She sits down with them, they eat in silence.

                     DOLORES
                  (maliciously)
          I heard you had some trouble today...

     Rusty stops eating. He looks at her sharply, hoping she
     won't go on. Suddenly Moms attention is drawn.

                     MOMS
          Trouble? What trouble? Is that how you
          got all beat up, why you were out all
          night?

                     RUSTY
          No trouble. Dolores didn't mean nothing.

                     MOMS
          What trouble?

                     RUSTY
          I tell you there's no trouble!

59   ANOTHER SHOT - THE GROUP

a tension building as Moms gets worked up again.

                    MOMS
          Why, why? What did I do to deserve
          this? A rotten brawler for a son, a
          daughter who runs with tramps, a
          husband...

                    RUSTY
                 (cuts in)
          Stop it, willya! Just once lemme come
          home and not have to hear all this
          damned bellyachin'! There ain't no
          trouble, I told you!

                    DOLORES
          I just want some fun, Ma...

                    MOMS
          Oh sure, yes yes yes, just fun, always
          fun. Is that what I brought you up to
          be, a street girl and a cheap hoodlum?

Rusty shoves back abruptly, throws his napkin on the table.

                    RUSTY
                 (yelling)
          Yeah, that's it, that's what you brought
          me up to be! A bum, a slob, a hoodlum...
          I'm gonna go out and rob a bank or kill
          a cop or mug an old lady...

                    MOMS
          Don't raise your voice to me!

                    RUSTY
                 (disgusted)
          Oh, forget it, just...forget it!

He slams out of the room. Dolores and Moms sit waiting,
and after two long beats there is the LOUD SOUND of the
FRONT DOOR SLAMMING. They sit a moment longer, Dolores
toying with her food. Finally, she shoves back her
chair, gets up.

                    DOLORES
          I lost my appetite.

She walks down the hall into a bedroom. She closes the
door. CAMERA HOLDS on Moms, MOVES IN to CLOSEUP: a tired
and confused woman. The SOUND of a rock n' roll record
LOUD from Dolores' bedroom, and now—the tears come.

                                        DISSOLVE TO:

60   THE STREET - ESTABLISHING - NIGHT

It is a different city at night. Not just darker, or colder,
but something deadly and menacing with its shadows, its pools
of light dropped by street lamps, surrounded by blackness.
Cars move down the street, sounds come from apartments, the
clanking of a garbage can, music...sounds of the city.

CAMERA ON RUSTY as he moves down the street TRUCKING WITH HIM.
He turns in at Cannon's.

SHARP CUT TO:

61   INT. CANNON'S MALT SHOP - NIGHT

EXT. CLOSEUP on PEPPER a very-well-built girl in capris and
shortie top, doing (the currently-popular) dance steps with
TIGER. Another couple, MARGIE and LOCKUP dancing also.
CAMERA PULLS BACK to find Rusty nudging his way through the
large crowd in Cannon's, to a stool at the end of the
fountain. The kids are friendly now. Rusty waves and nods.

62   ON CANNON

seeing Rusty, coming to him. He speaks above the din.

                    CANNON
          I'm thinking of having Congress repeal
          Friday night. Whyn't all these loafers
          go out and steal a aircraft carrier or
          something?

                    RUSTY
                    (grins)
          Then you'd be outta business.

                    CANNON
          I should get so lucky. Whaddaya want?
          No, don't tell me, a Coke, right?

Rusty nods. Cannon makes a face, goes to get it. CAMERA
HOLDS ON RUSTY as a hand drops on his shoulder. He turns
as CAMERA PULLS BACK to include Fish.

                    FISH
          Hey, man, what's shakin?

                    RUSTY
          Nothin'. You seen the sour apple?

                    FISH
          Candee?
                    (Rusty nods)
          He's out with Caroline in her old
          man's car. Hoo-hoo-hoo!
                              (CONTINUED)

62   CONTINUED:

CAMERA MOVES INTO 2-SHOT as Rusty laughs at Fish's remarks.

                    FISH
                 (continues)
What're you gonna do about tomorrow?

                    RUSTY
What ya think I'm gonna do: I'm gonna
be there.

                    FISH
All these nitwits're lookin' forward, man.
They ain't happy unless there's blood.

                    RUSTY
That's their problem.   You seen weezee?

                    FISH
                 (shakes head)
I think she cut out, man.   I got a feeling
she's scared worse than you.

                    RUSTY
I can't put her down for that.   But don't
get it in your head I'm scared.   Not of
that punk Candle.

                    FISH
Well, you outta be, man.   He's a rotten
operator, and you know it.   You seen
him in that bop with the Cherokees.   I
think that guy he was stompin' lost an
eye.

Rusty is about to speak when another song begins on the
juke box and PEPPER comes over to them.   She is a very
big-busted girl, and she is obviously on the make for
Rusty.

63   3-SHOT - RUSTY, FISH & PEPPER

as she slouches up to him, with a come-on attitude.

                    PEPPER
        Hi, Rusty.

                    RUSTY
        Hi, Pepper.

                    PEPPER
        Wanna dance?

                              (CONTINUED)

63   CONTINUED:

RUSTY
No.

PEPPER
(grabs his arm)
Aw, c'mon, Rusty, don't be a creep.
Dance with me...

Rusty shakes her off, annoyed. Cannon deposits drink, leaves.

RUSTY
G'wan, willya, beat it.

She moves away, angrily, finds another boy, dances in B.G.

RUSTY
(continues)
Whatta hog.

FISH
(nods agreement)
You got anything on tonight?

RUSTY
Nothin'. It's like the whole town's waiting
for the big show tomorrow.

Fish leans in close, speaks sotto voce.

FISH
Y'wanna turn on? Boy-O's got some
pot.

RUSTY
(uncertain)
I dunno, man, I'm on probation; the
fuzz bust the joint and they catch
me blowin' pot, I'll be in the farm
by next Friday.
(beat)
How much he want for it?

FISH
I dunno. Want me to check him out?

RUSTY
Okay. Just don't stand too close to
that cat. He stinks like a sewer.

Fish gets up, walks over to a booth in back. CAMERA HOLDS
TIGHT ON RUSTY and OVER HIS SHOULDER to Fish talking to Boy-O.

(CONTINUED)

63   CONTINUED:

Rusty does not turn around, but from the corner of his eye
he watches Fish and BOY-O, a slovenly little item with a face
like a ferret. In a few minutes Fish gives Boy-O some money,
and Boy-O reaches casually under the seat of the booth and
pulls free a small packet taped to the underside. He pulls
two cigarettes from the packet and gives them to Fish. Fish
returns to Rusty.

64   2-SHOT - RUSTY & FISH

as Fish hands one of the little brown hand-rolleds to Rusty.
They shield them from Cannon's sight. Rusty smells the weed.

                    RUSTY
          cheeew...man, how much did he want
          for this stink?

Fish holds up one finger.

                    RUSTY
                   (continues)
          A bean? He got a buck outta you for
          this garbage? Man, you must be high
          already.

He gives Fish a dollar in change. Then they casually get
up, walk nonchalantly to the rear alley door, and slip out
without anyone noticing as CAMERA GOES WITH THEM.

65   EXT. ALLEY - ESTABLISHING - NIGHT - HIGH SHOT

Rusty and Fish emerge from Cannon's back door. They find
a place behind a stack of old cartons, and light up. CAMERA
COMES DOWN SLOWLY AND AROUND to MED. CLOSEUP of the boys.
Sitting with backs to wall, they cup hands around the smoke
and puff deeply.

                    RUSTY
          Nothin'. This's all stems and leaves,
          man. Be been taken.

                    FISH
          Take it easy, give it a chance. Suck
          air with it, mix it good.

They puff a while longer. Fish exhales a long Aaaaahhhhh
of rising contentment. A moment later, Rusty too.

                    RUSTY
                   (softly, huskily)
          Yeahhhhh....

66   2-SHOT - RUSTY & FISH

as they sink into a dreamy state, not that far removed from
their normal manner to be noticeable, but still a little
more gentle, a little more sleepy, a little more slurred.

> FISH
> Mare-ee-wah-nahhhh! Oooooo...

> RUSTY
> Hey, Fish...?

> FISH
> Thass my name, man.

> RUSTY
> Where's Boy-O get this boo?

> FISH
> I'dunno, he's got a connection, some
> place I s'posse...oooo...

> RUSTY
> How come he's so filthy dirty alla time,
> man?

> FISH
> Cause he's a junkie, man, an' he spends
> all the bread he makes pushin', on his
> own dust. That cat's got a fifteen-buck-
> a-day habit...

> RUSTY
> His arm looks like a piece of swiss cheese
> from spikin'.

As they talk CAMERA OPTICALLY SOFTENS till they are in a
misty, dreamlike state, with the alley softer looking,
almost pleasant.

> RUSTY
> (continues)
> Hey, man, I wanna dance with that
> Pepper.

> FISH
> Aw, man, that hog? Whatta toad!

Rusty stumbles erect, puffing the last of the roach. He
drops it, and Fish grabs it up. Rusty moves like a sleep-
walker to the rear door of Cannon's, opens it. He goes
through, into a wall of noise and smoke and moving bodies.

67   MED. SHOT - ON RUSTY - TRUCKS WITH

as he moves through Cannon's. Over his shoulder as he
bumbles past one group, then another, shoving through; Pepper
in MID-B.G. his destination. The Beast suddenly sways into
his path.

                    BEAST
          Hiya, Rusty...

Rusty shoves past, as though sleepwalking, intent only on the
girl gyrating sexily in the middle of the dance area with
another boy. Rusty shoves through, grabs her. The other
boy resists, protesting. Rusty, dreamily, shoves him. The
boy stumbles back, falls over his own feet and a chair, and
goes down heavily. He sits staring wide-eyed at Rusty.
CAMERA CLOSES on Rusty dancing with the frightened Pepper.
In B.G. Cannon moving toward him steadily. Cannon grabs
him, tears him away from Pepper. They tussle awkwardly,
Rusty still smiling dreamily, till Cannon gets him by the
neck and the seat of the pants. He propels him forward.

                    CANNON
          That's it, boy! I like you, but
          nobody makes aggravation in Cannon's
          joint.

He duck-walks him through the customers to the front door,
opens it, and throws Rusty out the front door, Rusty still
grinning stupidly.

68   MED. SHOT - ON RUSTY - STREET - NIGHT

leaning against a car, Rusty hums to himself as though he's
way out there somewhere. CAMERA ON HIM as he starts walking,
whistling, erratically, going nowhere.

69   AEROFLEX INSERT - WHAT HE SEES - RUSTY'S POV

everything fuzzy, lovely, twisting and turning. Buildings,
cars, people, store windows, everything hazy and wild. A
man walking toward him, far away down the sidewalk, becomes
a cop, not noticing Rusty yet. CAMERA ZOOMS IN on cop...
a frantic tilt to the angle of focus, panic!

70   AEROFLEX ANGLES - WITH RUSTY
thru
74   as he bolts. He runs, down alleys, through hallways, over
fences, a mad Kafkaesque flight with CAMERA GOING all the
way. He stops, falls back against a brick wall, looks up.
Stars wheel overhead crazily, buildings shimmer and sway;
he plunges on again. Finally, CAMERA GOES OUT-OF-FOCUS,
leaving only the impression of movement remaining.

                              (CONTINUED)

70   CONTINUED:
thru
74   MUSIC BRIDGE thru de-focused footage. CAMERA COMES BACK-
        INTO-FOCUS in SILENCE. Rusty, sleeping on the ground, far
        below a great bridge that rises high overhead. SOUNDS of
        water lapping against a breakwater. A TUGBOAT HOOTS. Cars
        whip by on a highway nearby. Rusty lies there as CAMERA
        MOVES AROUND to look DOWN ON HIM. Gradually, he comes awake,
        shakes his head bringing back consciousness and reality.
        He rises to one elbow, runs a hand through his hair, and
        mumbles thickly, trying to rise.

                         RUSTY
                P-Pancoast...Mr. Pancoast...gotta see
                him.

        He starts to rise.

75   UP-ANGLE - RUSTY IN F.G. TO BRIDGE

        CAMERA LOOKS UP as he stands shakily, shooting TO BRIDGE
        above and behind him. CAMERA PULLS BACK & AROUND & HOLDS
        as Rusty stumbles away in distance. A tugboat hoots O.S.

                                        GO TO BLACK.

76   BLACK FRAME

        becomes CAMERA ON RUSTY ringing Pancoast's apartment doorbell.
        He rings insistently again.

                         RUSTY
                Mr. Pancoast! Hey, Mr. Pancoast!
                Answer y'bell--

        SOUNDS OF MOVEMENT from behind door. Door opens. Pancoast
        standing in socks, shirt open at the neck.

                         RUSTY
                Howdy, Pahder...

                         PANCOAST
                Rusty...what are you...doing...

                         RUSTY
                I come to talk. In my hour of need.

        He shoves past, stops dead. He stares.

77   REVERSE ANGLE - RUSTY'S POV - WHAT HE SEES

        sitting on the sofa is a pretty girl, her shoes off, curled
        relaxedly, but now staring wide-eyed at the disheveled boy.

                                        (CONTINUED)

77   CONTINUED:

The SOUND of a TV SET impinges; two drinks stand on the
coffee table. The girl is motionless at the intrusion.
SOUND of the DOOR CLOSING behind Rusty. Pancoast moves
around, into frame, staring at Rusty.

                    PANCOAST
                    (softly)
          It's pretty late, isn't it, Rusty.

78   ANOTHER ANGLE - THE SCENE

RUSTY in F.G. getting a long look at the girl, at the scene.

                    PANCOAST
                    (to girl)
          Jeanie, this is one of my students,
          Rusty Santoro. Rusty, this is a
          friend of mine, Miss Welsh. She's--

Rusty's expression changes, as he cuts Pancoast off.

                    RUSTY
          Man, you really had me fooled. All
          that crap about bein' straight arrow.
          You're just like me, fulla the same
          kinda jazz. And I went and got my
          tail kicked all over town...

                    PANCOAST
          Now wait just a minute--

                    RUSTY
          Wait? For what? Man, you're a big
          phoney like all the rest of them social
          workers. Holier than thou, and behind
          the scenes you're really cuttin' the
          mustard, aint'cha?

He starts toward door. Pancoast tries to stop him. Rusty
shrugs him off.

                    PANCOAST
          Listen, Rusty, I--

Rusty at the open door.

                    RUSTY
          Do as I say, teacher, not as I do. Bull!

He slams out violently. Pancoast turns back to the girl
with a helpless expression on his face. CAMERA MOVES IN
on him, HOLDS on his tortured face.

                              (CONTINUED)

78   CONTINUED:

PANCOAST
I never said I was anything else! I'm
human like anyone else...what do they
want from us...

CAMERA RISES away from him, standing alone and helpless in
the middle of the room, as his voice dwindles and CAMERA
GOES UP AND UP.

PANCOAST
(continues)
What the hell do I have to be to help
him? What...what...what...?

His VOICE FADES OUT as CAMERA GOES UP and we

SLOWLY LAP DISSOLVE TO:

79   INT. RUSTY'S BEDROOM - ESTABLISHING - MORNING

as CAMERA BEGINS TO COME DOWN from SAME ANGLE AS SCENE 78;
we have switched in the dissolve to Rusty's room, and as the
CAMERA DESCENDS we see Rusty stretched out on his bed,
spread-eagled in a fitful sleep, wearing only pajama bottoms.
It is as though he is crucified, a fitting counterpoint to
Pancoast's last helpless remarks. CAMERA CONTINUES TO
DESCEND SLOWLY giving us a prolonged view of Rusty on his
bed of nightmares, as NARRATION OVER:

NARRATOR
So this is your world, Rusty Santoro.
Fighting, running, emptiness, fear and
futility.

RUSTY
(hopefully)
Can't I ever get away from it? Can't
I ever break free?

NARRATOR
Today might be the day. You might get
killed today, Rusty.

RUSTY
No. No, I don't wanna die!

NARRATOR
Or you might kill. Have you ever killed
before? In all those rumbles...ever?

RUSTY
No!

(CONTINUED)

79   CONTINUED:

CAMERA COMES DOWN TO CLOSEUP of Rusty, sleeping on the bed.
As the O.S. RUSTY VOICE says "No!", simultaneously, he snaps
awake and lunges up INTO CAMERA for EXT. CLOSEUP saying:

                              RUSTY
                           (terrified)
              No!

80   ANOTHER ANGLE - ON RUSTY - MED. CLOSEUP

swinging his feet off the bed, he sits up, rubs his eyes.
What a helluva night! He gets up. Clothes thrown all over
the floor. The windowshade pulled down. He walks over,
grabs at it, and it rolls flopping to the top, letting in the
sight of the street...filthy rooftops, depressing rears of
buildings, cold-looking pavements. CAMERA FOLLOWS HIM as he
looks toward the battered bureau near the wall.

81   INSERT - THE BUREAU

CLOSE on the bottom drawer, closed tightly, though the other
drawers hang open partially, clothes sticking out.

82   FULL SHOT - RUSTY

as he starts toward the bottom drawer, stops, has a visible
battle with himself, then ignores it. CAMERA FOLLOWS HIM
as he looks closely into the mirror, checking out his puffy
lip and the cuts from being beaten; as he dresses; as he
takes a folded hankie from a top drawer and puts it in his
hip pocket; as he combs his hair in a carefully casual way.
When he is dressed, he pauses again, walks away from the
bureau.

83   INSERT - THE BUREAU

same as Scene 81

84   FULL SHOT - RUSTY

Same as Scene 82. As Rusty finally bends to one knee, pulls
open the bottom drawer, and rummaging under stacks of clothes,
takes out something that he conceals in his hand. He shoves it
up into his sleeve, then stands. CAMERA PULLS BACK to FULL
SHOT as Rusty stands poised, like a gunslinger, hands away
from his sides, body slightly stooped, bent at the knees,
legs apart. Then, with a smooth, catlike movement, he
shakes his arm, the knife concealed there drops into his
hand, and with a short, sharp sidewise movement he snaps
it open, raises it to striking position, fluidly. He stands
there a long beat, then breaks the knife, shoves it into his
boot-top, and kicks the bureau drawer shut. He goes to door.

85   LONG SHOT - DOWN HALLWAY

as bedroom door opens and Rusty emerges. Down the hall, to
the kitchen, can be seen Moms and Dolores. Rusty turns TO
CAMERA and moves toward us as CAMERA HOLDS over his shoulder.
Moms voice stops him. He does not turn around, but talks
into camera.

                    MOMS
          Don't you want breakfast?

                    RUSTY
          Not hungry. I gotta go.

                    MOMS
          Where? Where you got to go this early,
          and you didn't come home till a crazy-time
          last night?

                    DOLORES
          He's gotta go fight Candle, that's what
          he's gotta do.

                    RUSTY
          Shut up, Dolo!

                    MOMS
          Fight? Who he's gotta fight? You running
          in the streets again, Russell?

                    DOLORES
          My brother, the chicken!

                    RUSTY
          Dolores, please shut up, she's gettin' upset.

                    DOLORES
          Upset...yeah, me too! My brother's too
          chicken to fight...

                    MOMS
                 (hysterical)
          Oh my God, again! You'll die...! The
          police, Russell...!

                    RUSTY
          It's my life...if I'm gonna die...

He walks TOWARD CAMERA, reaches out, opens door, steps forward
again.
                    RUSTY
                 (continues)
          ...let me die my way!

He steps INTO CAMERA and SLAMS DOOR CLOSED TO BLACK.
                              FADE OUT.

FADE IN:

86   TRAVELLING SHOT - THE STREET - MORNING

as seen thru the WINDSHIELD of FISH'S CAR. Moving steadily
down the street, which is just gearing up for business. A
Saturday morning with fat old women shopping-bagging it,
and kids on stoops, and dogs, and shopkeepers haggling
over pennies. And Rusty walking along the sidewalk as the
car grinds to a halt beside him. CAMERA HOLDS as Fish leans
over to the open right-hand window.

                    FISH
        Hey, Rusty!

Rusty turns, comes over to the car.

                    FISH
                 (continues)
        Get in. They sent me for ya.

Rusty gets in, slams door.   Fish and Rusty look at each
other, but neither speaks.   Fish throws it into gear, the
car lurches forward.

87   LONG SHOT - THE STREET

as the car screeches away, turns a corner, and vanishes.

                              FAST WIPE TO:

88   THE GARBAGE DUMPS - ESTABLISHING - MORNING

SHOT ON HORIZON LINE sweeping the giant heaps of blazing
refuse, sending pillars of thick, ropey smoke up into the
cadaverous morning sky. CAMERA PANS ACROSS HORIZON and
BEGINS TO RISE. As it rises, we catch the outside edge of
a large circle of cars, all ringed with noses turned to
the center, forming a sort of wheel. BOOM SHOT RISING
till we are looking down into the center of the circle, with
boys and girls lounging about, smoking, jostling each
other, leaning on cars. A shout goes up from Pooch, standing
on the hood of one of the cars.

                    POOCH
        Here comes Fish!

CAMERA FOLLOWS his pointing, and in distance we see a
cloud of dust as Fish's car burns rubber zig-zagging into the
dumps.
                              CUT TO:

89   2-SHOT - CLOSEUP

PAST RUSTY & FISH in the front seat of the car, as it speeds
in a crazy pattern across the empty dirt-field toward the
group of cars and kids growing larger in the windshield.
PERSPECTIVE SHOT as they race madly for it.

CUT TO:

90   HIGH SHOT - THE CAR

speeding toward the group, CAMERA TRAVELLING ABOVE AND
BEHIND the car as it races almost into the center of the
wheel, suddenly applies brakes and skids wildly, slewing
sidewise and sending up a great wedge-shaped spray of dirt.
It grinds to a shuddering halt, and the drivers' door pops
open. CAMERA BOVE, HOLDING as Fish leaps out Doug Fairbanks
style.

> FISH
> Ta-ra-ta-<u>tahhhh</u>!

The door on the other side slowly opens and Rusty emerges as
CAMERA COMES DOWN AND AROUND to catch him in FULL SHOT.
CAMERA MOVES BACK as he walks toward us, as it holds his
face and expression as he enters circle.

91   REVERSE ANGLE

from behind Rusty as he marches into the center, toward
Candle, who stands waiting. The other kids begin to group
closer together as the showdown approaches. Rusty stops.
Beside Candle is Weezee. He has his arm around her. She
doesn't seem to object.

> RUSTY
> (to Weezee)
> I wondered where you'd gotten to.

> WEEZEE
> Rusty, I--

> CANDLE
> (cuts in)
> Forget it, he don't need no explanations.

> RUSTY
> (staring at Weezee)
> You're right, man. I don't.
> (beat)
> Any time you're ready.

92   3-SHOT - FISH, RUSTY & CANDLE

as Fish moves in between them.

>   FISH
>   This's gonna be by the rules. Apache-style.
>   Any objections?

>   CANDLE
>   Not by me. Ask the spick...maybe he wants
>   to use aircraft carriers at twenty paces.

The group laughs raucously. Rusty whips the hankie out
of his hip pocket, throws it to the ground at Fish's feet.

>   RUSTY
>   It's fine by me.

Fish picks up the hankie, motions to one of the boys to
come and help him. The group pulls together as Fish and
the other boy each perform the same operation on Rusty
and Candle:

They loosen the belts looped around each combatant's waist,
and making space in the back, Fish slips Rusty's right arm
through the belt as the other boy slips Candle's left arm
through the belt. Then they pull the belts tight again,
and buckle them, effectively pinning each combatant's arm
behind his back.

Then Fish takes the hankie--an extra-large red, figured
bandanna--and opens it full. Holding opposite corners,
he begins to "flip" the hankie, end-over-end (the way
kids do with a towel in a shower, when they "snap" the
towel at another bare-bottomed boy) until he has a long,
thin line of fabric. Candle and Rusty move closer, with
FISH BETWEEN THEM. CAMERA MOVES INTO EXT. CLOSEUP of their
faces as Candle and Rusty each take an end of the long,
twirled hankie in their mouths. They each pull in more fabric
with their teeth, holding it clamped in their mouths by
the strength of their bite. CAMERA PULLS BACK to FULL
SHOT of the combatants standing with the hankie dangling
between them. They begin to move back slowly, pulling the
bowed fabric tight between them. They reach the outer
edge of tension of the hankie, which leaves about half a
foot of empty space between them. Fish moves back.

>   FISH
>   On the count of three. One...

They tense, begin to crouch, the hankie pulled tight.

93   CLOSEUPS

CAMERA SNAPS FROM FISH TO CANDLE TO RUSTY as the count hits.

                         FISH
        Two...three! Go!

94   MED. 2-SHOT - RUSTY & CANDLE

as the count hits, Candle shakes his free arm and the switch
drops into his hand. He buttons it open with a vicious SNAP.
Simulataneously, Rusty ducks and reaches into his boot-top,
comes up with his own blade. NOTE: Rusty's knife is an 11-
inch Italian stiletto without a button. It is opened on a
gravity or "shake" principle. The movement is a fluid one
that whips the hand into striking position.

Even as it opens, Rusty swings widely at Candle's mid-section.
The other boy sucks in his belly and jumps back. The hankie
draws tighter. They circle each other, making idle cuts at
each other. The fact that Rusty is left-handed and Candle
is right-handed, puts each of them on the other's open side,
with the other hands locked behind the backs.

95   HIGH SHOT - THE SCENE

looking directly down on them, circling each other, slashing
and missing and slashing again. The kids moving idly at
the outside of the circle, yelling.

                        POOCH
        Don't drop the hankie, Candle! You'll
        lose!

                        FISH
        C'mon, Rusty, cut him, cut him!

                        ALL
        Go! Go! Go! Go! Go! Go!

They continue circling. Suddenly Candle lashes out, his
knife connects with Rusty's own knife-arm, opens it.

96   CLOSEUP - RUSTY

as his eyes widen in pain, he continues looking at Candle.
CAMERA COMES DOWN on the arm. The leather of the jacket
is neatly sliced, and the shirt beneath, and there is blood
on the arm. CAMERA PANS ACROSS the arm, to the hand,
down the length of the knife, across open space, to the
tip of Candle's knife, across his hand, his arm, and up to
his face where it HOLDS on his clenched teeth and jubilant
face. He has drawn first blood. The SOUND of the GANG
SCREAMING FOR BLOOD in the B.G.

97 UP-ANGLE - RUSTY & CANDLE

CAMERA LOOKING UP BETWEEN THEM as they circle above us, their
knives out in front of them, the hands making little circling
movements, the hankie stretched across the frame like a band
across the sky. They GRUNT and PANT without unclenching
their teeth. CAMERA GOES AROUND IN CIRCLE as it follows the
action from underfoot. Candle suddenly gives a sharp jerk
and there is the ~~xxxx~~ SOUND of FABRIC TEARING. Rusty moves
forward inexorably, slashing back-and-forth like a scythe,
winding the hankie tighter in his teeth all the while.

98 ANOTHER ANGLE - PAST CANDLE TO RUSTY

as they bend forward from the shoulders, putting their bellies
far out of swinging range. Their knife-tips are almost
touching and there is the frequent CLATTER of STEEL-ON-STEEL.
Candle's hand comes up and then down sharply, catching Rusty
across the wrist. Rusty drops his knife. Candle moves in
for the kill. An overhand slash. Rusty slips sidewise,
and Candle goes careening past, pulling the hankie tight.
Rusty yanks up on it with his teeth, almost pulling Candle
off-balance, and in the scuffle, regains his knife. In a
moment they are circling again. Circle, step, stop, circle,
step, stop...and constantly slashing, angling for an opening.
The ground is worn into a rough circle from their movement
around and around.

99 ANOTHER ANGLE - THE SCENE

as the kids scream their approval. Candle and Rusty circle
steadily. Suddenly Candle plunges forward and collides with
Rusty. They lock knife-hands and press against each other,
each trying to knock the other down. Candle drops his head
and butts Rusty in the chin. Rusty slips to one knee. Candle
draws back for the death-slash, and comes at Rusty with the
knife overhand. Rusty moves slightly, trips Candle with his
foot. Candle falls over, rolls, the hankie pops out of his
mouth. Rusty is on his feet instantly, the hankie dangling
from his mouth.

> ALL
> Kill him! Cut him! Jab him! Get him!

Candle makes a move to bring up his knife, but Rusty steps
quickly and plants a foot on the knife-hand. He jams his
foot down on the hand, then steps quickly and kicks the knife
away. Candle stares up terrified. Rusty slips down,
straddling Candle's body, one knee on either side. CAMERA
MOVES IN on the two boys and the knife, now DOMINANT IN THE
FRAME. Candle's face has gone flat with fear, and there is
a shine in Rusty's eyes. They stare at each other a long beat.

100   2-SHOT - CLOSEUP - RUSTY & CANDLE

Rusty straddling Candle's body.

> CANDLE
> (softly)
> Go on. Get it over with.

Rusty raises his knife and with all his might drives it down
--into the ground. Right beside Candle's head. Then, without
speaking, he snaps it off. Everyone stares. He throws the
broken blade from him. Still, he sits atop Candle, staring
down at him. Then, without malice, but with slow finality,
he begins slapping him across the face, open-handed, using
each slap to punctuate his speech. There is no anger in his
violence, only authority.

> RUSTY
> (slapping)
> I'm...through...with...you...

He stops slapping Candle, who lies there resting on his elbows.
He isn't hurt, but he has been shamed, beaten. Rusty rises.

> RUSTY
> (continues; with finality)
> I'm through. For good. Done.

He stands in the center of the ring, and slowly, the kids
begin to go back to their cars in twos and threes. He does
not move as a group of boys help Candle to his feet, and
--head hanging down--they help him to a car.

101   LONGER SHOT - BOOM - THE SCENE

CAMERA BEGINS TO RISE UP AND AWAY SLOWLY as the gang begins
its exodus. One after another they pile into cars and
go. Only Rusty standing alone remains, with Fish and his
car in the B.G. and Weezee, standing where she stood before.

> WEEZEE
> Rusty...?

He turns slowly. They don't move.

> WEEZEE
> (continues)
> I...I'm glad y'won? Huh?

He walks toward her and CAMERA COMES DOWN to CLOSEUP.

102   2-SHOT - RUSTY & WEEZEE

with Fish in B.G., waiting. Rusty comes to her.

> WEEZEE
> I'm--I'm sorry, Rusty...

> RUSTY
> (softly)
> It's not your fault.

> WEEZEE
> I didn't mean to run out on you.

> RUSTY
> Smoke can't help it if it goes up a chimney.

She looks at him without comprehension.

> RUSTY
> (continues)
> It's the way you're built, Weezee. You
> fold under pressure. I understand, but
> don't blame me if I don't want you around
> no more. Maybe some other guy won't mind
> it.
> (beat)
> Hey! Fish! Take her back?

> FISH
> Sure. Don't you need a lift?

> RUSTY
> I want to do some thinking.

He turns away from her. She looks at his back silently,
for a long beat; she tries to speak but nothing comes.
Then as CAMERA HOLDS ON RUSTY she walks to Fish and gets
into the car. As the car starts we

                                        CUT TO:

103   HIGH SHOT - THE DUMPS

the car pulling away in a cloud of dust. Rusty standing
alone, all alone. CAMERA BOOMS UP & BACK to show us the
smoking piles of refuse, the city in B.G. and the car
vanishing far away. And Rusty walking alone as NARRATION
OVER:

> NARRATOR
> Well, how does it feel, Rusty?

                                        (CONTINUED)

103   CONTINUED:

                    RUSTY'S VOICE O.S.
          I'm free! Man, I beat the game, I beat it!

                    NARRATOR
          You think so?

                    RUSTY'S VOICE O.S.
          Don't you?

                    NARRATOR
                    (cautiously)
          I hope so, Rusty. I hope so.

CAMERA CONTINUES TO PULL BACK & UP as Rusty walks away from
us as we:

                                        FADE OUT.

FADE IN:

104   CLOSEUP ON TV SET - SANTORO LIVING ROOM - DAY

CAMERA PULLS BACK to show Dolores sitting with feet up,
watching the set as it blares a teen-age rock n' roll dance
party show. She dips frequently into a bag of potato chips.
She turns to CAMERA AS IT PULLS BACK to show Rusty coming
in door behind her, tossing his leather jacket on sofa.
At the SOUND of DOOR CLOSING she leaps up, rushes to him,
kisses him.

                    DOLORES
          I heard! It's all over the turf!
          They said you really put him down.

                    RUSTY
          I'm a hero.

He flops into a chair. Dolores notices the slashed arm.

                    DOLORES
          You're cut!

                    RUSTY
          He got lucky. It don't hurt. I don't
          think it's bad.

                    DOLORES
          C'mon inna bathroom, I'll bandage it,
          before Moms sees it.

She pulls him up and CAMERA FOLLOWS as they go down hall
to the bathroom.

105   INT. BATHROOM – ESTABLSIHING

ON DOOR as it opens, Rusty and Dolores come in. She pushes
him down on the closed toilet seat and opens the medicine
chest over the sink. She takes out gauze and rubbing alcohol
and a tin of band-aids. She begins working over his arm.
Rusty watches her, and affection is evident in his expression.

> RUSTY
> (gently)
> Dolores, I'm worried about you.

> DOLORES
> You're worried about me! You come
> home in sections, and you're worried
> about me! Now that is too much!

> RUSTY
> No, I'm not kidding. I don't like you
> runnin' around with the Debs. Particul'y
> now since I'm outta the Barons.

> DOLORES
> You're the one got me into the Debs.

> RUSTY
> I know. But it was different then. A
> girl ain't safe in the turf if she ain't
> got a club backing her.

> DOLORES
> So I got a club backin' me.

> RUSTY
> Yeah, but it ain't no good. They're a
> buncha bums, Dolores, most of 'em.

> DOLORES
> You didn't think so a coupla months ago.

> RUSTY
> That was before.

> DOLORES
> So now, just because you hadda change of
> mind, I've gotta break with all my friends.

She swabs disinfectant on the cut. He winces slightly.

> (CONTINUED)

105   CONTINUED:

As the SOUND of a key turning in the FRONT DOOR comes to them,
they look at each other, and Rusty kicks the door shut. The
SOUND of the DOOR OPENING & CLOSING comes through the bathroom.

                    MOMS' VOICE O.S.
          Russell...Dolores...is anybody home?

                    RUSTY
          We're in here, Moms.

                    MOMS' VOICE O.S.
                         (jolly)
          What's going on, we have those Japanese
          kind of baths now? Hurry out of there,
          I'm putting lunch on.

                    DOLORES
          We're on the way, Moms.

SOUND of FOOTSTEPS going past, to the kitchen. Dolores
resumes her repairwork.

                    RUSTY
          You gotta stop goin' with them kids,
          Dolores. They're bad news.

                    DOLORES
          Let me alone, Rusty. I told you, they're
          my friends, and I'll do what I want.

                    RUSTY
          Not if I can help it!

She viciously applies a bandage to the cut.

                    RUSTY
                    (continues)
          Ouch! Take it easy!

Dolores shoves the things back into the chest, starts to
leave, turns back to him.

                    DOLORES
          No: you take it easy! I'm gettin' fed
          up with all this badgering.

She storms out of the bathroom, leaving the door open.
Rusty rolls down his sleeve, follows her exit.

106   LONG SHOT - FROM KITCHEN - DAY

DOWN HALLWAY as Rusty emerges from bathroom, walks down hall
and disappears into his bedroom a moment. He steps out,
pulling on a sweater to cover his slashed shirt and bandaged
arm. He walks TOWARD CAMERA and into kitchen. RECEDING
CAMERA PULLS AROUND as Rusty gets silverware from drawer,
lays it out. He sits down. Dolores comes from refrigerator
with butter dish, sits down also. Moms puttering, brings
mid-day food to table. She sits and they begin to eat.

107   3-SHOT - RUSTY & MOMS & DOLORES

at table, eating. Rusty and Dolores do not speak, and Moms
notices the animosity between them.

                    MOMS
          What's the matter with you two now?

                    RUSTY
          Nothing.

                    MOMS
          Always it's nothing. I'd hate to see you
          when it was a something.

                    DOLORES
          He's just playing big brother again, is all.

                    MOMS
          So what's wrong with that?

                    DOLORES
          He's getting to be my keeper.

                    RUSTY
          Forget it, let's just drop it.

They eat in silence for a few moments.

                    MOMS
                 (to Dolores)
          Where are you going tonight?

                    DOLORES
          Out.

                    RUSTY
                 (sharply)
          Don't start that jazz again. Moms ast
          Y'where you're goin'. So tell her. Exactly.

108 INTERCUTS - BETWEEN MOMS & RUSTY & DOLORES
thru
110 CLOSEUPS as the conversation ricochets back and forth.

                    DOLORES
                  (angrily)
          To a dance!

                    RUSTY
          The Barons dance? In the club rooms?

                    DOLORES
          That's right, in the club rooms back
          behind the bowling alley. You know
          anyplace else the Barons hold their
          dances?

                    MOMS
          Are you going with anyone we know,
          Dolores?

                    DOLORES
          Jeez, Moms, what <u>are</u> you, the FBI?

                    RUSTY
          Don't get salty, just answer.

                    DOLORES
                  (flaming)
          Alone, just by myself all alone, with
          some of the kids! Jeez!

                    RUSTY
          You know there's been trouble with the
          Butchers...I heard over at Cannon's they
          might try to bust that dance.

                    MOMS
          Who...what are the Butchers? Russell?

                    RUSTY
                  (still looking at
                   Dolores)
          They're another club. A bunch of trouble.
          There was a thing happened last week between
          one of their guys and a Baron...

                    MOMS
                  (frightened)
          What, what kind of thing...?

                              (CONTINUED)

108 CONTINUED:
thru
110 CLOSEUP INTERCUTS CONTINUE as conversation gets more heated.

                    RUSTY
          There was a fight over a girl...the
          Butcher xxxx pulled a zip gun and
          the Baron, he...backed off...and later...

                    MOMS
          Go on...what did he do...

                    RUSTY
          He backed off and waited till the Butcher
          came outside. He used a tire iron on him.
          He's in the hospital.

                    MOMS
          Oh my God.

                    DOLORES
          Now see what you done! You got her all
          upset, and she's gonna raise hell about
          me goin' to the dance! You and your big
          fat mouth!

                    RUSTY
          You wanna get cut up hanging around when
          there's gonna be trouble? Well, do you?

                    DOLORES
          I hate you! I really hate you!

     Rusty reaches out abruptly as we

                              SHARP CUT TO:

111 ANOTHER SHOT - ON DOLORES & RUSTY

     as he slaps her full across the mouth. She sits stunned.
     The tears don't quite come, though she is obviously overcome
     with fear and terror and pain.

                    RUSTY
          I...I'm...sorry...Dolores...I

                    MOMS
               (tries to placate)
          Dolores, you stay home with me...we'll
          take in a movie...we'll...

                              (CONTINUED)

111 CONTINUED:

Dolores sits unmoving.

> RUSTY
> I din't mean to hit you, honest.

> DOLORES
> You just can't leave me alone, can you.
> You just can't let me live my life the
> way I want to. You got me into the
> Debs, and now you won't let me alone!

As she speaks, her tone builds, builds, becomes more hysterical,
till finally she shoves her chair away. It topples with a
CRASH. She is shouting.

> DOLORES
> (continues)
> You just can't stand to see me have a
> little fun, can you? All the time
> jumping on me like I was some sort of
> a slut or something. I never see my
> old man, there's never enough money
> to do anything nice, or get any decent
> clothes...the only fun I have is with
> the Debs, and now I can't even have
> that.

She turns and runs to the hall. She stops, turns.

> DOLORES
> (raging, continues)
> I'm never comin' back here! Never! Never!

She races down the hall and SLAMS the FRONT DOOR behind her.
There is SILENCE in the kitchen and O.S. the echoing whisper
of the word Never Never Never Never hanging in the room like
dust.

112 ANOTHER ANGLE - ON RUSTY & MOMS

They sit silently.

> MOMS
> (like a child)
> Where will she go?

> RUSTY
> I don't know, Moms. She'll be back.
> Let her blow off steam.

113   LONG SHOT DOWN HALL TO KITCHEN

as Rusty shoves away from table as seen THRU DOORWAY. He
walks TOWARD CAMERA and turns into his bedroom, closes
door. CAMERA PANS to door. There is a beat of silence,
then the sound of MUSIC from a record player. CAMERA
MOVES IN toward kitchen, to Moms, at the table. For a
few seconds CAMERA HOLDS ON HER sitting there silently,
then she begins to sob, and drops her head into her arms.
The SOUND of MUSIC rises, as we

MATCH DISSOLVE TO:

114   MATCHING CLOSEUP OF KITCHEN - EVENING

it is now dark, Moms is gone, the SOUND of MUSIC still fills
the apartment. CAMERA RECEDES BACK DOWN HALL to CLOSEUP
ON RUSTY'S DOOR. Door opens, Rusty stands in doorway.

                    RUSTY
      Moms?
                    (beat)
      Anybody home?

No answer. He goes back into room. CAMERA FOLLOWS.

115   INT. RUSTY'S BEDROOM - EVENING

the record player is playing one rock n' roll number after
another from a spindle-full of 45s. They drop as Rusty
moves idly about the room. NARRATION OVER.

                    NARRATOR
      She'll be all right.

                    RUSTY'S VOICE O.S.
      Shut up, what the hell do you know?

                    NARRATOR
      Then why did you bring her into the club?

                    RUSTY'S VOICE O.S.
      You ever see what it's like for a girl in this
      neighborhood? The bums, the perverts, the
      gang kids? Don't be a moron. I had to.

                    NARRATOR
      That's nice music.

                    RUSTY'S VOICE O.S.
      Thanks a heap.

                    NARRATOR
      Like the music at the dance?

                              (CONTINUED)

Page 60 was as far as Ellison wrote before abandoning *Rumble*.
To find out what becomes of Rusty Santoro, read WEB OF THE CITY,
the novel upon which the screenplay was based.

HARLAN ELLISON* has been characterized by *The New York Times Book Review* as having "the spellbinding quality of a great nonstop talker, with a cultural warehouse for a mind." *The Los Angeles Times* suggested, "It's long past time for Harlan Ellison to be awarded the title: 20th century Lewis Carroll." And the *Washington Post Book World* said simply, "One of the great living American short story writers."

He has written or edited 76 books; more than 1700 stories, essays, articles, and newspaper columns; two dozen teleplays, for which he received the Writers Guild of America most outstanding teleplay award for solo work an unprecedented four times; and a dozen movies. *Publishers Weekly* called him "Highly Intellectual." (Ellison's response: "Who, Me?"). He won the Mystery Writers of America Edgar Allan Poe award twice, the Horror Writers Association Bram Stoker award six times (including The Lifetime Achievement Award in 1996), the Nebula award of the Science Fiction Writers of America four times, the Hugo (World Convention Achievement award) 8 ½ times, and received the Silver Pen for Journalism from P.E.N. Not to mention the World Fantasy Award; the British Fantasy Award; the American Mystery Award; plus two Audie Awards and two Grammy nominations for Spoken Word recordings.

He created great fantasies for the 1985 CBS revival of *The Twilight Zone* (including Danny Kaye's final performance) and *The Outer Limits*, traveled with The Rolling Stones; marched with Martin Luther King from Selma to Montgomery; created roles for Buster Keaton, Wally Cox, Gloria Swanson, and nearly 100 other stars on *Burke's Law*; ran with a kid gang in Brooklyn's Red Hook to get background for his first novel; covered race riots in Chicago's "back of the yards" with the late James Baldwin; sang with, and dined with, Maurice Chevalier; once stood off the son of the Detroit Mafia kingpin with a Remington XP-l00 pistol-rifle, while wearing nothing but a bath towel; and sued Paramount and ABC-TV for plagiarism and won $337,000. His most recent legal victory, in protection of copyright against global Internet piracy of writers' work, in May of 2004—a four-year-long litigation against AOL et al.—has resulted in revolutionizing protection of creative properties on the web. (As promised, he has repaid hundreds of contributions [totaling $50,000] from the KICK Internet Piracy support fund.) But the bottom line, as voiced by *Booklist*, is this: "One thing for sure: the man can write."

He lives with his wife, Susan, inside The Lost Aztec Temple of Mars, in Los Angeles.

CHRONOLOGY OF BOOKS BY
HARLAN ELLISON®
1958 – 2016

NOVELS:

WEB OF THE CITY [1958]

THE SOUND OF A SCYTHE [1960]

SPIDER KISS [1961]

RETROSPECTIVES:

ALONE AGAINST TOMORROW: *A 10-Year Survey* [1971]

THE ESSENTIAL ELLISON: *A 35-Year Retrospective* (edited by Terry Dowling, with Richard Delap & Gil Lamont) [1987]

THE ESSENTIAL ELLISON: *A 50-Year Retrospective* (edited by Terry Dowling) [2001]

UNREPENTANT: *A Celebration of the Writing of Harlan Ellison* (edited by Robert T. Garcia) [2010]

THE TOP OF THE VOLCANO: *The Award-Winning Stories of Harlan Ellison* [2014]

OMNIBUS VOLUMES:

THE FANTASIES OF HARLAN ELLISON [1979]

DREAMS WITH SHARP TEETH [1991]

THE GLASS TEAT & THE OTHER GLASS TEAT [2011]

GRAPHIC NOVELS:

DEMON WITH A GLASS HAND (adaptation with Marshall Rogers) [1986]

NIGHT AND THE ENEMY (adaptation with Ken Steacy) [1987]

VIC AND BLOOD: *The Chronicles of a Boy and His Dog* (adaptation by Richard Corben) [1989]

HARLAN ELLISON'S DREAM CORRIDOR, Volume One [1996]

VIC AND BLOOD: *The Continuing Adventures of a Boy and His Dog* (adaptation by Richard Corben) [2003]

HARLAN ELLISON'S DREAM CORRIDOR, Volume Two [2007]

PHOENIX WITHOUT ASHES (art by Alan Robinson and John K. Snyder III) [2010/2011]

HARLAN ELLISON'S 7 AGAINST CHAOS (art by Paul Chadwick and Ken Steacy) [2013]

THE CITY ON THE EDGE OF FOREVER: *The Original Teleplay* (adaptation by Scott Tipton & David Tipton, art by J.K. Woodward) [2014/2015]

BATMAN '66: *The Lost Episode* (adaptation by Len Wein, art by Joe Prado and José García-López) [2014]

SHORT NOVELS:

DOOMSMAN [1967]

ALL THE LIES THAT ARE MY LIFE [1980]

RUN FOR THE STARS [1991]

MEFISTO IN ONYX [1993]

COLLABORATIONS:

PARTNERS IN WONDER: *Collaborations with 14 Other Wild Talents* [1971]

THE STARLOST: *Phoenix Without Ashes* (with Edward Bryant) [1975]

MIND FIELDS: *33 Stories Inspired by the Art of Jacek Yerka* [1994]

I HAVE NO MOUTH, AND I MUST SCREAM: *The Interactive CD-Rom* (Co-Designed with David Mullich and David Sears) [1995]

"REPENT, HARLEQUIN!" SAID THE TICKTOCKMAN (rendered with paintings by Rick Berry) [1997]

2000^X (Host and Creative Consultant of National Public Radio episodic series) [2000–2001]

HARLAN ELLISON'S MORTAL DREADS (dramatized by Robert Armin) [2012]

AS EDITOR:

DANGEROUS VISIONS [1967]

NIGHTSHADE & DAMNATIONS: *The Finest Stories of Gerald Kersh* [1968]

AGAIN, DANGEROUS VISIONS [1972]

MEDEA: *Harlan's World* [1985]

DANGEROUS VISIONS (The 35th Anniversary Edition) [2002]

JACQUES FUTRELLE'S "THE THINKING MACHINE" STORIES [2003]

THE HARLAN ELLISON DISCOVERY SERIES:

STORMTRACK by James Sutherland [1975]

AUTUMN ANGELS by Arthur Byron Cover [1975]

THE LIGHT AT THE END OF THE UNIVERSE by Terry Carr [1976]

ISLANDS by Marta Randall [1976]

INVOLUTION OCEAN by Bruce Sterling [1978]

CHRONOLOGY OF BOOKS BY
HARLAN ELLISON®
1958 – 2016

SHORT STORY COLLECTIONS:

THE DEADLY STREETS [1958]

SEX GANG *(as "Paul Merchant")* [1959]

A TOUCH OF INFINITY [1960]

CHILDREN OF THE STREETS [1961]

GENTLEMAN JUNKIE
and Other Stories of the Hung-Up Generation [1961]

ELLISON WONDERLAND [1962]

PAINGOD *and Other Delusions* [1965]

I HAVE NO MOUTH & I MUST SCREAM [1967]

FROM THE LAND OF FEAR [1967]

LOVE AIN'T NOTHING BUT SEX MISSPELLED [1968]

THE BEAST THAT SHOUTED LOVE
AT THE HEART OF THE WORLD [1969]

OVER THE EDGE [1970]

ALL THE SOUNDS OF FEAR
(British publication only) [1973]

DE HELDEN VAN DE HIGHWAY
(Dutch publication only) [1973]

APPROACHING OBLIVION [1974]

THE TIME OF THE EYE (British publication only) [1974]

DEATHBIRD STORIES [1975]

NO DOORS, NO WINDOWS [1975]

HOE KAN IK SCHREEUWEN ZONDER MOND
(Dutch publication only) [1977]

STRANGE WINE [1978]

SHATTERDAY [1980]

STALKING THE NIGHTMARE [1982]

ANGRY CANDY [1988]

ENSAMVÄRK (Swedish publication only) [1992]

JOKES WITHOUT PUNCHLINES [1995]

ВСЕ 3ВУКN СТРАХА (ALL FEARFUL SOUNDS)
(Unauthorized Russian publication only) [1997]

THE WORLDS OF HARLAN ELLISON
(Authorized Russian publication only) [1997]

SLIPPAGE: *Precariously Poised,*
Previously Uncollected Stories [1997]

KOLETIS, KES KUULUTAS ARMASTUST MAAILMA SLIDAMES
(Estonian publication only) [1999]

LA MACHINE AUX YEUX BLEUS
(French publication only) [2001]

TROUBLEMAKERS [2001]

PTAK ŚMIERCI (THE BEST OF HARLAN ELLISON)
(Polish publication only) [2003]

DEATHBIRD STORIES (expanded edition) [2011]

PULLING A TRAIN [2012]

GETTING IN THE WIND [2012]

ELLISON WONDERLAND (expanded edition) [2015]

PEBBLES FROM THE MOUNTAIN [2015]

CAN AND CAN'TANKEROUS [2015]

COFFIN NAILS [forthcoming]

NON-FICTION & ESSAYS:

MEMOS FROM PURGATORY [1961]

THE GLASS TEAT: *Essays of Opinion on Television* [1970]

THE OTHER GLASS TEAT:
Further Essays of Opinion on Television [1975]

THE BOOK OF ELLISON
(edited by Andrew Porter) [1978]

SLEEPLESS NIGHTS IN THE PROCRUSTEAN BED
(edited by Marty Clark) [1984]

AN EDGE IN MY VOICE [1985]

HARLAN ELLISON'S WATCHING [1989]

THE HARLAN ELLISON HORNBOOK [1990]

BUGF#CK! *The Useless Wit & Wisdom of Harlan Ellison*
(edited by Arnie Fenner) [2011]

CHRONOLOGY OF BOOKS BY
HARLAN ELLISON®
1958 – 2016

SCREENPLAYS & SUCHLIKE:

THE ILLUSTRATED HARLAN ELLISON
(edited by Byron Preiss) [1978]

HARLAN ELLISON'S MOVIE [1990]

I, ROBOT: The Illustrated Screenplay
(based on Isaac Asimov's story-cycle) [1994]

THE CITY ON THE EDGE OF FOREVER [1996]

MOTION PICTURE (DOCUMENTARY):

DREAMS WITH SHARP TEETH (A Film About Harlan Ellison
produced and directed by Erik Nelson) [2009]

ON THE ROAD WITH HARLAN ELLISON:

ON THE ROAD WITH HARLAN ELLISON
(Vol. One) [1983/2001]

ON THE ROAD WITH HARLAN ELLISON (Vol. Two) [2004]

ON THE ROAD WITH HARLAN ELLISON (Vol. Three) [2007]

ON THE ROAD WITH HARLAN ELLISON:
His Last Big Con (Vol. Five) [2011]

ON THE ROAD WITH HARLAN ELLISON:
The Grand Master Edition (Vol. Six) [2012]

AUDIOBOOKS:

THE VOICE FROM THE EDGE: I HAVE NO MOUTH,
AND I MUST SCREAM (Vol. One) [1999]

THE VOICE FROM THE EDGE: MIDNIGHT IN THE SUNKEN
CATHEDRAL (Vol. Two) [2001]

RUN FOR THE STARS [2005]

THE VOICE FROM THE EDGE: PRETTY MAGGIE MONEYEYES
(Vol. Three) [2009]

THE VOICE FROM THE EDGE: THE DEATHBIRD
& OTHER STORIES (Vol. Four) [2011]

THE VOICE FROM THE EDGE: SHATTERDAY
& OTHER STORIES (Vol. Five) [2011]

ELLISON WONDERLAND [2015]

WEB AND THE CITY [2015]

SPIDER KISS [2015]

THE CITY ON THE EDGE OF FOREVER
(full-cast dramatization) [forthcoming]

THE WHITE WOLF SERIES:

EDGEWORKS 1: OVER THE EDGE
& AN EDGE IN MY VOICE [1996]

EDGEWORKS 2: SPIDER KISS
& STALKING THE NIGHTMARE [1996]

EDGEWORKS 3: THE HARLAN ELLISON HORNBOOK
& HARLAN ELLISON'S MOVIE [1997]

EDGEWORKS 4: LOVE AIN'T NOTHING BUT SEX MISSPELLED
& THE BEAST THAT SHOUTED LOVE
AT THE HEART OF THE WORLD [1997]

EDGEWORKS ABBEY OFFERINGS
(Edited by Jason Davis):

BRAIN MOVIES: *The Original
Teleplays of Harlan Ellison* (Vol. One) [2011]

BRAIN MOVIES: *The Original
Teleplays of Harlan Ellison* (Vol. Two) [2011]

HARLAN 101: *Encountering Ellison* [2011]

THE SOUND OF A SCYTHE *and 3 Brilliant Novellas* [2011]

ROUGH BEASTS: *Seventeen Stories
Written Before I Got Up To Speed* [2012]

NONE OF THE ABOVE [2012]

BRAIN MOVIES: *The Original
Teleplays of Harlan Ellison* (Vol. Three) [2013]

BRAIN MOVIES: *The Original
Teleplays of Harlan Ellison* (Vol. Four) [2013]

BRAIN MOVIES: *The Original
Teleplays of Harlan Ellison* (Vol. Five) [2013]

HONORABLE WHOREDOM AT A PENNY A WORD [2013]

AGAIN, HONORABLE WHOREDOM
AT A PENNY A WORD [2014]

BRAIN MOVIES: *The Original
Teleplays of Harlan Ellison* (Vol. Six) [2014]

HARLAN ELLISON'S ENDLESSLY WATCHING [2014]

8 IN 80 BY ELLISON (guest edited by Susan Ellison) [2014]

THE LAST PERSON TO MARRY A DUCK
LIVED 300 YEARS AGO [2016]

BRAIN MOVIES: *The Original
Teleplays of Harlan Ellison* (Vol. Seven) [2016]

Made in the USA
San Bernardino, CA
16 June 2016